Micro-Entrepreneurship and Micro-Enterprise Development in Malaysia:

Emerging Research and Opportunities

Abdullah Al Mamun
UCSI University, Malaysia

Mohammad Nurul Huda Mazumder
George Brown College, Canada

Noor Raihani Zainol
Universiti Malaysia Kelantan (UMK), Malaysia

Rajennd Muniady
New Era University College (NEUC), Malaysia

A volume in the Advances in Business Strategy and Competitive Advantage (ABSCA) Book Series

IGI Global
DISSEMINATOR OF KNOWLEDGE

Published in the United States of America by
IGI Global
Business Science Reference (an imprint of IGI Global)
701 E. Chocolate Avenue
Hershey PA, USA 17033
Tel: 717-533-8845
Fax: 717-533-8661
E-mail: cust@igi-global.com
Web site: http://www.igi-global.com

Library of Congress Cataloging-in-Publication Data

Names: Abdullah Al Mamun, 1977- author. | Mohammad Nurul Huda Mazumder, 1971- author. | Noor Raihani Zainol, 1984- author. | Muniady, Rajennd, author.
Title: Micro-entrepreneurship and micro-enterprise development in Malaysia : emerging research and opportunities / by Abdullah Al Mamun, Mohammad Nurul Huda Mazumder, Noor Raihani Zainol, and Rajennd Muniady.
Description: Hershey, PA : Business Science Reference, [2019] | Includes bibliographical references.
Identifiers: LCCN 2018054601| ISBN 9781522584735 (hardcover) | ISBN 9781522585152 (softcover) | ISBN 9781522584742 (ebook)
Subjects: LCSH: Small business--Malaysia. | Entrepreneurship--Malaysia. | Microfinance--Malaysia.
Classification: LCC HD2346.M3 A24 2019 | DDC 338/.0409595--dc23 LC record available at https://lccn.loc.gov/2018054601

This book is published in the IGI Global book series Advances in Business Strategy and Competitive Advantage (ABSCA) (ISSN: 2327-3429; eISSN: 2327-3437)

British Cataloguing in Publication Data
A Cataloguing in Publication record for this book is available from the British Library.

Advances in Business Strategy and Competitive Advantage (ABSCA) Book Series

ISSN:2327-3429
EISSN:2327-3437

Editor-in-Chief: Patricia Ordóñez de Pablos, Universidad de Oviedo, Spain

MISSION

Business entities are constantly seeking new ways through which to gain advantage over their competitors and strengthen their position within the business environment. With competition at an all-time high due to technological advancements allowing for competition on a global scale, firms continue to seek new ways through which to improve and strengthen their business processes, procedures, and profitability.

The **Advances in Business Strategy and Competitive Advantage (ABSCA) Book Series** is a timely series responding to the high demand for state-of-the-art research on how business strategies are created, implemented and re-designed to meet the demands of globalized competitive markets. With a focus on local and global challenges, business opportunities and the needs of society, the **ABSCA** encourages scientific discourse on doing business and managing information technologies for the creation of sustainable competitive advantage.

COVERAGE

- Joint Ventures
- International Business Strategy
- Business Models
- Adaptive Enterprise
- Foreign Investment Decision Process
- Competitive Strategy
- Balanced Scorecard
- Outsourcing
- Customer-Orientation Strategy
- Strategy Performance Management

IGI Global is currently accepting manuscripts for publication within this series. To submit a proposal for a volume in this series, please contact our Acquisition Editors at Acquisitions@igi-global.com or visit: http://www.igi-global.com/publish/.

The Advances in Business Strategy and Competitive Advantage (ABSCA) Book Series (ISSN 2327-3429) is published by IGI Global, 701 E. Chocolate Avenue, Hershey, PA 17033-1240, USA, www.igi-global.com. This series is composed of titles available for purchase individually; each title is edited to be contextually exclusive from any other title within the series. For pricing and ordering information please visit http://www.igi-global.com/book-series/advances-business-strategy-competitive-advantage/73672. Postmaster: Send all address changes to above address.

Titles in this Series

For a list of additional titles in this series, please visit:
http://www.igi-global.com/book-series/advances-business-strategy-competitive-advantage/73672

Analyzing the Relationship Between Innovation, Value Creation, and Entrepreneurship
Miguel-Ángel Galindo-Martín (University of Castilla-La Mancha, Spain) Maria-Teresa Mendez-Picazo (University Complutense of Madrid, Spain) and María-Soledad Castaño-Martínez (University of Castilla-La Mancha, Spain)
Business Science Reference • ©2020 • 374pp • H/C (ISBN: 9781799811695) • US $225.00

Handbook of Research on Increasing the Competitiveness of SMEs
Rafael Perez-Uribe (EAN University, Colombia) David Ocampo-Guzman (EAN University, Colombia) Carlos Salcedo-Perez (EAN University, Colombia) Lorena Piñeiro-Cortes (EAN University, Colombia) and Maria Del Pilar Ramirez-Salazar (EAN University, Colombia)
Business Science Reference • ©2020 • 550pp • H/C (ISBN: 9781522594253) • US $295.00

Leadership Styles, Innovation, and Social Entrepreneurship in the Era of Digitalization
Çağlar Doğru (Ufuk University, Turkey)
Business Science Reference • ©2020 • 449pp • H/C (ISBN: 9781799811084) • US $215.00

Business Reinvention for Ecosystem Value, Flexibility, and Empowerment Emerging Research and Opportunities
Soe-Tsyr Daphne Yuan (National Chengchi University, Taiwan)
Business Science Reference • ©2020 • 230pp • H/C (ISBN: 9781799815501) • US $155.00

Competitiveness, Organizational Management, and Governance in Family Firms
Cesar Camisón (University of Valenica, Spain) and Tomás González (University of Valencia, Spain)
Business Science Reference • ©2020 • 459pp • H/C (ISBN: 9781799816553) • US $225.00

Strategic Approaches for Conflict Resolution in Organizations Emerging Research and Opportunities
Siddhartha Bhattacharyya (RCC Institute of Information Technology, Kolkata, India)
Business Science Reference • ©2020 • 187pp • H/C (ISBN: 9781799817260) • US $195.00

For an entire list of titles in this series, please visit:
http://www.igi-global.com/book-series/advances-business-strategy-competitive-advantage/73672

IGI Global
DISSEMINATOR OF KNOWLEDGE

701 East Chocolate Avenue, Hershey, PA 17033, USA
Tel: 717-533-8845 x100 • Fax: 717-533-8661
E-Mail: cust@igi-global.com • www.igi-global.com

Table of Contents

Preface

This book mainly focuses on the key aspects of micro-entrepreneurial activities, and the effectiveness of supporting programs and policies on promoting micro-entrepreneurial activities in Malaysia. This book consists of six chapters, written by a team of academicians in this area of research. Basically, this book starts with the general socio-economic condition, followed by the relevant programs and policies that facilitate micro-entrepreneurial development in Malaysia. The subsequent chapters highlight the key issues of women micro-entrepreneurship, social capital and micro-entrepreneurship, entrepreneurial competencies, entrepreneurial knowledge and skills, entrepreneurial leadership, entrepreneurial motivations, entrepreneurial traits, women micro-entrepreneurs' quality of life and empowerment, and the future directions of micro-entrepreneurship development programs and policies in Malaysia.

Specifically, this book provides an in-depth understanding about the state of micro-entrepreneurial activities in Malaysia, followed by the critical review of current development programs and policies. Next, the main issues of promoting micro-entrepreneurial activities in Malaysia are also discussed.

Chapter 1 starts with the study context, started with the brief historical background including the political and demographic delays; followed by the economy and the changes of economic activities over the years; the poverty in Malaysia, including the history and measurements of poverty; and finally, an introduction to the Malaysian development policies and strategies. The next part of this chapter started with defining and understanding types and dimensions of poverty, followed by the origin of group based micro-credit programs focused on improving the socio-economic condition of the poor and low-income households. This chapter also presents the discussion regarding approaches of micro-credit, role of donors and investors, role of apex organizations, outreach of microcredit programs, impact of microcredit programs, and limitations of microcredit programs. Finally, this chapter presented the details of the programs and policies of the leading micro-credit organizations in Malaysia.

Chapter 2 presents a brief description regarding the types and characteristics of entrepreneurial activities in Malaysia. This chapter further illustrates the programs and policies initiated to promote entrepreneurial activities in Malaysia, followed by entrepreneurship and economic development in Malaysia, informal entrepreneurship in Malaysia, as well as characteristics of informal micro-entrepreneurship. Finally, this chapter provides future directions for micro-enterprises to propose initiatives that focus on developmental programs and policy-making in Malaysia. To introduce successful micro-credit programs, underlying organizations in emerging economies should be consistent in terms of cost-efficient operations without favoritism and political elements.

Entrepreneurship is a gateway to generate income so as to attain a more sustainable livelihood. Entrepreneurship has improved the aspect of employability among women in the Europe and Euroasia regions as they have begun to turn to self-employment and entrepreneurship as means of survival. Chapter 3 presents a brief description regarding women micro-entrepreneurs in Malaysia, and followed by the socio-economic effect of women micro-entrepreneurship upon the Malaysian economy. This chapter also depicts several characteristics of micro-enterprises owned and managed by women in Malaysia, and finally, the strength and shortcomings among women micro-entrepreneurs in Malaysia.

Social capital has been proven in many studies to correlate with economic development and increment in standards of living in a collective manner. Chapter 4 presents a brief description regarding social capital and micro-enterprises that narrowly focuses on the relationship between social capital theory and entrepreneurship. The chapter further portrays the varied dimensions of social capital, and followed by the status of social capital from the Malaysian perspective. Finally, the chapter ends with a discussion on the effect of social capital on competitive advantage, which has been presumed to be the most important aspect for micro-enterprises.

Entrepreneurial competency is the most influential contributing factor for rapid economic progression within many developed economies. Chapter 5 focuses on several selected entrepreneurial competencies and traits by investigating their influence on the performance and the sustainability of micro-enterprises owned and managed by low-income households. The key competencies and traits were selected after combing through a number of relevant theories and empirical studies that determined the effects of these traits and competencies on the performance and the sustainability of micro-enterprises.

The intervention of grassroots development initiatives embedded with microcredit programs have seen the emergence of the relationship between socio-economic development and women empowerment, thus suggesting a solid conceptual link to women's empowerment. Chapter 6 provides a discussion on the quality of life and women empowerment among low-income households in Malaysia. The focus is on how entrepreneurial development initiatives, rolled out by both the government and microcredit/developmental organizations, impact the quality of life and women empowerment of these households.

The purpose of this book is to disseminate the knowledge about micro-entrepreneurial activities among students, academicians, researchers, officials of development organizations, policy makers, and micro-entrepreneurs. This book can be helpful for business students (who are the potential micro-entrepreneurs or will be working in micro-enterprises in future) and academicians as the current academic curriculum does not emphasize on the practical aspects. For example, the advantages of the current development programs and policies, the effects of social capital, informal entrepreneurship, the influences of competencies and traits on micro-entrepreneurial activities performance. In fact, students are able to improve their knowledge and understanding about these aspects, which are expected to increase their intention to become entrepreneur. This book can benefit researchers as it provides a detailed discussion and review of empirical studies in different aspects of micro-entrepreneurial activities in Malaysia. Moreover, both governmental and non-governmental organizations are also able to foster entrepreneurial activities and improve the socio-economic condition of low-income households through various entrepreneurial activities. Remarkably, this book provides a complete guideline on new programs and policies that facilitate entrepreneurial activities in Malaysia.

Chapter 1
Entrepreneurial Development Initiatives

ABSTRACT

This chapter begins with a brief historical background including the political and demographic delays followed by the economy and the changes of economic activities over the years; the poverty in Malaysia, including the history and measurements of poverty; and finally, an introduction to the Malaysian development policies and strategies. The next part of this chapter defines and understanding types and dimensions of poverty, followed by the origin of group based micro-credit programs focused on improving the socio-economic condition of the poor and low-income households. This chapter also presents the discussion regarding approaches of micro-credit, role of donors and investors, role of apex organizations, outreach of microcredit programs, impact of microcredit programs, and limitations of microcredit programs. Finally, this chapter presents the details of the programs and policies of the leading micro-credit organizations in Malaysia.

STUDY CONTEXT: THE COUNTRY OF MALAYSIA

Malaysia is one of the emerging economies with its neighboring countries like Singapore, Thailand, Brunei, and Indonesia. As the geographical location of Malaysia is strategic with competitiveness, it attracts foreign companies to invest (PwC, 2017). According to the Department of Statistics Malaysia (2016), foreign direct investment (FDI) of Malaysia at the end of September

DOI: 10.4018/978-1-5225-8473-5.ch001

2017 valued RM558.7 billion. However, this modern concept of FDI did not exist previously and it caused many invaders to control Malaysia and its neighboring places. Early historians believed that during the early twenty first century, trading on the Strait of Malacca invigorated the economic and cultural linkages between China, South Asia, and the Middle East. At that time, Srivijaya was the most powerful kingdom ruling a large proportion of Peninsular Malaysia from the seventh to the fourteenth century. For Sabah and Sarawak, on the other hand, Brunei was the strongest political force until nineteenth century when the British colonization took place.

Malaysia was formed during the fifteenth century with the establishment of Malacca. At the end of the fourteenth century, Malacca, with its trading port and commercial and military power, became a commercial hub with cultural influences. In 1444, Muzaffar Shah advocated Malacca as a Muslim state. In the beginning of the sixteenth century, the European power was interested in the trading opportunity in Malacca. However, Portugal conquered Malacca in 1511. Throughout the sixteenth century, Portugal, Johor, and Aceh fought together. Finally, they agreed to establish a trade monopoly in the region. In 1641, the Dutch joined the battle and defeated the Portuguese and took control of this region (Library of Congress, 2016).

Later in 1785, the British entered this region and it was granted the island of Penang by the Sultan of Kedah. With the implementation of the free-trade policy, the island became the Peninsula's premier trade center. In 1819, the British East India Company and Tunku Hussain, a contender for the throne of Malacca, agreed that the British could settle in Singapore in exchange for formal recognition of Hussain as the Sultan of Malacca. Within a few years' time, Singapore became a central commercial hub because of its geographical location with support from free-trade policies (Library of Congress, 2016).

In 1826, British expanded their territory, joining the Peninsular territories of Malacca, Penang, Perai, Dindings (part of the state of Perak), and Singapore under a single administration, known as the "Straits Settlements". In 1870s, the British adopted a system of indirect rule over Malay states, which was the beginning of a centralized state. In 1896, the Malay rulers of three tin-producing states and Pangkor signed the Treaty of Federation to establish the Federated Malay States. Then, a different governing arrangement was made with other Malay states, which were more independent of British control than the Federated Malay States. In 1914, the Malay Peninsula was comprised of ten political entities, specifically the Straits Settlements, four Federated Malay States, and five Unfederated Malay States (Library of Congress, 2016).

Between the sixteenth and early nineteenth century, the development of Sabah and Sarawak was different from the Peninsula. The possible reason was the European involvement was relatively minimal. However, the situation changed in 1888 when the British agreed to provide protection for Sarawak, Brunei, and the British North Borneo Company (which administered the territory of Sabah) in exchange for control over their foreign policies. This situation contributed to the consolidation of Northern Borneo and its separation from the island's southern areas (Library of Congress, 2016).

At the end of nineteenth century, the Malaysian government stabled. Particularly, the tin and rubber plantation industries had flourished the economic in the country. Furthermore, Malay ethnicity began to emerge. Though Malays shared a common religion and language, their social identities were localized according to their own states. In the early 1900s, with the establishment of Malay cultural organizations and publications, Malays shared a common ethnicity, thereby forming a Malay nation (Library of Congress, 2016).

In 1941, Japanese forces attacked Singapore. On February 15, 1942, they occupied the Malay Peninsula and Singapore. During this period, racial tensions between Malays and Chinese increased. This was because Malays occupied most administrative positions while the Chinese were treated callously. In 1945, when the British resumed control over this region, the issue of racial tension influenced their political arrangements. Therefore, in 1946, the British proposed the Malayan Union plan, in which Singapore became a single colony while another colony was created from the separated Federated and Unfederated Malay States such as Penang and Malacca. Nevertheless, many Malays objected this plan, including the United Malays National Organization (UMNO), the first Malay political party formed in March 1946 (Library of Congress, 2016).

In 1948, the British decided to allow self-rule, but racial tensions were major obstacles. The British attempted to encourage national unity by having a dialogue between three ethnic groups: UMNO, the Malaysian Chinese Association (MCA), and the Malayan Indian Congress (MIC). The consensus of the dialogue was that the Malays would share political power with the non-Malays if the non-Malays were willing to improve the economic status of Malays. Based on this notion, a partnership known as "Alliance" was established from 1952 to 1955 among UMNO, MCA, and MIC whereby winning the municipal, local, and federal elections and thus emerged as an agent for unified Malayan interests. In October 1956, a Constitutional Commission produced a document that stated numerous compromises to satisfy all racial, religious, and linguistic concerns of Malaya's diverse population. In August 31, 1957, Malaya became an independent country (Library of Congress, 2016).

In 1959, Singapore requested its inclusion in the Federation of Malaya. They proposed an association to British that included Brunei, North Borneo (Sabah), and Sarawak. Nevertheless, pro-merger political parties won the elections in 1963. On September 16, 1963, the Federation of Malaysia came into existence. However, the Sultan of Brunei decided to remain independent. In August 1965, the officials from Singapore and the federal government of Malaysia agreed that Singapore to be separated from Malaysia. Ultimately, Singapore became independent on August 6, 1965 (Library of Congress, 2016).

After the separation of Singapore, the racial issues continued to simmer between Malays and Chinese that caused a racial riot in Kuala Lumpur. Unfortunately, this incident suffered from heavy casualties, primarily Chinese and Indians. The government declared a state of emergency and passed laws against questioning governing institutions and Malays' privileges. In 1972, UMNO established a partnership with the Pan-Malaysia Islamic Party (PAS) and renewed its ties with the MCA. This interracial coalition was named as the National Front (Barisan Nasional or BN), which won a large majority in the federal and state elections in 1974. From 1970s to 1980s, BN administration was successful in increasing the power of federal government over other state governments. As a result, aggressive measures were adopted to address economic inequalities among Malays (Library of Congress, 2016).

In 1981, Mahathir Mohamad became the Prime Minister. His primary attempts were to prevent official corruption and increase the power of elected officials. He ambitiously followed economic reforms, such as orienting the economy toward the production of export goods, promoting joint ventures to Asian firms, and privatizing many state industries (Library of Congress, 2016). Both UMNO and BN continued their election victories. In January 1999, Mahathir did a significant reshuffling, he appointed Abdullah Ahmad Badawi as his Deputy Prime Minister and Minister of Home Affairs. In November 1999, Mahathir advocated that he officially elected Abdullah as his successor. Mahathir retired in October 2003, and Abdullah became the next Prime Minister of Malaysia (Library of Congress, 2016).

Initially, Abdullah took substantial anticorruption efforts and terminated many government-funded projects. In the general election of 2004, the BN coalition won. Then, Abdullah was elected as the Party's President and the Prime Minister who continued growing the country's economic. In 2007, the opposition parties mounted BERSIH (a coalition comprising political parties and civil society groups) and started demanding for free and fairer elections. Finally, BERSIH's campaign paid off in parliamentary election in March 2008 after the BN won a simple majority of the seats in the national parliament. However, the BN failed to gain the two-thirds majority for the second time while the oppositions won five out of twelve state legislatures (Al Mamun, Malarvizhi, Hossain, and Tan, 2012).

On April 3, 2009, Dato' Sri Mohd Najib was appointed as the sixth Prime Minister of Malaysia. He launched a Government Transformation Programme to improve the quality and efficiency of public services and ensure that the government is transparent. The programme aimed to set Key Performance Indicators (KPI) to measure the performance of officials and agencies and the National Key Result Areas in order to define goals for specific components of public policy. Moreover, Dato' Sri Najib also introduced a New Economic Model to create a dynamic and supportive business environment. The objective of this model was to drive Malaysia towards a developed and high-income nation by 2020.

As proposed in the Tenth Malaysian Plan themed towards a high-income and advanced nation, Dato' Sri Najib stressed on the continuity of the Vision 2020, supported by the existing New Economic Model. Basically, the ten premises were:

1. Internally driven, externally aware
2. Leveraging on our diversity internationally
3. Transforming to a high-income nation through specialization
4. Unleashing productivity-led growth and innovation
5. Nurturing, attracting and retaining top talent
6. Ensuring equality of opportunities and safeguarding the vulnerable
7. Concentrated growth, inclusive development
8. Supporting effective and smart partnerships
9. Valuing our environmental endowments
10. Government as a competitive corporation

All premises were guided by the Five Strategic Thrust. In a nutshell, these thrusts were designed comprehensively to implement the ten aspirations. The five thrust were:

1. Designing government philosophy and approach to transform Malaysia using the National Key Results Area (NKRA) methodology
2. Creating a conducive environment for unleashing economic growth
3. Moving towards an inclusive socio-economic development

4. Developing and retaining a first-world talent base
5. Building an environment that enhances quality of life

For the first thrust, the Prime Minister introduced the philosophy of "One Malaysia, People First, Performance Now". To add, he launched the Government Transformation Program (GTP), Economic Transformation Program (ETP), and a five-year development plan which included the Eleventh Malaysian Plan. Particularly, the purposes of the NKRA were to reduce crime, fight corruption, improve student outcomes, raise the living standards of low-income households, and improve rural basic infrastructure and urban public transport.

In addition, the second thrust aimed at moving Malaysia towards a high-income economy by being competitive and specialized. Thus, the Prime Minister outlined 12 National Key Economic Areas (NKEAs) under the NKRA. These 12 key economic areas were:

1. Oil and gas
2. Palm oil and related products
3. Financial services
4. Wholesale and retail
5. Tourism
6. Information and communication technology
7. Education services
8. Electrical and electronic
9. Business services
10. Private healthcare
11. Agriculture
12. Greater Kuala Lumpur

To implement the NKEAs, Economic Transformation Unit (ETU) was established concurrently. Apart from the 12 key areas above, NKEAs focused also on high technology application platforms including high-end engineering, nanotechnology, and biotechnology. In May 2015, Dato Sri Najib launched the Eleventh Malaysian Plan, another transformation programme to realize the Vision 2020. This final plan looked at the development of people with the assistance of Malaysian National Development Strategy (MyNDS) to impact the economies positively in terms of Gross Domestic Product (GDP), job opportunity, cost of living, and family wellbeing. As a matter of fact, the ultimate outcome of this plan was to increase the national per capita income by USD15,000 in 2020. Specifically, the Eleventh Malaysian Plan emphasized on the macroeconomic outlook, aiming to achieve real GDP of 5%-6% per annum and create one million jobs. Similarly, the private sector investment was expected to grow more than 9.4% per annum, whereas the manufacturing and service sectors were expected to contribute over 17% to GDP. Furthermore, the inflation rate was estimated to be lower than 3%, while the full employment and government expenditure surplus were estimated to be lower than 2.6% of Gross National Income (GNI). In this particular plan, the Prime Minister introduced six strategic thrust and six game changers (Economic Planning Unit, 2004; Economic Planning Unit, 2010; Economic Planning Unit, 2015).

Six Strategic Thrusts:

1. Enhancing inclusiveness in an equitable society
2. Improving wellbeing for all
3. Accelerating human capital development for an advanced nation
4. Pursuing green growth for sustainability and resilience
5. Strengthening infrastructure to economic expansion
6. Re-engineering economic growth for greater prosperity

Six Game Changers:

1. Unlocking the potential of productivity
2. Uplifting B40 households in a middle-class society
3. Enabling industry-led technical and vocational education and training (TVET)
4. Embarking on green growth
5. Translating from innovation into wealth
6. Investing in competitive cities

Undeniably, these strategic thrust and game changers were achievable when they were supported by the transformation in the public service. In fact, the transformation should be productive, citizen-centric, and efficient in the service delivery. The public service was expected to have minimal bureaucracy, multi-skilled individuals, hierarchical and centralized, and more convenient services. Nonetheless, Dato Sri Najib realized that transformation was incomplete when the public service sector was not considered. Thus, five focus areas were identified. The first focus area was to enhance the service delivery by minimizing bureaucracy, expanding outreach, and increasing accountability. The second focus area was to lessen redundant roles and fraction among agencies, open exit doors for non-performers, and right sizing the public service. Then, the third focus area was to provide conducive working environment by implementing flexible work condition, upgrading public sector training, and empowering ministries and agencies. The next focus area was to enhance project management by working on the selection and allocation process for better results. To improve the project management among agencies, a team of professional personnel was crucial. The last focus area was to capitalize on local government for a better service delivery by incorporating local community and non-governmental organizations (NGOs), empowering local authorities, and increasing the outreach and service quality (Economic Planning Unit, 2004; Economic Planning Unit, 2010; Economic Planning Unit, 2015).

Demographic Characteristics

Malaysia is located in Southeast Asia. There are two distinct parts separated from each other by the South China Sea. The first part is the Peninsular Malaysia, which is bordered by Thailand to the north, the Strait of Malacca to the west, the Johor Strait to the south, and the South China Sea to the east. Another part is the northern portion of the Borneo, with the states of Sabah and Sarawak.

Size

The total land area of Malaysia is 329,758 square kilometers. Specifically, the land area in Peninsular Malaysia is 131,598 square kilometers, whereas the land area in Sabah and Sarawak is 198,160 square kilometers.

Climate

Peninsular Malaysia and East Malaysia, both north of the equator, are subject to have similar climates. Temperatures are uniform year-round with an annual average temperature of between 23° C and 34° C. From April to October, heavy rainfall is expected with annual southwest monsoons. In addition, the northeast monsoon is likely to occur from October to February. Also, humidity is high ranging from 80 percent to 90 percent.

Figure 1. Map of Malaysia

Natural Resources

The most economically significant natural resources in Malaysia include tin, bauxite, copper, gold, iron ore, natural gas, petroleum, and timber.

Environmental Factors

The frequent natural hazards in Malaysia are flash floods, landslides, and forest fires. Clearly, automobile discharge is the major source of air pollution in major cities. Oil and grease are the main issues of coastal and groundwater pollution.

Population

During the period from 1960 to 2016, the total population increased from 8 million to 31.7 million. The growth recorded 1.6 percent to 1.3 percent from 2011 to 2015. The dependency ratio is calculated by the number of children below 15 years old and the number of senior citizen above 65 years old to the number of individuals between 15 and 64 years old.

Education

The education system of Malaysia is divided into pre-school, primary education, secondary education, and tertiary education. Pre-school education is not mandatory for small kids as they are taken care by experienced and trained staffs in nursery or kindergarten. On contrary, children are compulsory to attend primary schools or government-funded schools. In actual fact, Bahasa Malaysia is the principal language of instruction, followed by English is the second language. Generally, Chinese and Tamil are used in primary education only.

In 2016, the number of pre-school enrollment increased by 6,356 as compared to 2015. Similarly, the number of primary school enrollment increased by 1,608 as compared to 2015. Apparently, the number of secondary school enrollment decreased by 22,125 as compared to 2015.

Health

Undeniably, the healthcare facilities in Malaysia are internationally recognized. Health indicators and infrastructure have improved significantly since independence. In particular, the high life expectancy at birth has also increased by over 10 years, which is driven by the rapid decline in infant, child, and maternal mortality. Moreover, common communicable diseases have been

Table 1. Population in Malaysia

	2012	2013	2014	2015	2016
Population ('000)	29,510	30,213	30,598	30,995	31,700
Growth Rate	1.5	2.4	1.3	1.3	1.5
Dependency Ratio	46.3	45.3	45.0	44.7	44

Source: Department of Statistics, Malaysia

Table 2. Education in Malaysia

	2015	2016
Pre-School Enrolment	527,030	533,386
Primary School Enrolment	2719044	2720652
Secondary School Enrolment	2181053	2158928

Source: Ministry of Education, Malaysia

under control. Conversely, the cases of non-communicable diseases (NCDs) increase due to the sluggish improvement in adult life expectancy.

In the last five years, there has been improvement in medical education system that decreases the doctor population in Malaysia. Gratefully, the health services at public hospitals are highly subsidized by the government. Since then, Malaysia has focused on "telehealth" and "telemedicine" services and built an "information technology-based" hospital to store patient data in a central database[1]. Recently, the Malaysian government has started promoting medical tourism through a national Entry Point Project and the Malaysia Healthcare Travel Council that is likely to provide growth opportunities in the healthcare industry of Malaysia.

Ethnic Groups

According to the Statistics Department of Malaysia (Department of Statistic Malaysia, 2017), 68.6 percent of the populations are Bumiputera, 23.4 percent are Chinese, 7 percent are Indian, and the remaining one percent is ethnic minorities. Since independence, the national identity has solidified with different ethnic categorizations.

Languages

Bahasa Melayu is the official language in Malaysia. Other spoken languages are English, Tamil, Telugu, Malayalam, Panjabi, Thai, Chinese (Cantonese, Mandarin, Hokkien, Hakka, and Hainanese). In Sabah and Sarawak, Kadazan and Iban are indigenous spoken languages, respectively.

Religion

Islam is the official religion in Malaysia and the freedom of religion is constitutionally guaranteed. In 2010, nearly 61.3 percent of the populations in Malaysia were Muslims, 19.8% were Buddhists, 9.2% were Christians, and 6.3% were Hindus. The remaining Malaysians believed in other religions.

MALAYSIAN ECONOMY: AN OVERVIEW

Malaysia, a middle-income country, has experienced rapid structural changes since independence. Before that, Malaysia was the world's largest producer for tin, rubber, and palm oil. With other raw materials, these three commodities thrived the country's economy. This is because the Malaysian government emulated other developed countries by emphasizing on manufacturing sector in the late 1960s and "Free Trade Zone Area" in the early 1970s. As a result, a trade-oriented economy with the focus of agriculture and mining commodities was turned into a more diversified export-oriented country. As such, export was the primary activity that marked a consistent GDP growth with more than 7% in conjunction with low inflation from the 1970s until 1990s.

This rapid economic growth continued until the Asian financial crisis took place in 1997, causing a massive external shock to the financial system in Malaysia. As a consequence, FDI declined at an alarming rate and the value of Malaysian Ringgit depreciated substantially from RM2.50 to USD1 to RM4.80 to USD$1 as the capital was withdrawn from Malaysia. Moreover, the composite index of Kuala Lumpur Stock Exchange declined nearly 400 points within several weeks. To minimize the effect of the consequential crisis, the Central Bank imposed capital controls and pegged the Malaysian Ringgit at RM3.80 to USD$1. Nonetheless, the financial sector suffered from substantial cutback as it was forced to merge. During the crisis, most ASIAN countries sought for financial assistance from the International Monetary Fund (IMF), except Malaysia. In this case, the demand for electronic goods in U.S increased the export of electronics components to help Malaysia recover from the crisis. The economic transformation also resulted in massive government spending and budget deficit in the following years after the crisis.

Today, Malaysia has a broad-based and diversified economy for the tenth consecutive year. The country's global trade exceeded RM1 trillion after an annual growth of 1.5% (2015: 1.0%) (Ministry of International Trade and Industry, 2016). The trade surplus stood at RM87.27 billion (2015: RM91.58 billion). Besides, the exports grew by 1.1% that recorded RM785.93 billion (2015: 1.6%, RM777.36 billion), while the imports recorded RM698.66 billion (2015: RM685.78 billion). According to the Ministry of International Trade and Industry (MITI), Malaysia was the 24th largest exporter and the 26th largest importer in the world. After independence, the Gross national Income (GNI) per capita income increased to RM41,567, while the poverty decreased from 0.6% in 2014 to 0.4% in 2016. In addition, the strong domestic economic

Table 3. Key economic indicators

	RM Million				
	Q3/16	**Q4/16**	**Q1/17**	**Q2/17**	**Q3/17**
GDP at 2010 prices	Q3/17	290,629	280,095	287,188	298,575
Agriculture	Q3/18	23,095	21,787	22,507	26,028
Mining and quarrying	Q3/19	25,456	25,096	24,405	23,756
Manufacturing	Q3/20	66,657	63,953	67,574	68,150
Electricity, gas and water	Q3/21	7,157	7,135	7,344	7,477
Construction	Q3/22	12,582	13,398	12,892	13,838
Wholesale and retail Trade, accommodation and restaurants	Q3/23	53,182	49,026	50,873	54,179
Transport, storage and communication	Q3/24	26,844	27,238	28,129	28,725
Finance, insurance, real estate and business Services	Q3/25	32,209	31,809	32,140	33,081
Other services	Q3/26	12,507	12,599	12,790	13,098
Government services	Q3/27	26925	23968	24484	26008

Source: Economic and Financial Data for Malaysia, Bank Negara Malaysia

fundamentals allowed a growth of 4.2% in 2016 and 5.6% in the first quarter of 2017. The growth was supported by robust private and public consumption in developing and emerging markets, leading to excessive external demand. To further grow, the government has driven Malaysia towards a developed nation by 2020 (Bank Negara Malaysia, 2017).

In order to realize the Vision 2020, the government made effort in increasing domestic demand. Initiatives were also taken to encourage private sector to boost the economic development. For foreign investment, the government reduced the corporate tax rates from 17% in 2007 to 26% in 2008. It also offered a 10-year tax exemption for venture capital companies that invested at least 50% of their investments in seed capital. In 2016, despite facing the global slowdown, Malaysia secured both FDIs and domestic direct investments (DDIs) successfully with a total of RM207.9 billion, indicating a growth of 11.3%. These investments were high quality projects and they underscored the sturdiness of the economy. Other than that, the inflow of FDIs provided the balance of 28.4% of the total private investments, employment, and technology transfer and business opportunities for small and medium enterprises (SMEs) as services providers or vendors. Thus, the FDI in the first quarter of 2017 recorded a rise of RM17 billion ringgit on account of higher earnings retained for reinvestment and the drawdown of intercompany loans (Bank Negara Malaysia, 2017).

Moreover, the government also made efforts in creating a dynamic service sector by targeting various sectors such as tourism, information and communication technology, logistic, Islamic finance, education, and healthcare (Economic Planning Unit, 2015). The service sector is the backbone of the national economy. Over the years, the service sector contributed to employment and investment opportunities. In 2015, the Services Sector Blueprint was designed to provide guidelines to the service sector in order to transform it to be more knowledge-intensive and innovation-led. This sector is projected to grow 6.8% per annum and provide 9.3 million jobs that will contribute 56.5% to the GDP by 2020. To illustrate, the growth rate of service sector to GDP (constant 2010 prices) was 6.6% in the third quarter of 2017, which was higher than previous quarter (1Q2017, 6.3%). Particularly, the performance of this sector was induced by wholesale and retail trade by posting 7.5%. Besides, data communication, computer services, and information services activities increased the information and communication sector to 8.8%. Nonetheless, the finance and insurance sector reduced from 5.1% to 4.2% in the preceding quarter due to the moderation in insurance sub-sector (Economic Planning Unit, 2004; Economic Planning Unit, 2010; Economic Planning Unit, 2015; Bank Negara Malaysia, 2017).

Apart from that, the manufacturing sector faced more challenges in 2016 due to the global economic slowdown, Ringgit depreciation, and volatility of oil prices. Despite all these challenges, many industries were able to experience positive growth with manufacturing ctompanies that strengthened performance. As there was a high demand for Malaysia's main exports from overseas, such as Electronics and Electrical products, food, and basic metal products, the manufacturing sector increased by 4.4% and contributed RM255 billion or 23% to the GDP growth in 2016. Then, there was an increase in the growth rate of GDP (constant 2010 prices) from 6% to 7% in the second quarter of 2017. Similarly, there was a growth of 8.7% in electrical, electronic, and optical products supported by higher production of semiconductors, integrated circui, and communication equipment. Furthermore, a growth of 5% was marked in petroleum, chemical, rubber, and plastic products as they were strengthened by a steady performance in refined petroleum product. Moreover, oils, fats, and food processing also showed a robust growth of 11.4% as compared to 10.4% in the preceding quarter, supported by refined palm oil products (Economic Planning Unit, 2004; Economic Planning Unit, 2010; Economic Planning Unit, 2015; Bank Negara Malaysia, 2017).

In a similar manner, the government took initiatives to transform agricultural sector into a commercial competitive sector. Currently, Malaysia is the main palm oil producer and exporter, further steps were taken to enhance value-added activities in this industry. The government also encouraged the private sector to invest in a large-scale commercial food production sector by establishing Permanent Food Production Park. In July 2009, an area of 4,339 ha was developed with 800 participants, yielding a production of 110,000 m.t worth RM113 million selling price (Yusoff, 2015). The agriculture sector also increased to 4.1% after a growth of 5.9% in the previous quarter as palm oil remained flexible after a double-digit growth of 10%. Meanwhile, livestock and other agriculture moderated to 4.5% and 1.5%, respectively. However, fishing rebounded to 0.3%, supported by aquaculture, which accelerated to 10.1% (Economic Planning Unit, 2004; Economic Planning Unit, 2010; Economic Planning Unit, 2015; Bank Negara Malaysia, 2017). Additionally, the growth in mining and quarrying sector reached RM23,756 million in the third quarter of 2017. The growth moderated on lower crude oil production, particularly in Sarawak and Peninsular Malaysia, as part of the global initiatives to reduce oil production. The growth rate of construction sector recorded a rise of 8.1% year-on-year in the third quarter of 2017, amounting RM34.5 billion. This development contributed to higher civil engineering activities in the petrochemical, power plant, and transportation segments (Economic Planning Unit, 2004; Economic Planning Unit, 2010; Economic Planning Unit, 2015; Bank Negara Malaysia, 2017).

In the first quarter of 2017, gross exports accelerated by 21.4% (4Q 2016: 2.8%). The sturdy growth in manufactured exports was attributable to high demand from all major trading partners, such as the U.S, China, and regional economies. Both semiconductors and E&E products were in high demand. Additionally, resource-based manufactured exports such as petroleum, chemicals, and chemical products were higher. On contrary, gross imports grew by 27.7% in the first quarter of 2017 (4Q 2016: 5%), especially for higher intermediate goods and imports of capital and transport equipment. Similarly, capital imports were driven by high-value items, including a floating structure, oil and gas vessels, and several aircrafts. Intermediate imports demonstrated higher growth with strong manufacturing export performance. As import growth outpaced export growth in the first quarter of 2017, the trade surplus was lower with a total of RM18.9 billion (4Q 2016: RM27.5 billion) (Economic Planning Unit, 2004; Economic Planning Unit, 2010; Economic Planning Unit, 2015; Bank Negara Malaysia, 2017).

In the first quarter of 2017, the current account surplus narrowed as a result of lower goods surplus with RM25.3 billion (4Q 2016: RM31.2 billion) and higher deficit in the services account. The goods surplus, as robust import growth outpaced export growth. The deficit in the services account recorded RM6.2 billion (4Q 2016: deficit of RM5.4 billion), which was attributable to higher payment for transportation services. Additionally, the net payment for construction services was higher as reflected in the pick-up in investments. The deficit in these categories was partly offset by a sustained net travel surplus of RM7.6 billion (4Q 2016: RM7.6 billion) (Economic Planning Unit, 2004; Economic Planning Unit, 2010; Economic Planning Unit, 2015; Bank Negara Malaysia, 2017).

The overall balance of payment position was favorable with a surplus for tenth consecutive years. In the third quarter 2017, the balance of payment marked a larger surplus of RM12.5 billion compared to RM9.6 billion in the previous quarter. The inflation is measured by annual percentage change in the consumer price index (CPI). In October 2017, CPI increased considerably because of higher price for transport (+12.1%), food and non-alcoholic beverages (+4.4%), restaurants and hotels (+2.7%), furnishings, household equipment and routine household maintenance (+2.6%), health (+2.4%), and housing, water, electricity, gas, and other fuels (+2.4%). Overall, CPI rose by 3.7 per cent from 115.7 to 120.0 in October 2017 in the corresponding month of the preceding year. On the other hand, the labour productivity rose 4.2% each year to RM82,456 after registering 4.0% (RM79,693) in the preceding. At the same time, the employment increased to 2.0% against 1.8% in the second quarter of 2017 (Economic Planning Unit, 2004; Economic Planning Unit, 2010; Economic Planning Unit, 2015; Bank Negara Malaysia, 2017).

POVERTY IN MALAYSIA

In Malaysia, poverty is conceptualized as an absolute and relative term. Both absolute poverty and hardcore poverty are measured by using quantitative money-metric measures in terms of the Poverty Line Income (PLI). A household is considered as poor when its gross monthly income falls below PLI. Further, relative poverty measures the inequality of the distribution among different ethnic groups in urban and rural areas. The official PLI has been calculated since 1976 based on food and other basic needs. The basic needs include education, recreation, transportation, communication, rental, fuel, power, clothing, footwear, and healthcare (Zin, 2007). The Institute of

Medical Research (IMR) developed the calculation of food per household based on the daily requirement of calories intake, which is 9,910 calories for household with five members. Conversely, the Department of Social Welfare measured the minimum requirement for clothing and footwear. All items were calculated based on the findings of Household Expenditure Survey, which measured the minimum level of expenditure among low-income households in Malaysia.

Basically, the government adjusts PLI to CPI. Because of the difference in the cost of living between Peninsular Malaysia and East Malaysia, the government measures PLI separately. Based on the PLI of 2007 (see Table 4), households in Peninsular Malaysia with gross monthly income below RM720 are considered as absolute poor households. In Sabah and Sarawak, the minimum income is RM960 and RM830, respectively. Normally, hardcore poverty is a condition in which average monthly household income is less than half of the PLI. In 2007, the government adjusted PLI for hardcore poor was RM430 in Peninsular Malaysia.

After independence, the poverty rate (proportion of households living below PLI) in Malaysia declined dramatically. Nearly half (49.3%) of the Malaysian households lived below the poverty line in 1970, subsequently it reduced from 16.5 percent in 1990 to 3.6 percent in 2007 in both rural and urban areas. The incidence of poverty in rural areas decreased from 14.9 percent to 13.5 percent in 2002 to 7.1 percent in 2007. Undeniably, poverty

Table 4. Poverty line income

Year	Peninsular Malaysia		Sabah		Sarawak	
	HH Income	Per-Capita	HH Income	Per-Capita	HH Income	Per-Capita
1987-1992	350	68	533	104	429	82
1993-1994	405	84	582	114	495	97
1995-1997	425	92	601	123	516	108
1998-2002	510	111	685	140	584	122
2003-2005	529	115	690	141	600	125
2006	661	150	888	171	765	166
2007	720		960		830	
2009-2015	460	760	630	1050	590	910

Note: HH – Household. Source: (Economic Planning Unit, 2004; Economic Planning Unit, 2010; Economic Planning Unit, 2015; Bank Negara Malaysia, 2017).

is high among agriculture, hunting and forestry workers in rural areas (Mid-term review of 9th Malaysian Plan, 2008).

Apparently, the decline in absolute poverty was the result of the government's efforts in implementing poverty eradication programmes including land improvement, development of agriculture-based and rural-based sectors, and other basic services and utilities (Economic Planning Unit, 2010).

The rapid economic development and government initiatives for hardcore poor significantly reduced the incidence of hardcore poverty in Malaysia. In 1995, the hardcore poverty in Malaysia was 2.1 percent, which declined to 0.7 percent in 2007. Unfortunately, the incidence of hardcore poverty was common in urban areas from 1999. In rural Malaysia, the rate declined from 2.6 percent in 2002 to 1.4 percent in 2007 (Mid-term review of the Ninth Malaysia Plan and Economic Report 2008/2009). In 2009, the overall poverty increased slightly to 3.8% (1.7% in urban; 8.4% in rural), then dropped drastically to 1.7 percent in 2012 (1.0 percent in urban; 3.4 percent in rural) and 0.6 percent (0.3 percent in urban; 1.6 percent in rural) in 2014. The percentage of poverty is higher in Sabah and Labuan, but an improvement was obvious as it decreased from 0.6% in 2014 to 0.4% in 2016. The poverty in the urban and rural areas also decreased to 0.2% and 1.0%, respectively. Generally, the incidence of poverty reduced with major improvement in Sabah from 4.0% in 2014 to 2.9% in 2016.

Table 5. Incidence of poverty in Malaysia

Year	'95	'97	'99	'02	'04	'07
Incidence of poverty (percent of population)						
Overall	8.7	6.1	8.5	6.0	5.7	3.6
Urban	3.6	2.1	3.3	2.3	2.5	2.0
Rural	14.9	10.9	14.8	13.5	11.9	7.1
Incidence of hardcore poverty (percent of population)						
Overall	2.1	1.4	1.9	1.0	1.2	0.7
Urban	0.9	0.4	0.5	0.3	0.4	0.3
Rural	3.6	2.5	3.6	2.6	2.9	1.4
Year	'09	'12	'14	'16		
Incidence of poverty (percent of population)						
Overall	3.8	1.7	0.6	0.4		
Urban	1.7	1.0	0.3	0.2		
Rural	8.4	3.4	1.6	1.0		

Source: (Economic Planning Unit, 2004; Economic Planning Unit, 2010; Economic Planning Unit, 2015; Bank Negara Malaysia, 2017).

To address the issue of hardcore poverty, a development programme was established to meet the specific needs among poor households, such as improving their ability to generate income and take advantage of employment opportunities, improving the quality of housing, providing food supplement, and supporting quality education. Specifically, this programme provides interest-free loan for hardcore poor members to purchase shares in unit trust scheme. Thus, the governmental, private sector, and NGO's, played a pivotal role in reducing the incidence of hardcore poverty in rural areas of Malaysia.

As stated in the ninth Malaysia Plan, the poverty reduction strategies aimed at eradicating poverty rate by 2020. Existing institutional mechanisms and social welfare programmes with access to credit facilities will enable the poor households to become involved in fruitful economic activities actively. After the implementation of the Tenth Malaysian Plan, the incidence of poverty was reduced to 3.8 percent in 2009 and 0.6 percent in 2014. Being said that, absolute income poverty group was eradicated substantially. Nevertheless, poverty existed in certain segments of society, rural-urban disparity, and income inequality. Particularly, poverty disparity was high among the minorities (0.9%) and Chinese (0.1%). The difference of poverty between urban and rural was noticeable where urban areas marked a 0.3% of the poverty incidence as compared to 1.6% in rural areas. In fact, Johor and Putrajaya had the lowest poverty incidence with zero incidences, while Sabah and Labuan recorded a poverty of 3.9%.

Besides the poverty disparity, the government was successful in eradicating absolute poverty. Next, it focused on relative poverty as outlined in the national development policy (NDP). Relative poverty is defined as earning an income of less than 40 percent of a country's median income. In fact, the Multidimensional Poverty Index (MPI) in the Eleventh Malaysian Plan is crucial for reducing relative poverty. Specifically, MPI measures the poverty in a broader perspective of income, education, living standard, and health. Even though relative poverty is perceived as a crude measure of poverty, it a simple measure to identify the number of households belongs to the low-income category.

MALAYSIA'S DEVELOPMENT PLANS

After independence, the government formulated a wide range of policies and plans to manage the economic development. The core policies were related to the philosophy of growth with equitable distribution, leading to poverty eradication and society restructure (Economic Planning Unit, 2004). The new economic policy (NEP) was introduced in 1970. It was operationalized and integrated as the outline perspective plan (1970-1990). Then, the plan was modified at a detailed level in the second Malaysia plan (1971- 1975). It continued to be the fundamental of the third Malaysian plan (1976-1980), fourth Malaysian plan (1981-1985), fifth Malaysian plan (1986-1990), sixth Malaysian plan (1991-1995), seventh Malaysian plan (1996-2000), eighth Malaysian plan (2001-2005), ninth Malaysian plan (2006-2010), tenth Malaysian Plan (2011-2015), and the eleventh Malaysian Plan (2016-2020). These economic plans deal with four major national challenges, referring to (1) creating a united nation among a diverse population of many races, religions and cultures (2) eradicating poverty (3) correcting the economic imbalance among the main racial groups, and (4) expanding the economy continuously and rapidly.

The NDP was introduced in 1991 and it focused on four major issues, specifically (1) the anti-poverty strategy towards hardcore poverty eradication and relative poverty reduction (2) an effective strategy to increase the involvement of the "Bumiputera" in the economy; (3) building a strong private sector by creating greater opportunities for growth, and (4) focusing on human resource development. The primary objective of proposing the shifts under two-pronged strategy of the NEP was to increase its effectiveness in poverty reduction. As a result, the poverty was reduced in 1990, further reduction was possible if the programme paid greater attention to the hardcore poor.

In 1991, Vision 2020 was introduced with nine strategic challenges that must be addressed. These challenges were (1) establishing a united Malaysian nation, (2) creating a psychologically liberated, secure, and developed Malaysian society, (3) fostering and developing a mature democratic society, (4) establishing a fully moral and ethical society, (5) establishing a mature, liberal and tolerant society, (6) establishing a scientific and progressive society (7) establishing a fully caring society and a caring culture, (8) ensuring an economically-just society, and (9) establishing a prosperous society (Government of Malaysia, 1991). The Vision 2020 was consistent with the components of NDP and NEP.

The National Economic Recovery Plan (NERP) was introduced in August 1998. The plan reviewed the policy after the 1997's financial crisis, identified the challenges to boost the economy, and minimized the impact of the crisis on poor people. The initial policy stabilized the economy through a tightening monetary policy by imposing fiscal restraint and introducing structural reforms in the financial sector. The plan identified six objectives through stabilizing the currency, restoring market stability, strengthening economic basics, continuing the equity, and stimulating affected sectors.

Although several poverty reduction strategies were proposed, the movements toward rapid economic development were critical. The economic growth generated high-pay employment opportunities and profitable micro and small-scale businesses opportunities to benefit the poor. In order to eradicate poverty, the government took a holistic approach by setting strategies and policies in the Tenth Malaysian Plan. It focused on enriching the bottom 40 households by improving the quality of life among rural households, enhancing economic participation of urban households, and raising household income through information and communication technology. This approach was successful in reducing Gini coefficient from 0.441 in 2009 to 0.401 in 2014. After the Eleventh Malaysian Plan was introduced, the Gini coefficient declined to 0.399 in 2016. In this particular plan, a policy was introduced, namely uplifting B40 households towards a middle-class society, which was expected to achieve zero poverty between 2015 and 2020, raise the income and wealth of B40 households, address the expensive cost of living, and enhance the delivery system of B40 households programme. Therefore, a novel MPI was developed to complement the existing PLI measurement.

STRATEGIES TO ERADICATE POVERTY

In 1970, NEP was the first clear and coordinated strategy introduced to reduce poverty. The poverty reduction strategy was an integral part of the NEP. Then, the NEP was replaced with NDP in 1991. Although some amendments were made, the fundamentals remained. In Vision 2020, it stressed on the importance of poverty reduction. Similarly, NERP was introduced in 1998 to address the problems of the poor as a result of financial crisis in 1997. The main objective of all public policies (NEP, NDP, Vision 2020, and NERP) was to eradicate poverty and minimize the income gap of different races within a given period of time. Thus, the government designed several strategies to increases the income among poor households.

Strategy 1: Concepts and Measurements

Initially, it is important to understand the definition and measurement of poverty. In Malaysia, absolute poverty is measured by the PLI. A household is considered poor when the gross monthly household income is below the PLI line. Absolute poverty is defined as a condition in which a household's gross monthly income is insufficient to purchase the minimum necessities required to survive. On contrary, hardcore poverty is defined as a condition in which a household's gross monthly income is less than half of the PLI. This definition was introduced in 1988 until 2006. In 2007, the government announced PLI specifically for hardcore poor, which is RM 430. Particularly, the relative poverty was linked to income disparity ratio of income groups, ethnic groups, and urban and rural population.

Strategy 2: Increasing Productivity and Diversifying Sources of Income

This strategy facilitated the poor to modernize their production methods and encourage them to take part in the mainstream of economic activities. As most poor households were involved in the agriculture sector, the government provided necessary support and opportunities for the poor, so they were involved in modern farming, non-farm/off-farm activity, or employment. In this regard, several innovative programmes were implemented.

1. Relocating the landless and other low-income poor with a new land development scheme to work in and eventually own the schemes.
2. Developing the existing agricultural land through rehabilitation and replantation of old commercial crops with new higher-yielding crops and better planting techniques.
3. Encouraging village industries and rural entrepreneurship to provide an additional source of non-agriculture income for poor farmers.
4. Enabling the farmers in double cropping, off-season cropping, inter-cropping, and mixed farming on the same land to increase their income.
5. Establishing farmers markets in urban areas where farmers can sell their products directly at cheaper prices.
6. Incorporating training and education programmes with agricultural and rural development projects to motivate participants to become productive farmers.
7. Providing industrial and vocational training as well as credit and other related supports to the rural people in order to enable them to get employed or start their own business.

Strategy 3: Targeting the Hardcore Poor

In NDP, the government introduced new policies to deal with hardcore poor. A special programme, "Development Programme for Hardcore Poor", was introduced in 1988. It profiled hardcore poor households to provide them additional opportunities to increase employability, income, better housing, food supplements, and educational assistance. Since 1992, Malaysia has been providing interest free loans for the Bumiputera (the major ethnic group among the hardcore poor) to purchase share in unit trust schemes.

Strategy 4: Improving the Quality of Life of the Poor

The government improved the quality of life among the poor through the provision of infrastructural and social services. For instance, piped water, electricity, roads, medical and health services, schools, and rural hostels.

Strategy 5: Provision of Welfare Assistance

This welfare assistance was designed for aged and disabled poor in the form of cash from the federal government and a case from Islamic Tithe Funds for Muslim poor.

Strategy 6: Maintaining Stable Prices

The government intervened the markets with a small number of food and other essential items. These interventions corrected market imperfections and unwarranted price increase to maintain a stable price for essential items that benefited the Malaysian consumers. The first intervention fixed a ceiling retail price for an item and provided subsidies to stabilize the price. Later, the government took action to eliminate supply blockage and facilitate larger imports of the item if necessary.

Strategy 7: Reducing and Eliminating Chargeable Income Rates for the Lower Income Group and the Poor

The income tax rates were reviewed several times to provide a bigger disposable income for those with the lowest income in Malaysia. In 1970, an individual with a chargeable income of RM 2,500 per year was subjected to a rate of six percent tax. By 2000, it will be expected to be zero percent.

Strategy 8: Involvement of Private Sector and Non-Government Organizations

The government also encouraged and assisted the private sectors and NGOs in reducing poverty. By working closely with one another, they can provide small business loans, industrial training, job opportunities, and educational support for children (Economic Planning Unit, 2004).

Technology for Micro Enterprise

According to case study conducted by Hairuddin found that micro enterprise in Malaysia faced challenge in adoption an information technology in business. This is due to the various cultural and perspectives in adoption IT specifically in *Batik* or handicraft industries. To date, Malaysian Handicraft Development Corporation plays a role to promote and market the batik abroad through national and international exhibitions (Haruddin, Noor, and Malik, 2012). Obviously, there are different views between micro batik entrepreneurs from east coast Malaysia and west coast. Micro entrepreneurs (Batik) in east coast are more traditional operating their business for daily living expenses. On the other hand, micro entrepreneurs in west coast prefer for creativity and take any initiative on new technology existence. Indeed, micro enterprise in Batik industry is one of the important contexts to adopt information technology (Nordin and Bakar, 2012). Yet, micro enterprises realize the challenge of batik industries to ensure continuity of traditional aesthetic attributes amongst the batik making business and imitation from the other competitors. In fact, most of micro enterprise being connected to the Internet, but they are still employee computer skills, application of web, databases and etc. Some of them are unfamiliar with Internet transaction due to privacy and security. In gaining competitive advantage, furniture industry as the best example for interesting case study in Malaysia. This case study demonstrates that Malaysia low-technology indigenous industries have moving forward in improving their quality and innovative design. Thus, furniture industries is able to expand business as one of the largest exporters of furniture in global. In addition, most of the innovative micro enterprise was mainly home grown in which 80% of them are fully own and manage by Malaysians (Rudie, 2013).

DEVELOPMENT INITIATIVES FOR POOR AND LOW-INCOME HOUSEHOLDS

The characteristic of poverty is multidimensional in terms of its causes, severity and solutions. Poverty is considered as a lack of food, shelter, representation, freedom, employment opportunities, and school accessibility. Basically, poverty prevents the poor from taking economic risk, seeing a doctor, and having clean water. In short, poverty is powerless as the poor can live less than a dollar a day. In general, material poverty is measured according to the consumption/income, and the solutions that eradicate poverty in order to improve the household's ability to earn. On the contrary, structural poverty refers to the chronic material poverty due to personal and/or social circumstances. It is associated with the average human resource development and the level of social bonding that facilitate mutual benefits (World Bank, 2010).

In most developing countries, commercial banks do not provide proper facilities to their poor clients. These banks impose strict rules and regulations to avoid poor or low-income clients that actually prevent them from improving their household income (McCarty, 2001; Pham and Lensink, 2007). The commercial banks design products and services that the poor cannot afford because the "*poor do not need financial services*". When dealing with the poor, the banks have to bear the high cost of small transactions, lack of traditional collateral, geographic isolation, and simple social prejudice. In Prahalad's (Prahalad, 2006) "*Fortune at the Bottom of the Pyramid*", he drew out some assumptions that were trailing behind the dominant logic of such commercial organizations. The assumptions include (a) the poor cannot utilize the products and services, and (b) the market of poor are not critical for a long-term growth and vitality. However, Prahalad (2006) disagreed with the first assumption through poverty penalty information. He mentioned that poor actually paid more money for the same service than the rich. Later, he destroyed the second assumption through a successful story about microcredit in his book "*Business success stories at the Bottom of the Pyramid*". Besides, in most developing countries, the microcredit policies failed to contribute to the self-sustained growth of the rural credit system and the poor. Particularly, some wrong assumptions were made, including (a) the rural poor did not have the capacity to save, (b) rural poor needed credit for a minimum rate of interest in relaxed terms, and (c) informal finance did not play a positive development role (Satish, 2001).

Normally, the poor and hardcore poor are provided with some financial services to improve their socio-economic status. These financial services are expected to improve their ability to start some small income-generating activities in order to move out of poverty (Abed, 2000). To encourage these poor households to invest and save, microcredit forced the governments, policy makers, and development organizations to re-evaluate their long-held assumptions about poor, expectations from the poor, and roles in the development process (Harris and Rajora, 2006). Basically, microcredit is a collection of banking practices that suit the needs of the poor and low-income earners by providing small loans and receiving small amount of saving deposits (Al-Mamun, Malarvizhi, Hossain, & Tan, 2012). This kind of service addresses the 'shortage of capital', which is usually faced by the poor. In fact, capital in terms savings or borrowings is important for all people with different income levels. It provides the time shifting services through 'borrow money now to solve current problem and pay the money back in future or save money now for an event in the future'. Specifically, it serves the poor and hardcore poor households and increases their productive capacity (Otero, 1999).

In 1976, Professor Muhammad Yunus started an action research. He designed a credit delivery system according to the needs and capabilities of the poor and hardcore poor households in rural areas in Bangladesh. At the beginning, Muhammad Yunus assumed that if they had access to credit, they were able to increase their profitability or diversify their economic activities that improved their household income. Then, he had lent a small amount of loan to these rural poor. Unfortunately, his first attempt was unsuccessful because of low repayment rate. Muhammad Yunus suspected the borrowers did not use the loan wisely. Perhaps, they were not trustworthy. Subsequently, he gave the second attempt by supervising the loans and selecting trustworthy clients. He successfully developed an effective model, known as 'Grameen Bank Model' that owened an iconic position in the world of microfinance (Hulme, 2008).

Grameen Bank provides credit to the poor women who represent their households. Most of its borrowers are illiterate with no experience in investing money in income-generating activities (Yunus, Moingeon, & Lehmann-Ortega, 2010). Since then, Grameen Bank designed a banking methodology according to the needs of financial services of the poor. It provides collateral free, group-based, doorstep financial services, and training and development in social bonding to enable the poor and hardcore poor households to utilize their skills for improving their socio-economic status (Yunus, Moingeon, &

Lehmann-Ortega, 2010). The features of Grameen Bank's credit delivery system includes:

1. **Focus on Hardcore Poor:** Grameen Bank's credit system designed effective selection criteria to reach its targeted poor households. This system provides financial services for the poor and hardcore poor households who are excluded from the formal financial sectors. The product and services are specifically designed to suit their socio-economic needs.
2. **Group-Based Design:** Potential members have to form their own group of five members with the same sex from the same neighborhood before they are allowed to participate. The purpose of having these criteria is to facilitate group harmony and participatory interaction.
3. **Joint Liability:** In group-based microcredit program, all clients have to share joint liability. For instance, when one of the members is unable to repay the loan, the remaining members will not receive loans until the full repayment of the defaulter's debt
4. **Small Weekly Repayment:** A small amount of installments are paid weekly. Loans are collected by the field workers at weekly center meeting. The centers are usually located near the client's residence.
5. **Special Loan Conditions:** A small amount of loan without collateral and legal action for self-selected income-generating activities.
6. **Social Development Agendas:** To raise social and political awareness, and empower women.
7. **Expansion of Loan Portfolio:** Besides giving credit for income-generating activities, Grameen Bank also designed other loans for housing, sanitary latrines, tube-wells, seasonal cultivation, and leasing equipment/machinery.

Approaches of Microcredit

The concept of microcredit is influenced by two schools; the Institutionalist School and the Welfarist School. First and for most, the Institutionalist School focuses on the development of a financially sustainable institution to serve the poor. The position of Institutionalist School is widely published by the World Bank, ACCION International, Consultative Group to Assist the Poor (CGAP), and Ohio State Universities Rural Finance Program (Dingue, 2005). However, the followers of the Institutionalist approach disagreed with the idea of dependency on subsidiaries because development agencies, non-governmental organizations (NGO), and the government of developing countries failed to alleviate poverty through subsidy credit. The reasons for this failure were high transactions cost, lack of household assets, institutions lacking saving mobilization, and high-level corruption. The failure of previous subsidized programs built the core arguments of Institutionalist thought. The arguments were (a) low-income households desire access to financial services, (b) only financially sustainable microcredit programs can provide significant impact on poverty alleviation, and (c) subsidized programs are inefficient to reach the poor and hardcore poor. According to the Institutionalists, the effect of poverty is attainable only if Micro Finance Organizations (MFOs) are financially self-sufficient and independent from any subsidized funding from donor or government. Examples of MFOs, which adopt Institutionalist approach, are Bank Rakyat Indonesia, Banco Solidario de Ecuador, and Uganda Microcredit Union.

Next, Welfarist approach focuses on the development of the poor households' socio-economic status. This approach provides financial services for the poor and hardcore poor households at a subsidized interest rate. MFOs that adopt this approach are heavily dependent on the government and donor subsidiaries. Although the long-term sustainability of MFOs is important, the households do not agree that avoiding donor subsidiaries is necessary to achieve that state. Examples of MFOs, which adopt Welfarist approach, are Grameen Bank Bangladesh, Amanah Ikhtiar Malaysia, FINCA in Latin America, and the majority of the MFOs in Africa and Asia.

To distinguish the differences of the aforesaid two approaches, Woller and Woodworth (2001) explained them in three different ways. The first difference is the service delivery methods by MFOs, particularly individual versus group based. Next, the second difference is the institutional structures, either with or without donor fund. The last difference is the population segment. Although microcredit is an instrument for both development and business purpose, the success of the microcredit is determined by the effectiveness of financial services on poverty alleviation (Dingue, 2005).

Objectives of Microfinance Organizations

Undoubtedly, the primary objective of employing Welfarist approach is to alleviate poverty. Most MFOs aim to improve the socio-economic status of the poor and hardcore poor households (Satish, 2001). In contrast, Institutionalist proponents argued that MFOs aim to achieve institutional financial sufficiency

(IFS), which provides sustainable financial services for the poor and hardcore poor households on a large scale (Dingue, 2005). Particularly, Khawari (2004) pointed out that the objectives of providing microcredit service as the "Triangle of Microfinance" are IFS, outreach, and impact.

To further discuss the objectives, financial sufficiency refers to a MFO's ability to break even the operational and capital cost. Then, outreach refers to how effective MFOs are able to provide financial services to the poor and the hardcore poor households. Particularly, the depth of outreach is the level of poverty outreach, whereas the breath of outreach is the number of poor participants in microcredit program. Due to the difficulties in measuring the depth of outreach in different countries, thus the breath is often used to indicate the outreach of microcredit programs. Lastly, impact is concerned about how microcredit programs affect the socio-economic conditions of the clients and household members.

To reiterate, the objective of adopting Institutionalist approach is to achieve financial sufficiency. Therefore, the followers have to lend a large amount of money. MFOs also have to increase loan size and breathe of outreach. When MFOs increase the minimum loan size, they create a barrier against the hardcore poor clients who do not have the capacity to use the entire loan, and then it reduces the depth of outreach. However, the only alternative is to increase the number of clients. When there is a positive response from existing clients, the number of poor and hardcore poor participants is expected to increase. To realize financial self-sufficiency, MFOs have to increase the number of clients, and design effective product and delivery methods that improve the socio-economic conditions of poor and hardcore poor households.

Apart from that, the main objective of establishing Welfarist MFOs is to improve the socio-economic effect of their products and services on a large number of poor and hardcore poor households. To make it possible, it is important for Welfarist MFOs to achieve financial sufficiency. Though the two approaches have different primary objectives, there are other two objectives MFOs have to achieve as stated in Khawari's (2006) 'Triangle of Microfinance'.

Role of Government

The government plays a vital role in building a sustainable financial system to alleviate poverty. Particularly, microfinance and development take place at an intersection between microfinance and the financial systems in a country

(Otero, 1999). It is accomplished when a MFO becomes a regulated institution. When MFOs become one of the aspects of formal financial system, they can get access to the capital market and capture some savings. Then, MFOs can increase their outreach (Otero, 1999). Besides, the government can also design some policies to promote healthy competition among all financial organizations and protect clients from being involved in fraudulent practices. Fundamentally, the objective of the regulations imposed by the government is to keep the fundamental features of the commercial financial market from the poor and MFOs. The regulations are expected to bring impact on the development and growth of MFOs that partially influence the poor and hardcore poor households (Gallardo, 2002). As suggested by Hubka and Zaidi (2005) the government can facilitate the development of sustainable MFOs through three specific practices.

1. **Eliminate Unfair Competition:** When the government owns financial institutions that provide financial services to the poor with a minimum or lower average interest rate, it actually creates unfair competition.
2. **Regulatory Reform:** For the MFOs, their regulatory reform should ensure that whether they are deposit-taking MFOs or non-deposit taking MFOs. MFOs that accept deposit must be regulated to protect the poor and hardcore poor clients from committing fraudulent practices. The key issues of regulatory reform include (1) permitting "credit-only" non-depository MFOs to lend freely without prudential supervision (2) abolishing financially repressive prudential regulations such as interest rate ceilings and high reserve requirements (3) adjusting prudential standards to reflect the specialized nature of microcredit such as high capital adequacy requirements, relaxation of unsecured lending limits and loan loss provisions, different loan documentation standards, waived restrictions on co-signers as borrowers, simplified reporting requirements, shareholder suitability, and diversification requirements on a case-by-case basis (4) revising bank branching rules that enable microcredit to reach remote areas (5) harmonizing taxation, and (6) allowing foreign equity participation in microcredit.
3. **Business Environments:** To improve the microcredit environment, the government should (1) focus on macroeconomic stability, (2) strengthen the banking system, (3) develop infrastructure in rural areas, (4) encourage the development of credit assessment mechanisms that improve credit information on borrowers and transparency of lenders, and (5) encourage

the establishment and streamlining of registration and titling systems for assets owned by poor rural and urban households.

Replication and Innovation

The replication of the successful MFO programs allows a quick start-up of new MFO through well-tested microcredit programs and delivery systems. When a new MFO is set up, the system is driven by the replication instead of a thorough analysis of needs and opportunities for the poor that exists in the communities where MFOs operate. Undeniably, the Grameen Bank is considered as one of the world's successful MFOs. The impact of the Grameen Bank's microcredit programs on borrowers and households encourages more donors, policymakers, NGOs and new MFOs to replicate the programs. The good practices of Grameen Bank's microcredit programs include peer selection, peer enforcement, credit discipline, timely repayment, repeat loans, and high repayment performance. However, the replication of the programs requires substantial adjustments to suit local conditions because the policy environments, legal frameworks, microcredit infrastructures, and other supporting conditions vary across all countries. In addition, it is important to adjust the innovation to suit the local conditions. Normally, replication may not threaten the innovation in better financial services.

Role of Donors and Investors

Both donors and investors play a vital role in growing MFOs. In particular, donors need to evaluate the financial system, whereas MFOs focus on the gaps that formal financial sectors and government agencies overlook. According to Helms (Helms, 2006), donors and investors have to promote innovation in products and services through research and development, strengthen the transparency of financial transactions, and build capacities for the existing MFOs.

Role of Apex Organizations

According to Vega (1998) and Levy (2002), an apex organization operates as wholesaler, second-tier organization, first-tier microfinance organization, or umbrella mechanism that builds the sustainable capacity for retailing MFOs. The operation of this organization is consistent with MFOs. It provides various services such as (a) wholesaling funds, (b) the distribution of the grants and subsidies on behalf of the donors and government, (c) screening and certification of MFOs, (d) operation of guarantee facilities, (e) guarantees for MFOs in raising funds in capital markets, (f) institution building support, and (g) prudential MFO regulation and supervision (Vega, 1998). Notably, the two central roles of apex organization are financial intermediation and market development (Vega, 1998). In intermediation role, it can intermediate funds from the government and donors. It offers institution-building support to new MFOs and existing financially unsustainable MFOs.

Widespread Product and Services Offered by MFOs

MFOs offer extensive range of financial services to the poor people. The services include group credit, individual credit, savings, micro-insurance, micro-leasing, micro-transfer, and micro-equity Micro-transfer involves remittance that is sent by migrants and expatriates back to their home countries (Levy, 2002), whereas micro equity refers to the provision of equity instead of credit to finance projects of the poor (Levy, 2002). However, these two concepts are still in their early stage of development. One of the most common services in microfinance revolution is lending. There are two types of lending: group lending and individual lending. Normally, group lending is widely practiced by the followers of the School of Welfarist. The borrowers are asked to form a group of three to seven members; each member is jointly liable for all loans. In other words, every member is held liable for his or her member's outstanding loan. In the Grameen model, payments are made immediately after the loan is given. It is due in a weekly basis and constant over the life of the loan. When a loan is repaid on time, the borrower is eligible for a larger loan as other group members have a good standing status. In the classic model, eight or more solidarity groups form a larger group, known as the "center". This large group gathers with a loan officer each week to perform all financial transactions. As indicated by Roodman and Qureshi (Roodman and Qureshi, 2006), "*given members' superior knowledge of the character and economic circumstances of friends and neighbors, they can do better than the lender at screening out risky borrowers prior to the loan decision and monitoring loan use after.*"

Individual lending, on the other hand, is practiced by the followers of the School of Institutionalist. It is built by the straight lending relationships with individual clients. The main difference between group lending and individual lending is that the individual lending offers smaller loans to the poor. It does not highly rely on traditional sources of marketable collateral and informal assessments of borrowers' backgrounds and business operations.

Basically, MFOs offer saving services to encourage the poor to save money for their future purpose such as marriage or funeral, survival of natural disaster, and business opportunity. The poor can save any amount they want at any time depending on the offer from MFOs. In fact, most MFOs prefer savings as the pre-requisite to approve loan.

Next, micro-insurance is the provision of insurance to low-income households. As mentioned by Ahuja and Jutting (2004), *the optimism that accompanies micro-insurance stems mainly from two different sources: the success of microcredit programs in improving the conditions of the poor in different parts of the world by enabling them through asset and/or skill formation to generate sustained income; and the growing recognition of the role that risk plays in the lives of the poor, and hence the need to increase the ability of the poor to cope with their various risks.* Poor people are vulnerable to risk, both in the form of natural calamities and regular illnesses and accidents[2]. With the aid of micro-insurance, the poor are able to receive life insurance, health insurance, disability insurance, livestock insurance, crop insurance, and unemployment insurance that lower their burden at the time of any occurrence. Grameen Bank provides micro-insurance for those who receive loans at least three times with some additional sources of income (Dowla, 1998).

Last but not least, financial leasing is a contractual arrangement between two parties, which allows one party to use an asset owned by the other in exchange for a specific periodic payment. There are three types of leasing: financial leasing, hire purchase, and operating lease. Micro leasing services are offered on an individual basis without prior list for leasing items.

Outreach of Microcredit Programs

Generally, outreach is divided into six aspects: cost, depth, breadth, length, scope, and worth. Actually, depth is central to the microcredit in poverty reduction. It is defined as the poverty level of the clients or the percentage of the poor. The role of microcredit in reaching the poorest becomes one of the most debated topics at present. The pith of the debate is to ensure that whether microcredit should target exclusively at the poorest or function as a complete financial system.

In addition, the breadth of outreach refers to the number of clients, to determine the sustainability of MFOs. The length of outreach is the time frame of the microcredit supplied, but it is difficult to measure. Thus, profit is a proxy that signals the ability to sustain the business over time. Moreover, the scope of outreach is the number of financial contracts supplied, depending on the market opportunities, available resources, management, and legal since credit is not the only microcredit service to clients. Next, worth refers to how microcredit services are valuable to clients. In particular, cost measures the value of these services according to price and transaction costs. Data about the depth and breadth of outreach are presented in Table 6.

According to the Microcredit Summit Campaign Report (2015), 3,133 microcredit institutions reported a total of 113,161,390 clients in 2005, with 81,949,036 were the poorest (half of them lived below their country's poverty line or below US$1 a day) when they received their first loan. Of these poorest clients, 68,993,017 (84.1 percent) were women. In 2006, 847 institutions submitted an Institutional Action Plan, accounting for 88 percent of the poorest clients being reported. Assuming five persons per family, the 81.9 million poorest clients reached by the end of 2005 affected some 410 million family members.

According to the Microcredit Summit Campaign Report (2015), a total of both microfinance borrowers and poorest borrowers grew between 2002 and 2007 at a compound annual growth rate of 14%. In the recent years (2009-2013), the total number of clients continued to grow at 2% per year, but the number of poorest clients declined at a rate of 2% per year. In 2013, there was an increase of 7.4 million borrowers as compared to 2012. The total number of poorest clients with outstanding loans continued to decline for the third consecutive year from 115.7 million in 2012 to 114.3 million in 2013. The total number of women clients with outstanding loans increased from 150.9 million in 2012 to 157.7 million in 2013. Concurrently, the total number of poorest women with outstanding loans decreased from 96.4 million in 2012 to 94.4 million in 2013.

3. Impact of Microcredit Programs

Microcredit programs create an extensive trust and expectation from academicians, policymakers, governmental and non-governmental development organizations, donors, and investors. Essentially, MFOs design products and services that meet the requirements of half of the world's poor

Table 6. Depth and breadth of outreach, 1997 to 2005

Year	Number of Institutions Reported	Total Number of Clients Reached (, 000)	Number of Poorest Client Reported (, 000)	% of Poorest (> USD 1)
1997	618	13,478	7,600	56.39%
1998	915	20,939	12,221	58.36%
1999	1,065	23,555	13,779	58.50%
2000	1,567	30,681	19,327	62.99%
2001	2,186	54,932	26,878	48.93%
2002	2,571	67,606	41,594	61.52%
2003	2,931	80,868	54,785	67.75%
2004	3,164	92,270	66,614	72.19%
2005	3,133	113,261	81,949	72.35%

Source: The Microcredit Summit Campaign Report [36]

Figure 2. Growth of total and total poorest borrowers (1997-2013)
Source: The Microcredit Summit Campaign Report

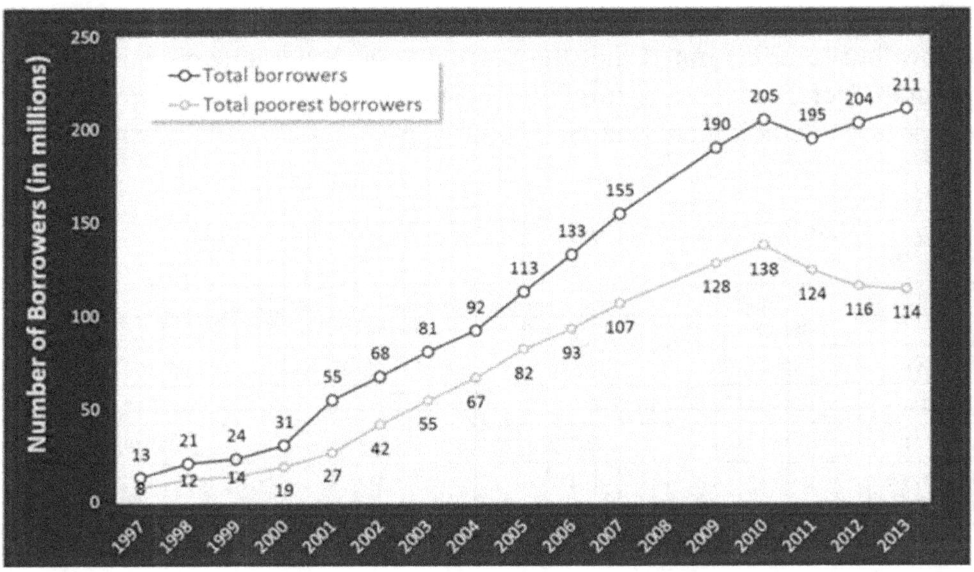

population (Abed, 2000). Microcredit is expected to reduce the poverty rate among clients and empower women clients. It is found to positively influence the socio-economic conditions of the borrowers in terms of household and microenterprise (Abed, 2000).

Mahabub Hossain conducted the first comprehensive impact study, entitled 'Credit for the Alleviation of Rural Poverty: The Grameen Bank in Bangladesh'. Hossain (1988) compared the Grameen's clients with other eligible non-clients. The findings revealed that Grameen's clients spent 8 percent higher on food intake than non-clients. He also highlighted the positive effect of capital accumulation. This increased the working capital invested in microenterprise owned by clients and their households. Clients who participated the program for more than three years, their fixed asset investment was 2.5 times higher than those who joined during the data collection. He also indicated a positive effect of Grameen's microcredit program on employment, about one third of the members started self-employed income-generating activities.

In addition, Sutoro (1990) measured the impact of Bank Rakyat Indonesia's microcredit program. The findings showed that clients who owned productive equipment increased by 26 percent, whereas those who owned business vehicle increased by 16 percent. Sebstad and Walsh (1991) conducted a study on K-REP and ISP borrowers. They discovered a lower impact on employment and microenterprise fixed assets. At the same time, they found a positive impact on enterprise sales. Moreover, they also found an increase in household expenditure and mixed impact on household income. Similarly, Neill, Davalos, Kiiru, Manundu, and Sebstad, (1994) discovered a 22 percent increase in employment and household security. Besides, Khandker and Chowdhury (1995) noted that the participation in Grameen's microcredit program increased the self-employment among the poor clients. Meanwhile, the access to credit increased their rural wages.

Table 7. Number of Borrowers Reported Each Year, 2009 to 2013

Year	Total Borrowers	Total Women Borrowers	Number of Poorest Borrowers	Total Poorest Women
2009	190,135,080	140,117,727	128,220,051	104,694,115
2010	205,314,502	153,306,542	137,547,441	113,138,652
2011	195,014,970	146,770,213	124,293,727	102,749,543
2012	203,672,249	152,477,064	115,747,387	96,386,285
2013	211,119,547	157,695,359	114,311,586	94,388,701

Source: The Microcredit Summit Campaign Report [36]

Mosley and Hulme (1998) researched BancoSol's borrowers in Bolivia and indicated that the enterprise income of the respondents increased by 91 percent. His findings revealed 39 percent of the borrowers were employed and 26 percent of them used the loan for buying new sewing machines. Mosley and Hulme (1998) did another impact study on two regional banks borrowers in India. He found a positive impact on the clients' household income. After they participated in microcredit program, they did not depend much on livestock income and their household assets increased. Besides, Mustafa Ara, Banu, Kabir, Mohsin, Yusuf, and Jahan (1996) discovered an improvement in coping capacity of the clients, which increased with the number of months as client and the total credit they received from BRAC – Bangladesh Rural Advancement Committee, Bangladesh. They reported an increase in household expenditure from an average of BDT419 per week for members participating 1-11 months to BDT528 for members participating more than 48 months. Also, the total market value of household assets owned by the members participating 1-11 months increased from an average of BDT10959 to BDT23230.

Next, Hossain (1988) did a longitudinal study, entitled 'Poverty Alleviation and Empowerment: The Second Impact Assessment Study of BRAC's Rural Development Programme'. The market value of non-land assets owned by the borrowers was 380 percent higher than the members of the comparison group. Moreover, 48.8 percent of the borrowers moved out of poverty as compared to 31.4 percent of the comparison groups. Actually, 27 percent of the BRAC clients were hardcore poor as compared to 37.2 percent of comparison groups. These findings indicated that the BRAC's microcredit program was beneficial to clients, especially the length of membership.

Khandker and Pitt's (1998) evaluation of microcredit program, entitled 'The Impact of Group-Based Credit Programs on Poor Households in Bangladesh: Does the Gender of Participants Matter', which was widely cited by many scholars. The program had a positive influence on borrowers and their families. The findings showed that the household consumption increased by BDT18 for every BDT100 provided for women borrowers, but the rate for male borrowers was BDT11. The poverty rate and hardcore poverty rate declined by 15 percent and 25 percent, respectively, among the households participating in BRAC's microcredit program for three years.

Although the literature unraveled that access to microcredit reduced the poverty rate, the finding was indirect. Jonathan Morduch disagreed with the Khandker and Pitt's (1998) finding from 'Does Microfinance Really Help the Poor? New Evidence from Flagship Programs in Bangladesh'. He criticized their use of econometric model which measured the impact of microcredit. Morduch (1998) argued that the model was likely to increase the program placement bias. Therefore, Morduch (1998) used their data and employed a different method to correct the selectivity bias. Morduch (1998) revealed that the participation in microcredit program did not increase the consumption and income significantly. At the same time, it did not reduce the poverty level.

In 2005, Khandker's article (Khandker, 2005) entitled "Micro-finance and Poverty: Evidence Using Panel Data from Bangladesh", he used a simpler model without excessive controversial estimates. For each additional BDT100 borrowed by the female clients, the annual household expenditure increased by more than BDT20. Also, there was an increase of BDT11.3 in food expenditures and BDT9.2 in nonfood expenditures. The findings showed a better implication than the Khandker and Pitt's (1998) study. Moreover, Khandker (2003; 2005) noted that the diminishing returns over time to borrowing had a more considerable impact than earlier loans.

In Bangladesh, Latifee (2003) highlighted that the effect of Grameen's loan on unemployment reduction among microcredit clients and their households was remarkable. He mentioned that about 90 percent of the borrower had an improvement in their standard of living. In 2002, the poverty rate of the borrowers also declined significantly, with over 46 percent borrowers crossed the poverty line. In 2005, Dunn (2005) conducted an impact study on 'Local Initiative (Microfinance) Project II' clients in Bosnia and Herzegovina. The findings indicated that microcredit positively influenced the household income, employment, business investment, business registration, and post-war transition. She also contended that participation in microcredit program significantly reduced the poverty rate of the clients from 51 percent in 2002 to 46 percent in 2004.

In a similar context, Hussain and Nargis (2008) completed their research, entitled 'A Welfare Economic Analysis of the Impact of Microfinance in Bangladesh', they measured the impact of microcredit on MFO clients. They found out that household income increased across all income percentiles for regular, occasional and non-participant groups. The average annual household income increased at an annual compound rate of 3.88 percent from BDT48195 in 1998 to BDT60546 in 2004. To compare the percentiles of annual household income between 1998 and 2004, the growth was recorded across all income strata. Such modification in household income distribution caused an upward shift in the curve of annual household income percentiles. Moreover, an impact study by Hoque (2008) entitled "Does Micro-credit Program in Bangladesh Increase Household's Ability to Deal with Economic Hardships?" indicating that participation in microcredit program improved the households' ability to deal with economic crisis. Rahman, Rafiq, and Momen (2009) noted that age, education, and the number of gainfully employed members positively influenced the household income and asset. In India, Panda (2009) pointed out a significant increase in borrowers' household income (11.41 percent). The asset position was 9.75 percent higher than those non-participants. This particular study found that the savings increased by 42.53 percent. Meanwhile, an increase was also recorded in annual employment days among the clients.

LIMITATIONS OF MICROCREDIT

Despite the advantages of microcredit programs, MFOs fail to reach a significant number of hardcore poor households (Abed, 2000; Matin and Begum, 2002). The majority of the hardcore poor households have limited access to microcredit services, especially those in Bangladesh. For instance, in Bangladesh, Hulme and Mosley (1998) estimated that 20 percent of the total hardcore poor households did not have access to any microcredit services. Rahman (1998) also mentioned that 24.5 percent of the services by MFOs in Bangladesh reached hardcore poor households. These findings were consistent with several studies (Rahman and Razzaque, 2000; Datta, 2004). In Malaysia, non-poor borrowers were benefited from the microcredit programs significantly (Nawai and Bashir, 2010; Mokhtar, 2011). However, hardcore poor households who did not participate in microcredit program due to inflexible attendance in center meetings fixed weekly repayment system, and compulsory savings (Abed, 2000). They were not confident in using the loan to increase their household income (Abed, 2000). Most microfinance borrowers lacked the knowledge about managing business income. They failed to distinguish between business and personal consumption. Hence, they allocated a large portion of their income for personal consumption, but not for business usage (Mokhtar, 2011).

Many MFOs do not have the vision to reach the hardcore poor households. They are either excluded in the group formation process required to access microcredit services or drop out of the microcredit program at an early stage (Abed, 2000; Matin and Begum, 2002). Undeniably, loan default becomes the main factor of voluntary and involuntary dropouts (Datta, 2004). Hardcore poor who gave up the program as they had problems with their entrepreneurial capacity, physical inability and credit risk. Although only a few hardcore poor participated in the microcredit program, they were included accidentally rather than systematically (Datta, 2004). As mentioned by Hasan (2003), group-based conventional microcredit models are not applicable to reach the hardcore poor.

MICROCREDIT IN MALAYSIA

Since 1987, Malaysia has provided microfinance services to improve the socio-economic condition of the poor and low-income households. The government encourages the development of private sector and state-based programs to provide the poor and low-income households with small-scale financial services (Mokhtar and Ashhari, 2015). According to the Malaysian Muslim law (Sharia Law), microfinance institutions are not allowed to charge interest on loans that should be replaced with the administrative fees (Mokhtar and Ashhari, 2015). The below sections presents the details of the leading development organizations in terms of objectives, products and services, and level of outreach.

Tabung Ekonomi Kumpulan Usahawan National

Tabung Ekonomi Kumpulan Usahawan National (the Economic Fund for National Entrepreneurs Group), also known as TEKUN, is an agency under the Ministry of Entrepreneur Development and Cooperatives, Malaysia. TEKUN was founded after the resolution of the Penang Bumiputra Economic Convention in 1994. By adopting a simple, efficient and free-of-charge capital distribution system, the small Bumiputera entrepreneurs are able to get access to business financing. In 1995, Universiti Sains Malaysia (USM) implemented a pilot project of Venture Fund Economics Group, the Malaysian government expanded the project throughout the country to benefit those small Bumiputera entrepreneurs. To succeed this project, the National TEKUN Foundation, currently known as TEKUN was established on 9 November 1998 under the Ministry of Entrepreneur and Cooperative Development (MECD). The operation commenced on February 1, 1999.

Essentially, TEKUN provides financing services to the Bumiputera's to support their startup and development of small-scale economic activities. In 2008, TEKUN's programs and policies were revised to be transformed into a strategic entrepreneurial institution. The new direction and re-branding were expected to meet its objectives in line with the government's aspiration to establish the Bumiputera Commercial and Industrial Community (BCIC). In 2008, the Young Indian Entrepreneurs Development Scheme (SPUMI-Special Program) was introduced to the Indian community under the new policy, with the purpose of increasing the number of Indian entrepreneurs. TEKUN is an institution, under the purview of Ministry of Agriculture and Agro-Based Malaysia, providing business and income-generating opportunities, business capital financing, guidance and support services, and web entrepreneurs.

TEKUN Strategy – 2011

1. Ensuring that the funds are disbursed to the borrowers who own and manage businesses. They should be given a priority to adopt an effective method.
2. Enhancing and intensifying its efforts to collect debts effectively and aggressively.
3. Developing the integrity, efficiency, and productivity of the employees.
4. Ensuring that the TEKUN's businessmen are successful. They have a good relationship with the TEKUN's officers, followed by the establishment of TEKUN business community club.
5. Strengthening the delivery system, structure, and operating procedures of the National TEKUN with strong corporate governance.
6. Developing TEKUN funds and establishing the Economic Development Trust People One Malaysia.
7. Establishing strategic alliance between TEKUN and departments, agencies, NGOs, institutions, and corporations.

TEKUN's Entrepreneurial Development Center - Roles and objectives:

1. Providing information on the services provided for the development of entrepreneurs by the Ministry and agencies and fostering the entrepreneurial spirit and culture among Malaysians.
2. Providing information on business opportunities and income-generating activities that can be pursued by the natives.
3. Becoming a reference center, service, and support to both existing entrepreneurs and potential entrepreneurs.
4. Becoming a center to create networking with the existing entrepreneurs.
5. Becoming a center for various activities and events in the development of local entrepreneurs.

TEKUN's Products and Services

TEKUN offers six different types of financing schemes to micro-entrepreneurs. The value of the loans starts from RM100 to RM10,0000. These loans benefit both male and female small-medium scale entrepreneurs between 18 and 65 years old. The modes of loan repayment are weekly, monthly or semi-annually, depending on the business nature and TEKUN management's decision.

To apply the loan, the application form can be obtained from the local TEKUN Office, TEKUN National Entrepreneur Development Center, TEKUN Mobile, or TEKUN service counter. Completed form must be submitted to TEKUN office in the same parliamentary location as where the business premise is located, together with the applicant's passport sized photo, copies of identity card for both applicant and spouse, copies of valid license/permit/business registration, a photo of business premise, copy of bank statement, copy of utility bill of the business and proposal, quotation or purchasing requisitions if required. The application will be verified in the regional office and sent to Head Office for approval. The approval process takes 14 working days.

TEKUN's Outreach

TEKUN has operating offices throughout Malaysia. In September 2017, a total loan of RM4.9 billion were disbursed and benefited 395,753 borrowers in Peninsular Malaysia alone. There were 310,594 borrowers from Peninsular Malaysia, accounting for RM3.94 billion of loan disbursed. The TEKUN Nasional aimed to fund RM500,000 to 40,000 entrepreneurs in 2017. In August 2017, RM41.6 million were disbursed to 2,669 entrepreneurs. Besides, TEKUN also targeted women entrepreneurs, thus allocating RM50 million to provide them start-up loans to run business in collaboration with the professional associations and bodies.

AGROBANK

AGROBANK provides holistic financial services and banking facilities to cater to the needs of customers with savings activities, banking services, loan facilities, insurance coverage, and advisory services. It is a government-linked-company under the Minister of Finance Incorporated. The bank's

Table 8. Different types of TEKUN loan schemes

Loan Schemes	Details	Instalments	Amount (RM)
TEKUN Nasional Financial	Small loan Medium loan	Up to 5 years Up to 10 years	RM10000-RM50000 RM50000-RM100000
Teman TEKUN	1.Group concept (5 members regardless of their sex) 2. Age between 18-65 years old 3. Have a specific business location	Up to 5 years	Max RM50,000
Temanita TEKUN	1. Group concept (5 members regardless of their sex) 2. Age between 18-65 years old 3. Have a specific business location	Up to 5 years	Max RM50,000
Kontrak-I	Finance contracts and direct supplies obtained from the federal government, state government, government agencies, and statutory bodies.		RM1000-RM100000
Ar-Rahnu TEKUN	The client/entrepreneur pledge gold product or jewellery based on the types of gold accepted as collateral for the financing granted.	6 months	RM100-RM100000
Indian Community Entrepreneur Development Scheme (SPUMI)	1. Indian and Malay citizen. 2. Age between 18-60 years old 3. Have a specific business location	Up to 65 years	Above 20000

Source: TEKUN (https://www.tekun.gov.my/ms/)

financing of the agricultural sector is driven by a policy from the Ministry of Agriculture and Agro-based Industries.

AGROBANK is a continuity of the former Bank Pertanian Malaysia Berhad (Agricultural Bank of Malaysia) with 40 years' experience in agricultural banking. It has an excellent track record in producing successful entrepreneurs. The vision of AGROBANK is to become the leading bank which focused on the agricultural sector. Meanwhile, its mission is to provide financial services for agro-entrepreneurs, micro, small and medium-scale entrepreneurs, and other individuals according to the market demands and customer needs through prudent financial management.

Table 9. TEKUN's Outreach

	Total Borrower	Total Branches	Total Loan Disbursed
Kedah	42,108	16	479,485,832
Perak	28,616	23	335,148,700
Kelantan	34,329	14	429,517,000
Terengganu	35,029	9	439,080,200
Pahang	29,298	15	339,759,500
Selangor/KL	44,225	28	660,282,750
Negeri Sembilan	17,314	7	234,571,500
Melaka	11,830	7	175,315,700
Pulau Pinang	18,205	11	213,630,400
Perlis	6,855	3	80,476,600
Johor	42,785	26	555,349,400

Source: TEKUN (https://www.tekun.gov.my/ms/)

AGROBANK's Products and Services

AGROBANK has designed two uncollateralised financing programs: Modal Usahawan 1Malaysia (MUS1M-*i*) and Paddy-*i* (Tawarruq). To enjoy its microfinance service, applicants need to prepare some supporting documents such as a photocopy of identification card, proof of business operations (business registration, license and permit), payment slips, utility bills, and other relevant documents. Then, the application form and supporting documents are sent to the nearest AGROBANK branch. The application for microfinance has to be approved by the Head of Micro Business Section within six working days. The details of the products are given in Table 10.

AGROBANK's Outreach

According to the AGROBANK'S 2009 annual report, the total disbursement of Micro ESP-I financing in December 2009 was RM 212.46 million, with 11,619 borrowers. However, the total approval for Micro ESP-I funding was RM 255.93, with 13,375 borrowers. The total collection for Micro ESP-I was RM 6.99 million.

Table 10. AGROBANK loan schemes

Loan Schemes	Details	Eligibility	Instalments	Amount (RM)
MUSIM	Provision of credit facilities to micro-entrepreneurs to undertake agriculture and agro-based activities that involve production, processing, services, marketing, and consumer needs.	Malaysian citizen aged 21-60 years on the date of application.Micro-entrepreneur with more than one year experience.Possess approval Guarantor required No collateral required	Up to 60 months	Max RM50, 000.00. Financing limit up to 100% of the total cost and subject to credit evaluation.
Paddy-i	Finance working capital for rice planting activities in a paddy field, which is certified by the government agencies.	Malaysian farmers who registered with BERNAS or the government agencies. Age between 18 to 70 years on the expiry of the financing period. No legal obstacle No collateral required	Minimum: six (6) months Maximum: seasonal review, not exceeding five (5) years	Minimum: RM1,000 Maximum: RM50,000

Source: AGRO Bank (http://www.agrobank.com.my/home/corporate-info/about-agrobank/)

Lembaga Kemajuan Ikan Malaysia (LKIM)

Lembaga Kemajuan Ikan Malaysia (Malaysia Fisheries Development Board) started under the Act 49, Malaysia Fishers Development Board Act 1971. The vision of LKIM is to become a pioneer in the National Fishermen and Fisheries Industry Development. Meanwhile, the mission of LKIM is to create a developed, independent, and progressive fishermen community. Specifically, LKIM aims to increase production, ensure the national fish supply is sufficient, comply with standards, provide modern and integrated fishery infrastructure facilities, and create competent human resources. Besides, LKIM offers both financial and non-financial assistance to the fisherman. Apart from coordinating and processing the fisherman loan facilities and other financial activities, LKIM helps in designing, assisting, and implementing different programs for fishermen community and associations. It also helps the fishermen in monitoring subsidies, allowances, and insurance. Most importantly, LKIM plays a crucial role in eradicating poverty of fishermen by providing assistance to build houses.

LKIM LOANs

Fishermen's Fund Program is an interest free loan fund designed for fishermen to increase their income and productivity. The purpose of providing this fund is to buy and replace the unused boats, engines, nets, emergency loan, and working capital project marketing.

Fishermen Loan Scheme - LKIM offers five different schemes to the fishermen, but some of the schemes are interest free. All the loan schemes help the fishery sector to increase efficiency and eradicate poverty. The eligibility to apply for any of the loans is clear-cut. The applicant must be a member of Area Fishermen Association (PNK) with a valid vessel license. He or she must perform self-run fishing activities and sell sea products to PNK.

Payment Methods and Application

Eligible fishermen will receive their living allowance monthly through the bank accounts such as AGROBANK, CIMB, Malayan Banking Berhad, and National Savings Bank. The payment will be made through the Responsibility Center (RC) in the office of the State LKIM. The application form can be obtained from all the PNK and State LKIM offices. Once the form is completed, it can be submitted to the nearest PNK that is responsible for loan consideration and confirmation process. After that, those successful applications are passed to the Community Development and Fisherman Institution Secretariat (PMN) at the LKIM Headquarter for further process.

LKIM Outreach

LKIM located its 88 branches according to parliamentary division and serves both in east and west Malaysia. The total borrower of LKIM 2017 reached to 98,608 with a value of RM 78,497,775.14 loan being disbursed.

Amanah Ikhtiar Malaysia (AIM)

AIM was initiated by the Center of Policy Research, USM as an applied research in 1986. This project named "Projek Ikthiar", which replicated the microcredit model developed by Grameen Bank in Bangladesh. The project had a few changes in the procedures to fit the model into the Malaysian rural context. This particular project tested the effectiveness of group-based

Table 11. LKIM Non-financial assistances

Name	Functions	Tasks	Program
Fisherman Community Development Section	Designing and implementing fisherman development programs. Helping the poor fisherman to get modern equipment. Designing, implementing, assisting, and supporting the fisherman group program.	Planning, identifying, and monitoring the economic improvement programs of fisherman communities. Planning, implementing, and monitoring the fisherman entrepreneurship training courses. Monitoring and coordinating the GIATMARA-LKIM cooperation programs for special fisherman children. Coordinating programs involving the NGOs-LKIM.	Aktiviti Kumpulan Wanita Nelayan (KUNITA) Aktiviti Kumpulan Belia Nelayan (KUBENA) Aktiviti KOR Tani Tabung Bencana Alam Nelayan
Fisheries Institutional Development Section	Helping fishermen association in planning economic activities. Monitoring and regulating the economic projects that are in progress. Monitoring the monthly progress report and providing annual performance report for fishermen association. Improving the management of fishing association toward an efficiency administration. Planning and implementing training programs.	Assisting and mobilizing the fishermen association in the economic growth through business activities. Supervising the performance report of fishermen economic development projects. Assisting the fishermen development management in achieving an efficient administration through fishermen training programs. Planning and managing the projects, trainings, seminars, and workshops to fishermen.	Hari Nelayan Peringkat Negeri. Hari Nelayan Peringkat Kebangsaan. Konvensyen Hari Nelayan. Malaysia Agriculture, Horticulture and Agro tourism International (MAHA). Program Kepimpinan Nelayan.
Fisherman Help Section	Planning, implementing, and coordinating the implementation of subsidized to fishermen. Coordinating subsidized diesel requirement for fishing activities. Regulating subsidized diesel sales center. Managing, monitoring, and controlling the aid or incentives to target groups.	Implement fishermen subsistence allowances. Supervising the eligibility of fishery subsistence allowances every month. Supervising fisherman insurance registration. Supervising the payment of insurance compensation to fishermen.	The payment of fishery subsistence allowance in cash.
Fisheries Poverty Eradication Section	Planning, implementing, and coordinating the fishery-housing programs. Planning, implementing, and coordinating the Azam Tani Program.	Monitoring the movement of program expenses. Updating the participants of Azam Tani data.	Providing assistance for the construction of fisherman home. Grand aid under the Azam Tani program.

Source: LKIM (2017)

Table 12. LKIM loan schemes

Loan Schemes	Details	Eligibility	Loan Period	Amount (RM)
Sea Fishermen Loan Scheme (SNEP)	To finance activities in the fisheries sector to increase the efficiency of boats, equipment, and existing traditional fixtures towards innovative technology.	- Being a member of PNK - Owning a valid vessel license. - Performing self-run fishing activities - Selling sea products to PNK	6 Years	Min. RM1000 Max. RM25000
Deep Engine Fishermen Loan Scheme (SNED)	To finance activities in the fisheries sector, especially for deep engine according to zones: A, B, and C.	- Being a member of PNK - Owning a valid vessel license. - Performing self-run fishing activities - Selling sea products to PNK	6 Years	Min RM5000 Max. RM70,000
Commercial Fishermen Loan Scheme (SNEK)	To finance projects related to fishing, production, processing, and marketing such as the use of input materials or products.	- Being a member of PNK - Owning a valid vessel license. - Performing self-run fishing activities - Selling sea products to PNK		
Fishermen Housing Loan Scheme (SPEN)	To provide hire purchase scheme to finance house purchase for housing projects developed/financed by LKIM / KPLB/ State Government / Federal	- Being a member of PNK - Owning a valid vessel license. - Performing self-run fishing activities - Selling sea products to PNK		
Fishermen Development Institute Loan Scheme (SPIN)	To provide loan service for the fishermen association to finance economy projects related to fisheries, aquaculture, and processing activities.	- Being a member of PNK - Owning a valid vessel license. - Performing self-run fishing activities - Selling sea products to PNK	8 Years	Min RM 10000 Max. RM 3000000

Source: LKIM (2017)

Grameen's microcredit approach on poverty reduction in the rural areas of North West Selangor for two years. According to Gibson and Kasim (1994), the founder of 'Projek Ikthiar' intended to identify whether the Grameen Bank's approach caused a further substantial decline in hardcore poverty in rural Peninsular Malaysia that complemented the existing poverty reduction programs. This project provided benevolent loans to at least 300 very poor households and maintained a standard repayment rate of 90 percent. This is one of the characteristics of Grameen Bank's approach.

In June 1988, the project had 448 members. A study, with a sample of 178 clients, showed that the average monthly household income before the participation was RM173 or RM29 per capita per month, which was far below the poverty line income (household income per month RM200 and RM40 per capita). In 1988, an internal impact study was conducted on 100 old borrowers and 100 recent borrowers. The finding showed that about 70

Table 13. LKIM outreach

	Total Borrower	Total Branches	Total Loan Disbursed
Kedah	9,196	5	14,675,657.80
Perak	14,275	7	15,650,924.50
Kelantan	4,660	4	3,006,757.250
Terengganu	7,046	10	1,576,966.63
Pahang	2,865	4	5,445,411.21
Selangor/KL	5,100	5	3,947,160.90
N9/ Melaka	1,739	5	1,784,274.00
Johor	10,247	9	6,544,616.75

Source: LKIM (2017)

percent of the clients had their household income increased. The average increase of the female clients was higher (RM113 per month) than the male clients (RM63 per month). The repayment rate for the female clients was 95 percent, which was higher than the overall repayment rate. When 'Projek Ikthiar' was institutionalized, the female clients were prioritized to receive financial services for their households (Gibbons and Kasim, 1990).

As Projek Ikhtiar successfully reduced the poverty of at least 300 poor households and achieved the expected repayment rate of the women borrowers, it was a successful project. In 1987, this research was institutionalized as a registered private trust, named "Amanah Ikhtiar Malaysia". The establishment of AIM was sponsored by the regional agency of Asia and Pacific development Center (APDC), a government agency under Economic Developing Planning Unit (EPEN), USM, and Islamic Economic Development Foundation (YPEIM). This trust was expected to reduce rural poverty through the provision of small loans for income-generating purpose for poor women. AIM is a non-governmental organization which provides microcredit services to the poor and hardcore poor households in Malaysia, irrespective of their race, religion and political ideology (Gibbons and Kasim, 1990).

Client Selection Process

AIM designed a cost-effective way to select potential clients, who are households with a gross monthly household income below the PLI. Basically, these households are considered poor. Based on the PLI in 2007, households who earn gross monthly income below RM720 are considered absolute poor in Peninsular Malaysia. For Sabah and Sarawak, the absolute poor households are those who earn monthly household income of RM960 and RM830, respectively.

Group Formation

Before participating in AIM's microcredit program, potential clients have to form a group of five with the same gender. In addition, the members must live in the same neighborhood with similar socio-economic status. All members must be approved by AIM. Then, the members will be trained by AIM's officers, followed by a verbal certification test. A chairperson leads each group. Then, the chairperson selects a leader to administer the center. Ikhtiar Centers consist of two to ten groups. The income-generating projects are decided by the members based on their skills, knowledge and abilities. Although the loan is provided for each member, all members must agree to bear collective responsibility for every decision in terms of loan application approval and project implementation.

AIM's Microcredit Schemes

AIM provides a small amount of loans to the poor and hardcore poor households in order to improve their socio-economic status. The AIM's microcredit programs essentially provide credit without collateral or guarantor, with no legal action if the borrowers fail to settle their payments. The cost of applying the loan is nearly zero because all transactions are taken place at the center meetings near the client's house. The microcredit approach is a small repayment system that requires weekly payment through center meetings. The loan is provided for individual members before those borrowers form a group and agree to bear responsibility collectively.

As AIM's microcredit scheme aims to provide loans for income-generating activities, it provides loans to support non-economic activities as well. In 2017, the economic loans were i-Mesra, i-Srikandi, and i-Wibawa whereas the non-economic loans were i-Bistari and i-Sejahtera.

First and foremost, the IKHTIAR Mesra or I-Mesra loan is the first loan for newly joint clients who are involved in income generating activities. The first loan is given as a trial loan with lower than RM2,000. The repayment must not be more than 50 weeks. Clients who successfully repay the first loan

Table 14. Types of capital financing

Loan Schemes		Details	Amount (RM)
Economic (general loan)	I-Mesra I-Srikandi I- Wibawa	Continuously Continuously Continuously	RM1,000-RM10,000 RM12,000-RM20,000 RM5,000
Non-economic (social loan)	I-Bestari I-Sejahtera	Educational loan Multi-purpose loan	RM1,000-RM5,000 RM1,000-RM10,000
Recovery loan	I-Penyayang	To provide for those who fail their projects because of health problems or natural disasters	RM1,000-RM5,000
	Management Fees: Group Savings:	10% for all loan RM1-RM5 per week	

Source: AIM (http://aim.gov.my)

are entitled to get subsequent loans with an additional amount of RM1,000. The maximum amount is RM10,900.

In addition, the IKHTIAR Srikandi or I-Srikandi is similar to I-Mesra. However, the main difference is the amount I-Srikandi offers. This loan is provided for clients who show good progress in using their I-Mesra loan. In this scheme, the amount is doubled every time until it reaches the maximum limit of RM20,000. The clients cannot apply I-Mesra and I-Srikandi loans concurrently.

Next, IKHTIAR Wibawa or I-Wibawa loan is a short term loan provided to fulfil a business or project opportunity for a specific period of time. This loan is specifically provided for clients who have a good repayment record and a successful record in economic activities. The total amount of I-Wibawa loan is RM5,000. Clients can apply the loan for several times as long as the previous outstanding loan is fully settled. They can apply this loan together with both I-Mesra and I-Srikandi concurrently.

In 2003, AIM introduced I-Penyayang to revive the economic activities that are destroyed by natural disaster, theft, cheating, or mismanagement. The "Skim Pembiayaan Pendidikan" (Education Loan Scheme), known as I-Bistari, is provided for clients who need financial resources to support their children's education. The maximum amount of loan is RM1,000 while the maximum is RM5,000. Besides, the "Skim Pembiayaan Perumahan" (Housing Loan Scheme), also known as IKHTIAR Sejahtera or I-Sejahtera, is famous for its multiple purposes. This loan (up to RM 10,000) is provided for clients to repair houses, buy furniture and amenities, spend on investment, or save for Haj fund and/or Trust share.

Table 15. AIM's development programs and courses

Name	Tasks	Program	Objective program
Sahabat Teras	To provide entrepreneurship short-term courses involving around 120,000 people	Risk Management Awareness Workshop	To enhance the understanding and skill related to assessment. To enhance the understanding of design, implementation, and monitoring the risk management plan. To reveal workshop participants by definition of terminology and the key process in management risk.
Strengthening Entrepreneurship	To upgrade business activities	Retreat Program Opportunity to Generate Income	To ensure that all AIM staff and members understand the priority of AIM operation, identify issues, and make plans more effectively. To provide a platform to help poor and low-income people. To disclose the information regarding the implementation of the handicraft training programs.
Sahabat Berjaya	Keep going and be independent with target 20,000 members	Sales Carnival Program Explore Program	To brief the AIM members and introduce its role to the community.

Source: AIM (http://aim.gov.my)

Basically, AIM provides different workshops, short courses, and training programs to help people generating their income. Table 15 provides detailed information about different programs and their objectives.

Beside credit, AIM also encourages its clients to save through compulsory saving or group fund. The compulsory saving is between RM1 to RM15 for each member every week. Meanwhile, the group fund, known as 'Tabung Kumpulan (TK)', is established to foster saving habit among the poor and hardcore poor participants. This fund is used to provide short-term loan to the group members when they need.

AIM's Outreach

AIM provides its services, particularly for Sabah, Kelantan and Kedah being the poorest states in Malaysia. It has 93 branches in Peninsular Malaysia with a total borrowers of 279,841, amounting RM10,838,854,993 loan disbursed in 2017.

Yayasan Usaha Maju (YUM)

YUM is a Grameen Trust funded micro-finance partner organization in Malaysia. Since its inception in June 1995, YUM has reached more than 10,000 families through its poverty alleviation programs. In 1988, it started as a government agency, Projeck Usahamaju (PU), implemented by the Rural Development Corporation. Therefore, the State Government of Sabah decided to institutionalize PU to form YUM in 1995 because of its excellent performance of lifting its members out of poverty. At present, YUM has 23 branches, with one branch located in every district of Sabah.

YUM's Objectives

1. To reduce the incidence of poverty in Sabah through microcredit program to enable the poor to venture into profitable economic activities.
2. To increase the minimum income to RM1,000 per month within three years
3. To disburse loans amounting RM30 million per year
4. To ensure loan repayment rate of 98 percent per year
5. To recruit 1,000 new members per year
6. To provide training for 50 staffs per year.

Table 16. AIM's outreach

	Number of Borrowers	Number of Branches	Total Loan Disbursed
Kedah	53,458	17	3,15,189,170
Perak	38,730	12	1,861,151,980
Kelantan	49,356	15	3,580,721,468
Terengganu	32,198	9	2,108,819,155
Pahang	30,804	12	1,142,678,670
Selangor/KL	29,171	13	998,708,700
Melaka	20,312	7	599,284,450
Johor	25,812	8	547,490,570

Source: AIM (http://aim.gov.my)

YUM Loan Schemes

YUM offers three types of loan to its members. The first type is general loan. It is offered to YUM members as start-up capital or additional capital to finance existing activities. The second type is general Loan 2. It is extended to YUM members who are successful in crossing over the poverty line income. The third type is group fund loan. It is an additional loan package for YUM members for various purposes. Apart from these loan services, YUM offers compulsory saving (RM2 per week), group saving fund, and emergency fund.

Bank Rakyat

Bank Rakyat was established on 28 September 1954 under the Cooperative Ordinance 1948. In 2002, Bank Rakyat was transformed from a conventional bank to Syariah based banking system which further encouraged profit generation. It is an organization under the Malaysian Ministry of Domestic Trade, Cooperatives and Consumerism, fulfilling the mission of the ministry in consolidating the cooperative sector as a main pillar of the country's economic growth. The products and services ranging from consumer bank, commercial financing, saving, investment to financial plans to satisfy a wider customer base.

Bank Rakyat is the biggest Islamic Financial Institution in Malaysia with a total asset of RM92.29 billion. It recorded pre-tax and pre-zakat profit of RM2.01 billion for the financial year ending December 2015. Bank Rakyat operates 147 branches in Malaysia, 95 Ar-Rahnu X'Change, and 960 automated teller machines (ATM) and cash deposit machines (CDM).

Mikro-i MUsK and Micro Enterprise Fund (MEF)

Basically, both Mikro-i MUsK and MEF finance schemes provide funding for hawkers and micro enterprises to expand their business. Particularly, it provides working capital and capital expenditure for micro enterprises without collateral and guarantor. Under this scheme, the financing amount is between RM1,000 to RM50,000 with a financing rate of 8.25% to 12.56% per annum. This plan is designed for businesses related to agriculture, services, manufacturing, retailing, and trade. The finance is transferred directly to the members of cooperative/hawkers and Petty Traders Association. The repayment method is done through savings account deduction or ATM. The financing period should be more than five years that requires approval from the Central Bank of Malaysia.

Requirement

1. Malaysian citizen
2. Member of cooperative/hawkers and Petty Traders Association
3. Aged between 18 and not more than 65 years old at the end of financing
4. Place of residence is within the business vicinity
5. Being a self-help group member with a good repayment record (arrears are not more than 4 weeks).

Mikro-I ME2

This plan offers finance to micro enterprises as working capital in purchase/ payment for service or stocks related to the nature of the business. It acts as capital expenditure in buying fixed assets for the enterprise. The maximum finance is up to RM50,000 with a financing period between three months to a maximum of five years. The financing margin is up to 90% of the working capital and/or capital expenditure. In this plan, a guarantor is required except for private limited companies, and collateral is not necessary. The financing rate is fixed at 5% per annum.

Requirements

1. Malaysian citizen
2. Aged between 18 and less than 65 years old at the end of financing
3. Involved in micro enterprise on a full-time basis.
4. Having business license/permit/business registration.
5. Business types:
6. Sole proprietorship
7. Limited
8. Private limited
9. Partnership
10. Eligible business sectors:
    a. Manufacturing and manufacturing-related services
    b. Service (except insurance and finance)
    c. Agriculture (agro-based products)

11. The business does not contradict any Syariah Laws.
12. The business has operated for more than six months.
13. Approved by SME Corp to apply Bank Rakyat's finance.
14. Having a Bank Rakyat's saving account.
15. Having a good credit record and is not blacklisted.

Bank Simpanan Nasional (BSN)

BSN is a service that started in Selangor and Perak in the late 19th century. This bank became a saving bank network under the Malaysian Postal Services Department or Post Office Savings Bank. In 1974, this network served more than 2.5 million depositors with an accumulation of assets worth RM537 million. BSN was officially structured on 1 December 1974 and launched on 5 December 1974. Then, the management power was transferred from the Postal Services Department to the Board of Directors. Initially, postal department acted as agent, where BSN operated through 526 post offices and 135 postal mobile units. The management had a mission to build lifelong and meaningful relationships with their customers by providing savings and investment opportunities, inculcating savings habits, and supporting the nation's economic development through the bank's funds investment. After experiencing continuous growth, BSN was listed in the Malaysian Book of Records for having the largest network of banking agents.

BSN offers two types of micro finance, specifically conventional and Islamic. There are three schemes in conventional finance: BSN Micro (TemaNiaga), BSN Micro (TemanMesra), and BSN Microplus. In Islamic finance, there are BSN Micro-I (TemaNiaga-I Murabahah) and BSN Micro-I (TemaNiaga-I Tawarruq), based on the Murabahah concept. All these schemes were introduced in 2007 to provide financial facilities to micro-enterprises and self-employed individuals with the most convenient manner. The aim of BSN's micro finance is to upgrade micro-enterprises to small and medium-sized enterprises (SMEs).

BSN Micro (TemaNiaga), BSN Micro (TemanMesra), BSN Micro-I (TemaNiaga-I Murabahah & BSN Micro-I (TemaNiaga-I Tawarruq)

Above micro finance schemes provide loan amounting RM5,000 to RM50,000 for one to five years, primarily for micro-enterprises specializing in manufacturing and retail sectors. These schemes come with a 6.83% interest rate.

Eligibility

1. Malaysian citizens aged 21-60 years old.
2. Micro-enterprise or self-employed individuals.
3. Having a valid business license/registration
4. Running a business for at least 2 years.
5. Without guarantor or with guarantor earning at least RM2, 000 per month.
6. Guarantor should be a business partner/director/shareholder (if applicable)

BSN Microplus

BSN Microplus is a loan scheme which assists micro and small business entrepreneurs to grow their businesses in retail, manufacturing, and services. Loan amounting from RM50,000 to RM250,000 for between one to seven years.

Eligibility

1. Applicant meets the definition of micro and SME by the National SME Development Council.
2. Satisfactory financial track record(s) with BSN and/or any other financial institution.
3. Business has been operating in the same line of activity/industry for at least 3 years.

Table 17. Required documents for BSN micro finance

For Individual Applicants	For Guarantor
2 copies of NRIC (front and back).	2 copies of NRIC (front and back).
A copy of business registration or business license.	Original and copy of pay slip (for past 3 months).
Bank statements for the past 6 months (if applicable).	A copy of income tax statement (if applicable).
A copy of account passbook including a BSN account (if applicable).	A copy of EPF statement (if applicable).
Other documents related to the business (e.g. utility bills, business premise's tenancy agreement	Confirmation letter from the employer (if applicable).
Sales records for the past 6 months (if applicable)	

Source: BSN (www.mybsn.com.my)

4. Being an existing BSN's micro finance customer.
5. The majority of the company's shareholders or the business proprietors are Malaysian.
6. Possessing a valid registration certification and license from the Companies Commission of Malaysia (CCM) or local government authorities/bodies.

Required Documents

1. Copy of identity card or passport of Director(s)/Guarantor(s)/Proprietor(s), whichever is applicable
2. Copy of business registration certificates/licenses (CCM, Form A/B, Form 24 & 49 and M&A or any similar forms under the Companies Act 2016)
3. Audited financial statement for the last two (2) financial years and the latest management account financial statement.
4. Company's bank statement for the last 6 months.
5. Company's profile
6. List of existing credit facilities and financing arrangements.
7. List of major suppliers/buyers and list of creditors/debtors.
8. Particulars of existing charges (if any). For property charges, submit valuation report and copy of the title.
9. Any other information and documents required by the Bank

The application process for both conventional and Islamic micro finance is same. Completed form and documents need to be certified by a bank or the surety's employer, and then submitted to a BSN's micro finance center. Verification and approval takes six working days from the date of submission. Unsuccessful applicants can appeal, which requires two working days to process.

IMPACT MICROCREDIT IN MALAYSIA

The first impact study was conducted by the founder of AIM, Sukor Kasim and Gibbons in 1988 and published in 1990 (Gibbons and Kasim, 1990). This study determined whether the replication of the Grameen Bank's microcredit model was effective in Malaysia. This study also measured the differential impact of access to microcredit among both male and female clients. Looking at both first and third time borrowers, the role of access to credit on household income was examined. A total of 178 members were chosen in the pilot branch in the north-west Selangor, Malaysia.

This first impact study discovered a significant increase in client's monthly household income from an average of RM142 per month before the program participation to RM220. This showed a 55-percent increase in their monthly household income. Similar to Grameen bank, Gibbons and Kasim's study showed that 84 percent of the female clients had an increase in their monthly household income of an average of RM136. The overall average increase in income was RM113. In contrast, only 65 percent of the male borrowers had an increase in their household income of an average RM65. The overall repayment rate was 78 percent, which was lower than 97 percent of repayment rate achieved by the Grameen Bank. It was also noted that the target repayment rate set by Project Ikhtiar was 90 percent. However, the repayment rate was 95 percent for the women borrowers. The overall average income for male borrowers was RM63, nearly half of their female counterparts (Gibbons and Kasim, 1990).

Apart from the first impact study, the second internal impact study (1990) was conducted by AIM's research and development unit in July 1990. A sample of 200 households was selected comprising 100 first time borrower, 50 active borrowers from the first study, and 50 non-participants. The second impact study covered three branches located in the northern Seberang Perai, southern Seberang Perai, and north-west Selangor. This study showed an improvement in the household's social-economic status. To further illustrate, around 98 percent of the households had an increase in their household income as compared to 70 percent in the first study. The pilot branch recorded an 88-percent increase in household income compared to a 56-percent of increase in the previous study. The overall increase was 77 percent compared to 45 percent in the first study, with an average increase of RM4668 per year or RM391 per month (see Table 10). The per capita monthly income increased from RM40 to RM73. Moreover, the average household size also declined while the average number of working members per household increased from 1.94 to 2.61. In conclusion, the second study showed that the access to credit further increased the household income, which was consistent with the first study.

In mid-1990, the Malaysian government initiated an impact assessment study of AIM's microcredit schemes, carried out by a team of Social Science and Economic Research Unit (SERU) (1990), Prime Minister Department. The objectives of this impact study were (1) to evaluate the AIM's credit delivery mechanism to their target clients, (2) to evaluate the AIM's achievements in poverty reduction and determine the improvement in quality of life while seeking out positive self-development traits among participants, and (3) to evaluate the cost effectiveness of the AIM's programs on poverty reduction.

In August 1990, AIM had 20 branches in six states with 2083 members. SERU impact study selected samples from three branches in an earlier study with additional two branches in Kedah. A total of 396 active clients who completed their first loan were selected. To evaluate the targeting procedure, SERU (1990) checked both the housing index mechanism and PLI. It discovered that 83 percent of the members' total housing score was less than 10, thereby qualifying the first basic means-test of a total housing score of 10 points or less. The ultimate eligibility test was a total household income of less than RM250. The finding revealed that 80 percent of the AIM's client's household income was lower than RM250. On the per capita basis, 78 percent of them were eligible. The findings also confirmed that the effectiveness of AIM's methodology. As the findings were congruent with the first two studies, SERU impact study noted that the overall household income was doubled (from RM197.78 per month to RM465.66 per month) after participating in the AIM's microcredit schemes. Clearly, half (RM229) of the income was generated from microcredit. For poverty reduction, 63 percent of the clients crossed the national poverty line income. Those clients who were selected from older branches in Selangor and Penang had better record than those from the two younger agriculture-based branches in Kedah. Besides, SERU also looked into the impact of the ownership and quality of housing, type and quality of household assets, agricultural land, and savings on the participant's quality of life. Undeniably, an increase in household income enabled the participants to improve their housing conditions. As the household savings increased from RM33.11 to RM211.25, subsequently it increased expenditure on food, nutrition, education, and reinvestment. In terms of cost effectiveness, with an operating cost of RM7056, AIM managed to release 249 poor families from poverty (SERU, 1990).

Then, the third internal impact study was conducted by the AIM's research and development department in 1994. The objectives of this study were to assess the nature of trust's outreach of clients into their microcredit programs, evaluate the impact of microcredit on the clients' socio-economic conditions, and study the cost effectiveness of microcredit operation. A total of 13 older branches (operating for at least two years) from six states were selected. At that time, AIM had an outreach of 9401 members in 33 branches, with 5401 members were active borrowers. The total disbursement of RM 4143965 was recorded with an outstanding balance of nearly RM 2 million. A stratified random sampling technique was applied to select 265 households from 5,401 borrowers with subsequent loans. Concurrently, a control group of non-participating poor was also included. This study collected data on a weekly basis (household income, savings, and expenditure patterns) by introducing daily entry throughout the year. However, many research problems were discovered when the data were collected on a daily basis. In fact, only 152 households (57 percent) completed their daily income expenditure patterns (Third Internal Impact Study, 1994).

The third study (Third Internal Impact Study, 1994) confirmed the non-monetary impact of microcredit on poor household. This study showed an improvement in the owner occupancy houses to 85 percent compared to 80 percent prior to the Ikhtiar loans application. The use of electric household products also showed a slight improvement. Then, the ownership of agricultural land improved from 3 percent to 40 percent due to the return received from microcredit. In terms of nutritional quality, 58 percent of the households perceived an improvement, 34 percent of them did not notice a change, and the remaining had no opinion. In the meantime, the voluntary savings among the poor also increased. This study also demonstrated a 72-percent increase in household income from an average of RM309 per month to RM532 as compared to RM223 before the program participation. As a result, this study found a direct positive relationship between level of income and utilization of loans. In other words, when more loans were used for income-generating activities, thereby earning higher income (Third Internal Impact Study, 1994).

In 2000, the Center for Policy Research (Rahman, 1998) conducted an impact study funded by AIM. The objectives of this external impact study were to measure (1) What proportion of the trust's members actually is from the four states? (2) How and what members can be benefitted from microcredit and how much variation is there among the four states? (3) What is the cost benefit ratio to the borrowers spent on the trust's operations among the four states? (4) How efficient are the trust's operations between the state and center? How can efficiency be increased? (5) What improvement in the trust's loan portfolio and operations makes the services more attractive or beneficial to its potential members? Are there variations among four states? (6) What kind of new loan products improve the return to the borrowers and how subsequent loan is stimulated?

In 1993, AIM extended their operations through 34 branches in eight states of Peninsular Malaysia. These 34 branches had 1306 centers, with 5249 groups and 25470 members. Of 34 branches, this study investigated

16 of them in Kedah, Perak, Kelantan, and Terengganu. Four branches were selected from each state and one center per branch was chosen. This study collected data from active borrowers, non-participating poor households, non-borrowing members, and former AIM clients or dropouts. Data were collected in the form of opening inventory (a profile of sampled households in the first interview), daily income and expenditure survey, and closing inventory (similar to opening inventory, the data were collected at the end of the collection). The finding showed that 77 percent of the non-participating poor were below poverty line, with 32.7 percent were hardcore poor and 23 percent were able to move out of poverty without microcredit. On the other hand, of 244 active and inactive members and dropouts, 57 percent of them were no longer poor, 33 percent of them were moderately poor, and 11.5 percent remained hardcore poor.

The findings of non-monetary measurement ascertained a corresponding impact such as net worth value of all assets and quality of life. The opening inventory of non-participating poor showed a net worth of all assets of RM7181, which was higher than the non-borrowing borrowers and dropouts (RM4938) and active borrowers (RM6865). The closing inventory showed that the access to microcredit made a tremendous increase in net worth of assets recorded as RM20541, compared to RM15303 for inactive and dropout clients and RM11340 for non-participating poor. These active borrowers also managed to generate non-monetary benefits overtime compared to non-participating poor. The benefits included piped water, toilet facilities, housing conditions, electricity supply, walls and roofs, land, and savings.

In 2004, another impact study was carried out by Salma (2004) from USM. She intended to analyze the modus operandi, strategy, philosophy, and outreach coverage of PPRT (Program Pembangunan Rakyat Termiskin) and AIM to determine which program reached higher number of targeted households and examine why poor households were not members of any programs. The effect was measured using both 'before and after' method and 'with and without' method. The finding showed that the household income, expenditure, savings, and assets increased among both AIM and PPRT participants compared to non-participants. In a nutshell, the increase in AIM clients was higher than PPRT clients. This particular study concluded that the microcredit program had direct and stronger contribution to income generation than non-microcredit program like PPRT (Salma, 2004).

Al-Shami, Majid, Mohamad, and Rashid (2017) investigated the impact of AIM productive loan on women household welfare and empowerment. Their study collected data from 495 old and new borrowers and found that micro-credit had a positive influence on borrowers' household income and personal assets acquisition. However, this study was only limited to urban areas rather than both urban and rural areas. A similar study by Al-Shami, Razali, and Rashid (2017) found out that the effect of AIM on women empowerment in urban Malaysia was similar because microcredit had positive influence on monthly income, thereby the household income. Samer, Majid, Rizal, Muhamad, Halim, and Rashid, (2015) collected data from 780 old and new AIM clients comprising both rural and urban borrowers in Selangor and Melaka, Malaysia. The finding supported that microcredit positively influenced household income. Besides, Al-Mamun and Mazumder (2015) collected data from eight randomly selected AIM's urban branches and seven randomly selected AIM's rural branches. They collected completed data from 281 poor rural clients and 242 low-income urban clients. As a result, they found that AIM's microcredit program increased household income, simultaneously, reduced both poverty rate and level of economic vulnerability.

AUTHOR CONTRIBUTIONS

All authors were involved in collecting relevant information and literature review, and writing this chapter.

CONFLICTS OF INTEREST

The authors declare no conflict of interest.

ACKNOWLEDGMENT

This research was funded by the Ministry of Higher Education, Malaysia under the grant entitled "Developing a Comprehensive Rural Entrepreneurship Model for Poverty Eradication (REMODE)" (R/NRGS/A01.00/00047A/006/2014/000149).

REFERENCES

Abed, F. H. (2000). *Micro-credit, poverty and development: the case of Bangladesh*. Retrieved January 22nd, 2016 from https://www.questia.com/magazine/1G1-84894333/micro-credit-poverty-and-development-the-case-of

Ahuja, R., & Jütting, J. (2004). Are the poor too poor to demand health insurance? *Journal of Microfinance*, *6*(1), 2–11.

Al-Mamun, A., Malarvizhi, C. A., Hossain, S., & Tan, S. H. (2012). Examining the effect of microcredit on poverty in Malaysia. *ASEAN Economic Bulletin*, *29*(1), 15–28. doi:10.1355/ae29-1b

Al-Mamun, A., & Mazumder, M. (2015). Impact of microcredit on income, poverty, and economic vulnerability in Peninsular Malaysia. *Development in Practice*, *25*(3), 333–346. doi:10.1080/09614524.2015.1019339

Al-Shami, S., Razali, R., & Rashid, N. (2017). The Effect of Microcredit on Women Empowerment in Welfare and Decisions Making in Malaysia. *Social Indicators Research*. doi:10.100711205-017-1632-2

Bank Negara Malaysia. (2017). *Developments in the Malaysian Economy*. Retrieved November 30th, 2017 from https://www.bnm.gov.my/files/publication/qb/2017/Q1/p3.pdf

Center of Policy Research. (2000). *Impact of Banking on Rural Poor in Peninsular Malaysia*. University Science Malaysia.

Datta, D. (2004). Microcredit in rural Bangladesh: Is it reaching the poorest? *Journal of Microfinance*, *6*(1), 56–81.

Department Of Statistic Malaysia. (2016). *Current Population Estimates, Malaysia, 2014 – 2016*. Retrieved November 28th, 2017 from https://www.dosm.gov.my/v1/index.php?r=column/cthemeByCat&cat=155&bul_id=OWlxdEVoYlJCS0hUZzJyRUcvZEYxZz09&menu_id=L0pheU43NWJwRWVSZklWdzQ4TlhUUT09

Department of Statistic Malaysia. (2017). *International Investment Position, Third Quarter 2017*. Department of Statistics Malaysia. Retrieved November 26th, 2017 from https://www.dosm.gov.my/v1/index.php?r=column/cthemeByCat&cat=87&bul_id=QnBwekg1VmNlcnVGbjVOaEJiMEhmdz09&menu_id=azJjRWpYL0VBYU90TVhpclByWjdMQT09

Dingue, P. (2005). *Building inclusive micro-lending program to support social and economic development in Cameroon* (M.Phil thesis). Department of Regional Economic and Social Development, University of Massachusetts Lowell.

Dowla, A. (1998). *Micro leasing: the Grameen Bank experience*. Program for Research on Poverty Alleviation, Grameen Trust.

Dunn, E. (2005). *Impact of Microcredit on Clients in Bosnia and Herzegovina*. Foundation for Sustainable Development of the Federation of Bosnia and Herzegovina and Republika Srpska Development and Employment Foundation.

Economic Planning Unit. (2004). *Malaysia: 30 Years of Poverty Reduction, Growth and Racial Harmony*. Economic Planning Unit, Prime Minister's Department in Scaling up Poverty Reduction: A Global Learning Process and Conference, Shanghai.

Economic Planning Unit. (2010). *Tenth Malaysian Plan*. Retrieved November 28th, 2010 from https://www.pmo.gov.my/dokumenattached/RMK/RMK10_Eds.pdf

Economic Planning Unit. (2015). *The Malaysian Economy in Figures 2015*. Economic Planning Unit, Prime Minister's Department. Retrieved November 28th, 2017 from http://www.epu.gov.my/sites/default/files/2015.pdf

Gallardo, J. (2002). *A framework for regulating microfinance institutions: The experience in Ghana and the Philippines*. Academic Press.

Gibbons, D. S., & Kasim, S. (1990). *Banking on the rural poor in Peninsular Malaysia*. Center for Policy Research, University Science Malaysia.

Government of Malaysia. (1991). *Malaysia: The Way Forward*. Kuala Lumpur: National Printing Department.

Hairuddin, H., Noor, N. L. M., & Ab Malik, A. M. (2012). Why do microenterprise refuse to use information technology: A case of batik microenterprises in Malaysia. *Procedia: Social and Behavioral Sciences*, *57*, 494–502. doi:10.1016/j.sbspro.2012.09.1216

Harris, R., & Rajora, R. (2006). *Empowering the poor: Information and communications technology for governance and poverty reduction: A study of rural development projects in India*. UNDP Asia-Pacific Development Information Programme.

Hasan, M. E. (2003). Implications of financial innovations for the poorest of the poor in the rural area: Experience from Northern Bangladesh. *Journal of Microfinance*, *5*(2), 101–137.

Helms, B. (2006). *Access for all: building inclusive financial systems.* Washington, DC: CGAP. doi:10.1596/978-0-8213-6360-7

Hoque, S. (2008, January 10). *Does Micro-credit Program in Bangladesh Increase Household's Ability to Deal with Economic Hardships?* Munich Repack Personal Archive, Paper No. 6678. Retrieved November 11st, 2008 from http://mpra.ub.uni-muenchen.de/6678/

Hossain, M. (1988). *Credit for the Alleviation of Rural Poverty: The Grameen Bank in Bangladesh.* Research Report No. 55, International Food Policy Research Institute (IFPRI), Washington, DC.

Hubka, A., & Zaidi, R. (2005). *Impact of Government Regulation on Microfinance, Prepared for the World Development Report 2005: Improving the Investment Climate for Growth and Poverty Reduction, World Development Report no- 31438.* The World Bank.

Hulme, D. (2008). *The Story of the Grameen Bank: From Subsidised Microcredit to Market-based Microfinance.* BWPI Working Paper 60, Brooks World Poverty Institute.

Hulme, D., & Mosley, P. (1998). Microenterprise finance: Is there any conflict between growth and poverty alleviation? *World Development*, *26*(5), 783–790. doi:10.1016/S0305-750X(98)00021-7

Hussain, G., & Nargis, N. (2008). A welfare economic analysis of the impact of microfinance in Bangladesh. Department of Economics, University of Dhaka, Nilkhet, Dhaka, Bangladesh.

Khandker, S. R. (2003). *Microfinance and Poverty: Evidence Using Panel Data from Bangladesh.* World Bank Policy Research Working Paper 2945.

Khandker, S. R. (2005). Microfinance and poverty: Evidence using panel data from Bangladesh. *The World Bank Economic Review*, *19*(2), 263–286. doi:10.1093/wber/lhi008

Khandker, S. R., & Chowdhury, O. H. (1995). Targeted Credit Programs and Rural Poverty in Bangladesh. World Bank.

Khandker, S. R., & Pitt, M. (1998). The impact of group-based credit programs on poor households in Bangladesh: Does the gender of participants matter? *Journal of Political Economy*, *106*(5), 958–996. doi:10.1086/250037

Khawari, A. (2004). *Microfinance: Does it hold its promises? A survey of recent literature* (Unpublished Paper). Hamburg Institute of International Economics, Hamburg, Germany.

Latifee, H. I. (2003). *Microcredit and Poverty Reduction.* International Conference on Poverty Reduction through Microcredit, Taksim-Istambul.

Lembaga Kemajuan Ikan Malaysia. (2017). Retrieved July 24th, 2017 from http://www.moa.gov.my/dana-nelayan-lkim

Levy, F. (2002). *Apex institutions in microfinance. Consultative Group to Assist the Poorest.* CGAP.

Library of Congress. (2016). *Country Profile: Malaysia.* Library of Congress – Federal Research Division. Available at https://www.loc.gov/rr/frd/cs/profiles/Malaysia.pdf

Matin, I., & Begum, A. S. (2002). *Asset-ing the extreme poor: Experiences and Lessons from a BRAC Project. In RED BRAC Economic Studies, XVIII.* Dhaka, Bangladesh: BRAC.

McCarty, A. (2001). Microfinance in Vietnam: A survey of schemes and issues. Hanoi, Vietnam: Department for International Development (DFID) and the State Bank of Vietnam (SBVN).

Meagher, P. (2002). *Microfinance Regulation in Developing Countries: A Comparative Review of Current Practice*. IRIS Center, University of Maryland.

Microcredit, S. C. R. (2015). *Microcredit Summit Campaign.* Available at https://stateofthecampaign.org/read-the-full-2015-report/

Ministry of International Trade and Industry. (2016). *25th MITI Report 2016.* Retrieved November 28th, 2017 from http://www.miti.gov.my/miti/resources/MITI%20Report/MITI_REPORT_2016.pdf

Mokhtar, S. H. (2011). *Microfinance Performance in Malaysia* (Unpublished Doctoral Dissertation). Lincoln University, Christchurch. New Zealand.

Mokhtar, S. H., & Ashhari, Z. M. (2015). Issues and Challenges of Microcredit Programmes in Malaysia. *Asian Social Science*, *11*(26), 191. doi:10.5539/ass.v11n26p191

Morduch, J. (1998). *Does microfinance really help the poor? New evidence from flagship programs in Bangladesh. Research Program in Development Studies*. Woodrow School of Public and International Affairs.

Mosley, P., & Hulme, D. (1998). Microenterprise finance: Is there a conflict between growth and poverty alleviation? *World Development, 26*(5), 783–790. doi:10.1016/S0305-750X(98)00021-7

Mustafa, S., Ara, I., Banu, D., Kabir, A., Mohsin, M., Yusuf, A., & Jahan, S. (1996). *Beacon of Hope: An Impact Assessment Study of BRAC's RDP' Research and Evaluation Division*. Dhaka: BRAC.

Nawai, N., & Bashir, M. S. (2010). *Evaluation of micro credit program for poverty alleviation: A case of Amanah Ikhtiar Malaysia (AIM)*. Retrieved from http://ddms.usim.edu.my/handle/123456789/1555

Neill, C., Davalos, M., Kiiru, W., Manundu, M., & Sebstad, J. (1994). *The Kenya Rural Enterprise Programme under Cooperative Agreement*. GEMINI Technical Report No. 77.

Nordin, R., & Bakar, S. S. A. (2012). Malaysian batik industry: Protecting local batik design by copyright and industrial design laws. *International Journal of Business and Society, 13*(2), 117.

Otero, M. (1999). Bringing development back into microfinance. *Journal of Microfinance, 1*(1), 8–19.

Panda, K. D. (2009). Participation in the group based microfinance and its impact on rural households: A quasi-experimental evidence from an Indian State. *Global Journal of Finance and Management, 1*(2), 171–183.

Pham, T. T. T., & Lensink, R. (2007). Lending policies of informal, formal and semiformal lenders. *Economics of Transition, 15*(2), 181–209. doi:10.1111/j.1468-0351.2007.00283.x

Prahalad, C. K. (2006). *The Fortune at the Bottom of the Pyramid*. Pearson Education India.

Process Waterhouse Coopers. (2017). *Greater Kuala Lumpur: Bride between Asia and the world.* ProcewaterhouseCoopers organization in Malaysia. Retrieved from https://www.pwc.com/my/en/assets/publications/170703-greater-kl-bridge-between-asia-and-the-world.pdf

Rahman, A., & Razzaque, A. (2000). On reaching the hardcore poor: Some evidence on social exclusion in NGO programmes. *Bangladesh Development Studies*, *26*(1), 1–35.

Rahman, H. Z. (1998). *Bangladesh: Dynamics of rural poverty*. Paper presented at International Conference on Poverty, Dhaka, Bangladesh.

Rahman, S., Rafiq, R. B., & Momen, M. A. (2009). Impact of microcredit programs on higher income borrowers: Evidence from Bangladesh. *International Business & Economics Research Journal*, *8*(2), 119–124.

Roodman, D., & Qureshi, U. (2006). Microfinance as business. *Center for Global Development*. Retrieved March 23rd, 2017 from https://www.cgdev.org/files/10742_file_Microfinance_as_Business.pdf

Rudie, I. (2013). Ethnic Experience and Global Horizons: Batik Entrepreneurs on a Tourist Beach in Malaysia. In Embedded Entrepreneurship: Market, Culture, and Micro-Business in Insular Southeast Asia (pp. 29-59). BRILL.

Salma, M. (2004). *A Comparative Case Study on Outreach and Impact of Ikhtiar Loan Scheme and Special Program for Hardcore Poor in Seberang Perai Pulau Pinang* (M.Phil Thesis). University Science Malaysia.

Samer, S., Majid, I., Rizal, S., Muhamad, M., Halim, S., & Rashid, N. (2015). The Impact of Microfinance on Poverty Reduction: Empirical Evidence from Malaysian Perspective. *Procedia: Social and Behavioral Sciences*, *195*, 721–728. doi:10.1016/j.sbspro.2015.06.343

Satish, P. (2001). Institutional alternatives for the promotion of microfinance: Self-Help groups in India. *Journal of Microfinance*, *3*(2), 44–49.

Sebstad, J., & Walsh, M. (1991). *Microenterprise credit and its effects in Kenya: an exploratory study. Report prepared for USAID AFR/MDI and S&T/WID*. Washington, DC: Coopers and Lybrand.

Second Internal Impact Study. (1990). *Impact Assessment Report*. Research and Development Unit. Amanah Ikhtiar Malaysia.

SERU. (1990). *Impact Assessment Report*. Research and Development Unit. Amanah Ikhtiar Malaysia.

Sutoro, A. D. (1990). *KUPEDES Development impact survey: briefing booklet. BRI, Planning*. Research and Development Department.

Third Internal Impact Study. (1994). *Third Impact Study*. Research and Development Unit. Amanah Ikhtiar Malaysia.

Vega, G. C. (1998). *Microfinance Apex Mechanisms: Review of the Evidence and Policy Recommendations. CGAP-OSU Research Project on Microfinance Apex Mechanisms*. Department of Agricultural, Environmental and Development Economics, The Ohio State University.

Woller, G. M., & Woodworth, W. (2001). Microcredit and third world development policy. *Policy Studies Journal: the Journal of the Policy Studies Organization*, *29*(2), 265–266. doi:10.1111/j.1541-0072.2001.tb02090.x

World Bank. (2010), *Overview: Understanding, measuring and overcoming poverty*. Retrieved February 19th, 2010 from http://go.worldbank.org/RQBDCTUXW0

Yunus, M., Moingeon, B., & Lehmann-Ortega, L. (2010). Building social business models: Lessons from the Grameen experience. *Long Range Planning*, *43*(2), 308–325. doi:10.1016/j.lrp.2009.12.005

Yusoff, N. (2015). Food production and management in Malaysia. *International Journal of Humanities and Social Science Invention*, *4*(8), 41–48.

Zin, M. H. R. (2007). Understanding the formation of the revised poverty line in Malaysia. *Academia (Caracas)*, *70*, 21–39.

Chapter 2
Entrepreneurship in Malaysia

ABSTRACT

This chapter presents a brief description regarding the types and characteristics of entrepreneurial activities in Malaysia. This chapter further illustrates the programs and policies initiated to promote entrepreneurial activities in Malaysia, followed by entrepreneurship and economic development in Malaysia, informal entrepreneurship in Malaysia, as well as characteristics of informal micro-entrepreneurship. Finally, this chapter provides future directions for micro-enterprises to propose initiatives that focus on developmental programs and policy making in Malaysia. To introduce successful micro-credit programs, underlying organizations in emerging economies should be consistent in terms of cost-efficient operations without favoritism and political elements.

ENTREPRENEURIAL ACTIVITIES IN MALAYSIA

Entrepreneurship has a significant role in determining the progression of economy in a nation. In fact, it is one of the many essential factors that appear to aid in creating jobs and boosting the economic growth of a country. On top of that, entrepreneurship plays a crucial role in establishing small- and medium-sized enterprises (SMEs), apart from enhancing productivity. Therefore, it is utmost important for policy makers to devise effective programs and policies towards encouraging its fellow citizens in becoming successful entrepreneurs. As such, governments across nations have begun taking initiatives and implementing viable strategies to facilitate entrepreneurship by promoting

DOI: 10.4018/978-1-5225-8473-5.ch002

entrepreneurship activities among their societies as entrepreneurship, unquestionably, is a solution in eradicating poverty.

The Malaysian government has reckoned the importance of entrepreneurship, and thus, has been providing necessary support to mould entrepreneurs. With that, promoting entrepreneurship appears to be one of the integral transformation agendas to achieve the high-income nation status by 2020. The government has introduced several policies, such as the New Economic Policy (NEP) and the Malaysia Plans (MP), through which entrepreneurial activities and cultures are given emphasis. The Malaysian government places special attention to entrepreneurship as a way to assist and to upgrade the industrial structure in the attempt to create industries for future generation. Most of these programs ultimately lead to increment in productivity for entrepreneurs and indirectly generate entrepreneurs with higher-income.

Entrepreneurship has varied roles across nations depending on the varying stages of economic development (Van Stel, Carree, & Thurik, 2005). Therefore, it is important to identify economic activities, which in turn, helps to determine the opportunities that lay within the economic system (Ahmad and Seymour, 2008). The Global Entrepreneurship Monitor (GEM) is a distinctive project, where a standardized methodology is applied to assess entrepreneurial activities across the globe. The GEM model, considering the national economic growth as a major dependent variable, provides information pertaining to the impact of entrepreneurship upon growth, aside from indicating entrepreneurship attitudes, activities, and growth, which are influenced by the many factors of entrepreneurial environments, for instance, availability of finance, government policies, government programmes in aiding new and growing firms, education and training, research and development transfer, commercial and professional infrastructure, internal market openness/barriers to entry, access to physical infrastructure, as well as cultural and social norms (Ahmad and Xavier, 2012).

Hence, it is crucial for the Malaysian government to participate in the GEM project as it reveals both positioning and improvement accordingly. For instance, the GEM has classified actions taken by entrepreneurs at various phases of their business duration, such as nascent entrepreneurship, new business ownership, Total Early-Stage Entrepreneurial Activity (TEA), and established business ownership, as depicted in Table 1.

Malaysia has been acknowledged as an Asian country that supports entrepreneurship by providing its people both finance and physical infrastructures (SME Corporation Malaysia, 2016), as projected in the

Table 1. Entrepreneurial activities in Malaysia (% of population aged 18-64)

Entrepreneurial Activities	2015	2016
Nascent entrepreneurship rate	0.8	2.0
New business ownership rate	2.3	2.8
Total Early-stage entrepreneurial activity (TEA)	2.9	4.7
Established business ownership rate	4.8	4.7
Discontinuation of businesses	1.1	14.6
Necessity-driven (% of TEA)	13.7	16.1
Improvement-driven opportunity (% of TEA)	67.0	59.4

Sources: GEM (2016; 2017)

Malaysian TEA rate outcome, which exhibited a hike to 4.7% in 2016, in comparison to 2.9% in 2015. This reveals that more Malaysians are getting interested in entrepreneurial opportunities and innovative initiatives. Furthermore, the data presented in Table 1 demonstrate that the initial phase of entrepreneurial activities are mostly driven by opportunity, instead of necessity, thus indicating that Malaysian entrepreneurs are opportunity-driven, motivated by better income, and risk-takers, apart from wanting to be independent through start-ups (SME Corporation Malaysia, 2016).

The perception among Malaysians that entrepreneurship is a bad career option is beginning to take a shift all together. In 2016, agreement to the notion that entrepreneurship as a good career choice displayed a rise to 44.1%, in comparison to 39.3% in 2015. This increment in percentage may reflect the slight rise of 0.5% for the new business ownership rate in 2016, when compared to 2015. This also means that Malaysians are coming out of their shells of being satisfied with steady income through employment and turning into entrepreneurs themselves (SME Corporation Malaysia, 2016).

PROGRAMS AND POLICIES

A number of scholars have asserted in their studies that entrepreneurship works as an engine that drives the economy forward (Shamsudin, Al Mamun, Nawi, Nasir, & Zakaria, 2016) for both developed and developing economies [8]. The Malaysian government, as such, has encouraged its people to get involved in entrepreneurship. In fact, vast programs and policies, such as entrepreneurship funds, physical infrastructure, and business advisory support, have been implemented to motivate people to become entrepreneurs. During the era of British colonization, the economic activities were isolated by ethnic groups, which led to economic inequalities. So as to avoid such inequalities, the government has established the *Rural Industrial Development Authority* (RIDA) in 1951, which was later renamed as *Council of Trust for the Indigenous People* (MARA) to encourage entrepreneurship among those bearing the status Bumiputera (Fong, 1990). In 1971, the Malaysian government launched the NEP following the unfortunate racial clashes that took place on 13th May 1969 in the attempt to achieve national unity by eradicating poverty and restructuring the society so as to correct economic imbalances among races (Gomez, 2003). Based on several reports, this policy appeared successful as the poverty rate dipped from 49.3% in 1970 to 16.5% in 1990 in Peninsular Malaysia (Federation of Malaysian Manufacturers, 2010). Following NEP, the *National Development Policy*, which was introduced in 1991, emphasized on growth with equity that allowed all Malaysians to take part in economic activities, so as to ensure political stability and national unity (Shamsudin, Al Mamun, Nawi, Nasir, & Zakaria, 2016). Later in 2010, the government devised a new policy called New Economic Model (NEM) in its mission to attain the 'developed country' status by 2020. Additionally, this policy highlights the need to expand entrepreneurship in creating a competitive domestic economy (Federation of Malaysian Manufacturers, 2010). The Malaysian government has taken initiatives at grass-root level in order to develop Malaysia as an entrepreneurial nation. As such, the National Entrepreneurship Institute (INSKEN) has introduced Young Entrepreneurs Program (PUM) in 1989 for secondary school students to cultivate the seed of entrepreneurship at a very young age. In recent years, INSKEN has also implemented other entrepreneurship programs, for example, Program Usahawan Bimbing Usahawan (Coaching by Industry Players) where a minimum of 70% of training modules are developed and delivered by industry players and professionals in a series of seminar, training, and coaching, as well as Program Pembangunan Permulaan Perniagaan (Start-Up Business Accelerator Program) that targets university graduates who venture into businesses (Shamsudin, Al Mamun, Nawi, Nasir, & Zakaria, 2016). INSKEN also organises programs for existing entrepreneurs who wishes to improve their business structure. The names and details of several established programs devised specially for entrepreneurs are presented in Table 2.

Additionally, the Kedah State Development Corporation (PKNK), which is supervised by the Ministry of Finance, has been promoting numerous entrepreneurial programs. They provide assistance in becoming more

Table 2. Programs initiated by INSKEN

Name	Details
INSKEN Meet the Bisceptor	Provide consultancy services and information reference centres
INSKEN Business Training (IBT)	Business-oriented training programs INSKEN runs the IBT program as follows: Action Business Plan 1. How to Get Halal Certification 2. Bookkeeping for Small Business 3. Business Budgeting 4. Business Model Canvas 5. Develop Business Standard Operating Procedure 6. Marketing and Sales 7. Social Media Marketing
INSKEN Business Coaching (IBC)	INSKEN conducts the IBC program as follows: 1. Develop an SOP for Spa Business 2. Exploring Export Markets Through Contracted Business 3. Designing and Developing a Car Workshop Business 4. Road to Hypermarket

Source: INSKEN (2017)

competitive, apart from organising training and coaching sessions to university graduates and entrepreneurs who are keen to venture into franchised business.

The Malaysian government has also been emphasizing entrepreneurship via small- and medium-enterprises (SMEs). In order to strengthen and to promote SMEs from the light of economy, the government has allocated SME financing fund that is worth RM2 billion at 13 Islamic banks throughout the

Table 3. Programs initiated by PKNK

Activities	Details
Business Development	• Promotions and Expo • Sales Carnival • Travel incentives seek domestic and foreign business opportunities • *Hypermarket* promotion • Business match
Tunas Niaga Program (Protune)	Nurturing and cultivating entrepreneurship at the secondary level in collaboration with the Malaysian Ministry of Finance and the Malaysian Ministry of Education
Survey / Seminar Training Program	• Women's Development Program • Merchant Training Program and Hawkers • Business Advisory Services Program • *Coaching and Mentoring* Program • Product and Packaging Quality Improvement Course • Halal Development Program
Local Franchise Development Program	Identifying competitive local businesses to be developed as franchisor and franchisee Introductory seminar, training, and coaching sessions are provided to university graduates and entrepreneurs who are keen to venture into franchised business

Source: PKNK (2017)

nation, including 2 percent of profit rebate. In order to achieve high-income economy by 2020, the established SMEs would require competitiveness, efficiency, and effectiveness. In the attempt to address this challenge, the government has initiated the Economic Transformation Program (ETP) in 2010, where several projects have been introduced to upgrade retailers and automotive workshops (Economic Transformation Program, 2017). For instance, the Small Retailer Transformation Program (TUKAR), which was launched in 2013, has been expected to contribute approximately RM5.58 billion to the country's gross national income (GNI) and to generate 51,540 job opportunities by 2020, while the Automotive Workshop Modernization (ATOM) is aimed to contribute as much as RM1.1 billion to the Malaysian GNI upon transforming 500 workshops nationwide (Food and Fertilizer Technology Center-Asia Pacific, 2015).

In addition, to support of SMEs, the Malaysian Government offers microcredit facilities, training sessions, and other programs through TEKUN Nasional and Amanah Ikhtiar Malaysia (AIM), which are both government institutions. The government places a lot of emphasis upon women entrepreneurs as well, hence resulting in a substantial increment of entrepreneurial activities carried out by women (Mutalib, Arshad, Ismail, & Ahmad, 2015). Along with AIM and TEKUN, several other government agencies that offer adequate training and workshops to enhance entrepreneurial skills among women are listed in Table 4, as follows:

Apart from supporting the women, the government also offers support for all entrepreneurs, in general. As such, several agencies, such as Global Innovation and Creativity Centre (MaGIC), 1Malaysia Entrepreneurs (1MeT), Ministry of Youth and Sports (MOYS), MITI, and others, share similar objective to encourage the people to be more entrepreneurial in developing an entrepreneurial nation as envisioned in Vision 2020.

The Development of Micro Enterprise in Malaysia

The essence of Malaysia micro enterprise was began in early 1970s in line with the implementation of the New Economic Policy (NEP) in 1971. The purpose of this policy is to reduce socioeconomic disparity among races in the country and eradicating poverty amongst the *Bumiputeras*. In order to achieve this purpose, government encourages ownership of businesses/ enterprises. The term of *Bumiputra* is broadly used in Malaysia that refers to indigenous people of the Malay Archipelago (Jamak, Salleh, Sivapalan, &

Table 4. Programs initiated by government agencies for entrepreneurship among women

Government Agencies	Programs
Ministry of Women, Family and Community Development (MWFCD)	Single Mother Skill Incubator(I-KIT) Women Entrepreneurs Incubators (I-KeuNita) Women Capacity Development Program Women Entrepreneur Launching Grant Women Taxi Program Women Economic Development (WEDA) Program 1AZAM (1Aim)
Ministry of Agriculture (MOA)	Women Fisherman Group Project (KUNITA)
Malaysia External Trade Development Corporation (MATRADE)	Women Exporters Development Program (WEDP)
Perbadanan Nasional Berhad	Women/Graduate Franchise Program
Small and Medium Industrial Development Corporation (SMIDEC)	Provides financial assistance to entrepreneurs, also known as special assistance schemes

Source: Mutalib et al., [16]

Table 5. Programs initiated by the government

Government	Programs
Global Innovation and Creativity Centre (MaGIC)	Pre-Accelerator Bootcamp Corporate Entrepreneurship Responsibility Distro Camp MaGIC Educ8 Global Accelerator Program
1Malaysia Entrepreneurs (1MeT)	National Blue Ocean Strategy (NBOS)
The Ministry of Youth and Sports (MOYS)	Offers courses, such as basic entrepreneurship in labelling and packaging technology, Smart Partnership, Smart Financial Manager, and Technical Agriculture.
Ministry of International Trade and Industry (MITI)	The Groom Big Program - nurtures, grooms, and develops entrepreneurs to become competitive, resilient, and sustainable SMEs in domestic and global markets Vendor Development Program (VDP) - develops SME entrepreneurs to become competitive suppliers and manufacturers of component/services at domestic and global markets. Outreach program - disseminates information regarding facilities/incentives provided by the Ministries and Agencies to entrepreneurs *Satu Daerah Satu Industri* program (SDSI) - formulates action plan for promotion and devises marketing strategies for products and services - monitors performance and enhances implementation of promotion and marketing programmes for products and services - assists expansion of market at domestic and international levels for products and services through some activities, such as Showcase SDSI

Sources: MaGIC (2017), 1MeT (2017) MOYS (2017), MITI (2017)

Figure 1. SMEs vs overall GDP growth
Source: SME Corporation (SME Corporation, 2017a)

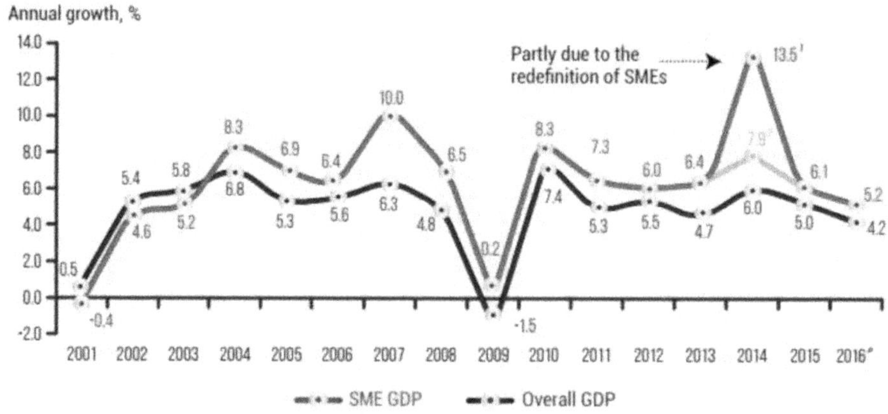

[1]Growth based on 2014 New SME Definition versus 2013 Old SME Definition
[2]Growth based on 2014 New SME Definition versus 2013 New SME Definition
p: preliminary

Abdullah, 2012). Thus, after 30 years of the program, the government further implements Malaysian Industrial Master Plan (IMP1-IMP3). As reported by Malaysian Department of Statistic, majority of Malaysian companies are contributed by micro enterprises compared to the other enterprises. The development of micro enterprise is in line with micro financing approach. This is due to micro financing function to provide finance to micro enterprise, as well as medium and small enterprises. The growth of micro financing led to the development of micro enterprise to access the formal financial systems in expanding their business activities (Hamdan, Othman, & Hussin, 2012). In addition, in 2006, the introductory of micro finance framework with combination of Bank Negara Malaysia and FIs, as one of the effort by government to enhance support for micro enterprises. Micro enterprises in Kelantan are higher than the other states in Malaysia.

ENTREPRENEURSHIP AND ECONOMIC DEVELOPMENT

Entrepreneurship has a significant function in "*maintaining a country's international competitive power, economic development, employment, and standard of living*" (Neergaard, Nielsen, & Kjeldsen, 2006; Berglann, Moen, Røed, & Skogstrøm, 2011). In fact, the aspect of entrepreneurship has been considered as the push factor for economic and social development across the world (Audretsch, 2003; Pokrajac, Dondur, Grbić, & Savanović, 2011; Dawson and Henley, 2012) Several studies have proven that over the years, entrepreneurial activities that derive from entrepreneurial talent and motivation appear to be the reason for successful growth of some economies (Baumol, 1993; Durmaz, Platt, & Yigitcanlar, 2010; Mokyr, 2013).

In Malaysia, the contribution of SME businesses to the progression of economy is definitely inevitably. Aside from providing job opportunities, SMEs substantially contribute to the prosperity of multinational magnates. They enhance the industry through their creativity and innovation. In fact, it is the unique contribution of an entrepreneur that dictates the performance of a firm (OlyNdubisi, & Iftikhar, 2012). According to the SME Corporation (2017a), 98.5% of Malaysian businesses are comprised of SMEs and they appear to be a significant backbone of the Malaysian economy (World Bank, 2016). Amongst them, mostly are associated to the services sector (89.2%), mainly in wholesale & retails, followed by manufacturing (5.3%), construction (4.3%), agriculture (1.1%), and mining & quarrying (0.1%) (SME Corporation, 2017b). Besides, despite of facing external and domestic challenges, the SME GDP in Malaysia remained resilient and rose at a more moderate pace of 5.2% in 2016, when compared to 6.1% in 2015, due to support by domestic demand, tourism activities, and supportive policies implemented by the Government. In fact, the SME GDP managed to, astoundingly, surpass the overall Malaysian GDP growth of 4.2% in 2016.

Entrepreneurs play a major role in contributing to and developing the economy of a nation. Many economists and politicians believe that entrepreneurs appear to be the notable contributors of economic growth and job creation, which emerges as the reason for many countries to seriously promote entrepreneurial activities (Audretsch, & Thurik, 2001; Reynolds, Carter, Gartner, Greene, & Cox, 2002). Entrepreneurs are not only linked with economic growth through establishment of new firms that creates new economic opportunities (Wennekers, Thurik, Buis, 1997; Floss and Klein, 2010; Ahlstrom, 2010; Du, Guariglia, & Newman, 2015), but they are also linked to wealth distribution (Schumpeter, 1999; Cumming and Suret, 2011). Not just halting there, entrepreneurs have directly contributed in diminishing poverty (Saini and Gurjar, 2001; Bruton, Ketchen, and Ireland, 2013).

The Malaysian Department of Statistical presents that the unemployment rate increased drastically in 1990, as illustrated in Figure 2, mainly due to unstable Malaysian economy. Nevertheless, the figure decreased dramatically after 5 years. Next, starting from 2000 to 2010, a rise in unemployment rate

Figure 2. Malaysian unemployment rate
Source: SME Corporation (2017b)

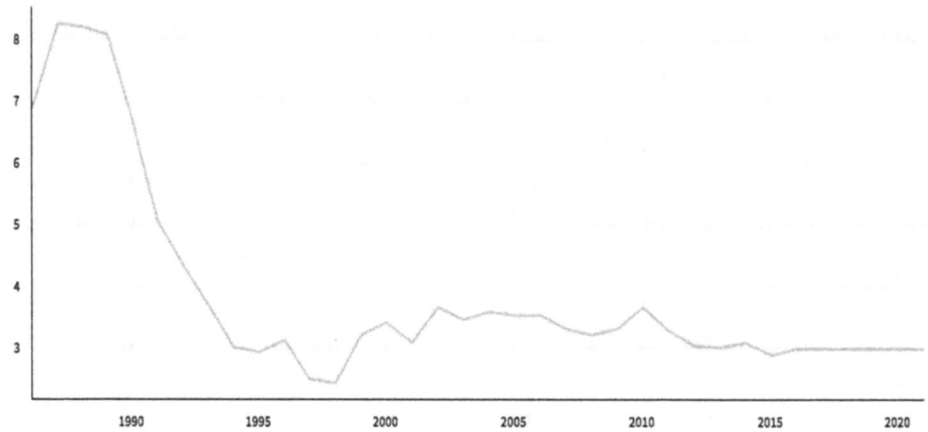

Figure 3. Employment share of SMEs to total employment (%)
Source: SME Corporation (2017b)

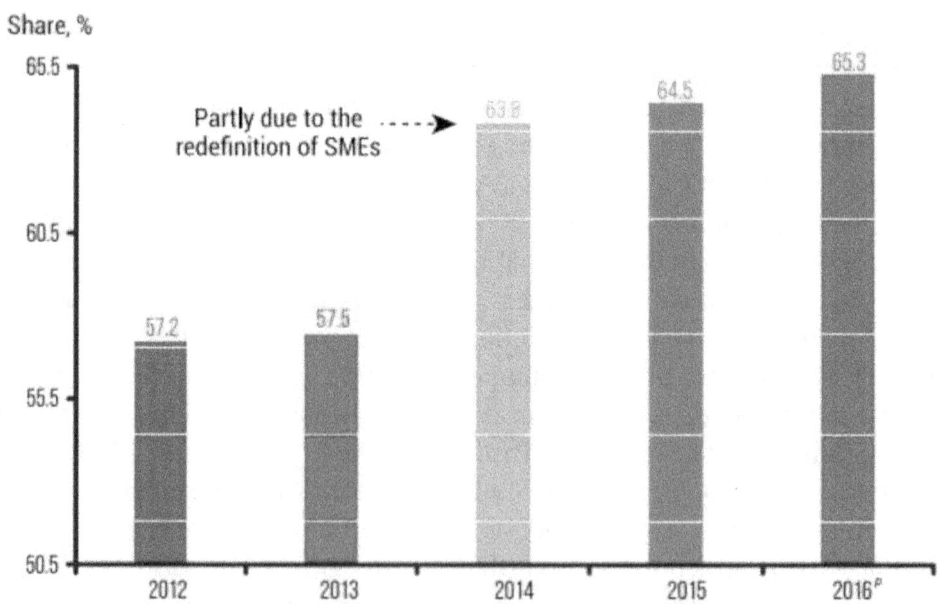

was projected by 0.5 percentage points. Due to this problem, the Malaysian government has taken a definite step to promote entrepreneurship. By 2015, the unemployment rate saw a decrease at 3.2 percent and this has been expected to remain until year 2020. Furthermore, Figure 3 displays that due to the expansion of employment of SMEs, a growth of 2.1% was noted in 2016, which summed up to 6.7 million workers, resulting in the share of SME employment to the total employment increment from 64.5% in 2015 to 65.3% in 2016, thus successfully achieving the SME Master plan target of 65.0% of SME employment to the total employment by year 2020.

Overall, one could say that entrepreneurs create social wealth out of the total economic value created. This happens when markets fail to cater to specific social needs or when the government agencies fail to provide fundamental amenities, such as welfare and basic education among poor nations (Venkatamaran, 1997). After recognizing the role of entrepreneurship, the General Assembly of the United Nations Organization approved a resolution in 1993 upon acknowledging entrepreneurship as an economic and social force that increases the living standards throughout the world. Besides, the United Nation urges their member countries to build and to implement policies towards encouraging entrepreneurship amongst the society (Slaughter, 1996; Kidd, 2008).

INFORMAL ENTREPRENEURSHIP IN MALAYSIA

Several scholars have determined the links associated to production that fall under the realm of informal sector in an economy. Finally, a consensus among scholars suggests that any enterprise with particular characteristics, such as ease of entry into the industry, dependence on local resources, family ownership, small-scaled operations, labour intensive, adaptive technology, skills acquired outside of the formal sector, unregulated and competitive markets, as well as firms established through informally organized activities; is classified as an informal economy player (Hart, 1973; Bangasser, 2000). Informal entrepreneurs operate at a very small scale, hence becoming a barrier for them to exploit economies of scale in specialization, innovation, and investment in fixed capital (Amin, 2011). For such entrepreneurs, staying small is not only a strategy, but also in part of a forced condition that is implied by financial constraint (DeSoto, 1989).

The economy in Malaysia was badly affected by the Asian financial crisis in 1997-1998. Economic development slumped and unfortunately, investments failed to recover the terrible crisis. At the time of the economic crisis, most people began migrating from rural area to urban cities for job opportunities. Such pressing scenario pushed people to venture into business, especially within the informal sector (Idris and Siwar, 2003; Kerr and Kerr, 2011; Kleemans, 2014) as a solution to escape from poverty (Klassens, 2010). Furthermore, people were also found to engage in informal economic activities due to deficit, unemployment (Gerxhani, 2004) tax evasion, changes in non-wage costs, labour regulations (Chong and Gradstein, 2007) preferences and incompetency among workers (Kasseeah and Trandayen-Ragoobur, 2015), non-reliance with minimum legal binding (Gerxhani, 2004), as well as complications in occupational and productivity of businesses within the formal sector (Chong and Gradstein, 2007).

Those involved in the informal economy are those who failed in securing a job in the formal sector (Istrate, 2012). Moreover, some get involved in the informal sector on a part-time basis in order to earn additional income. In Malaysia, several types of informal trades are in existence, for example, cart-vending, hawking (at night/day market), home-based online businesses, small stores, vendors, roadside cobbling, pedal rickshaw driving, and domestic home-helpers, all of which reflect a structuralize perspective due to the genre of jobs conducted by informal entrepreneurs, especially among developing nations (Lund and Srinivas, 2000) Informal enterprises can be found in various locations that deal with different types of goods manufactured differently, but all are licensed in the same way as informal business. Although it is compulsory for anyone who wants to open a business, regardless small or large, to register with Suruhanjaya Syarikat Malaysia (SSM), a regulatory authority for firms (Suruhanjaya Syarikat Malaysia, 2017) informal businesses are exempted from such procedures. Informal businesses only need to be registered with the district council in their respective states in order to obtain a license, as SSM approval is only required for formal business registrations in Malaysia (Suruhanjaya Syarikat Malaysia, 2017).

In addition, entrepreneurs who operate within the informal economy are considered as informal entrepreneurship. Keith Hart (1973), a social anthropologist, appears to be the first to use the term 'informal; in a research that identified this sector as predominantly the urban service-providing sector within the context of Third World, which works outside the formal institutional arrangements (Chakraborty, 2010). Informal economy incorporates the processes of producing goods and services that are not legitimate and do not entail any right to compete with the goods and services of the formal sector, for instance, petty trade, subsistence production, and small-scaled commercial production (Harris-White and Sinha, 2007). Additionally, Buehn (2012) asserted that informal economy, generally, is characterized by unregistered, unregulated, and untaxed businesses and service enterprises, which are engaged in small-scale production activities and various street-vending operations. Furthermore, scholars appear to classify such informal economy into varied industries, including manufacturing and services, but excluding strictly illegal activities, such as prostitution or drug trafficking and/or personal activities, such as providing domestic-help (World Bank, 2006). On top of that, several scholars coined 'informal economy' as underground economy, shadow economy, irregular economy, unobserved economy, and hidden enterprises (Webb, Bruton, Tihanyi, & Ireland, 2013). According to Hart (1973) and Johnson, Kaufmann, & Zoido-Lobaton, 1998) informal economy or unofficial sector consists of economic activities that are taxable, but are, not reported to the state statistical office or tax authorities, although registered as a legal business. Informal entrepreneurs are considered as necessity entrepreneurs, even as those who failed to find alternative employment opportunities, and therefore, secure employment in the informal sector (Kasseeah, & Tandrayen-Ragoobur, 2015). Informal entrepreneurs, in precise, reflect unprivileged and unfortunate pawns within an exploitative global economic system, in which work turns to be more precarious and poorly paid with every passing day. Interestingly, although informal entrepreneurship is perceived as a highly insecure and an unstable job with long hours of work under poor working conditions without legal or social protection and limited access to credit and bargaining power (Lund and Srinivas, 2000); the same informal sector happens to contribute significantly towards Malaysian economic growth, development, and prosperity (Ministry of Women, Family and Community Development, 2014).

CHARACTERISTICS OF INFORMAL MICRO-ENTREPRENEURSHIP

Naturally, informal entrepreneurs make use of local resources and sell at local markets, which differ from globalists, who use any level of resources; be it international product sources and markets (Spring, 2009). In this view, informal entrepreneurship appears to be a direct by-product at the advent of a deregulated open world economy (Castells and Portes, 1998). Thus, they range from street sellers to home-based micro-enterprise owners [66] involved with informal self-employed entrepreneurial activities (Das, 2003). Researchers have further characterized them as independent while operating in the informal sector (Suhaimi, Al Mamun, Zainol, Nawi, Permerupan, & Malarvizhi, 2016) where they do not only initiate a business independently, but also take all matters related to business into their hands.

Shaw and Shiu (Shaw and Shiu, 2002) claimed that behavioral intentions, for example, venturing into entrepreneurship, are strongly influenced by one's personal values. In the context of informal entrepreneurship, Maloney (2004) and Yamada (1996) revealed that entrepreneurs who enter the informal sector by choice attempt to grab available business opportunities, while initiating a business enterprise and managing all risks and barriers that come their way. Besides, the literature concerning informal entrepreneurship offers a number of insights to a more detailed look at the fundamental characteristics of informal entrepreneurs, as technically less-efficient taxpayers, who need not abide by formal labor market regulations (Boughzala and Kouki, 2003).

From a different stance, Islam, Khan, Obaidullah, & Alam (2011) highlighted that entrepreneurial attributes consist of demographics, personal traits, entrepreneurial orientation, and self-efficacy projected by entrepreneurs. Self-confidence and determination are significant entrepreneurial personality traits among informal entrepreneurs. Personality traits consist of the representative forms of opinions, feelings, and performances that make a person unique from the rest (Boz and Ergeneli, 2014). On the other hand, self-efficacy refers to one's entrepreneurial readiness in running a business. Self-efficacy provides the foundation of one's motivation that may affect his/her beliefs if a certain goal could be achieved. According to scholars, a significant correlation is established between self-efficacy and entrepreneurial intention (Islam, Khan, Obaidullah, & Alam, 2011; Carsrud and Brännback, 2011). These traits can influence one's intention and entrepreneurial effort in the informal economy related to exploiting opportunities, which others may fail to recognize or choose not to pursue. Furthermore, self-efficacy is a significant determinant of career interests, goals, choices, and performance. As for entrepreneurial orientation, a number of researchers have defined it as a combination of independency, innovativeness, autonomy, risk-taking, pro-activeness, competitiveness, aggressiveness, and self-motivation (Islam, Khan, Obaidullah, & Alam, 2011) which serves to facilitate informal entrepreneurs in running business operations successfully.

Interestingly, a majority of informal entrepreneurs are represented by the younger generation and women participants with limited education background, when compared to formal entrepreneurs (Amin, 2011). This signifies that gender, age, and education level appear to have some significance to entrepreneurial background to participate in the informal sector (Spring, 2009). According to Zengyu, Nandialath, Kassim Alsayaghi, & Esra Karadeniz (2013), demographic factors, such as age, gender, income, education level, and working experience, emerge as significant characteristics of informal entrepreneurs. Nevertheless, Williams (2007) depicted that informal entrepreneurs do not only set up their own business using the skills gained from their work experience, but also, at times, as a result of some hobby or interest that they crave for outside their formal environment. Finally, a positive mind-set of joining the informal sector by ignoring the structure of relegation representation reflects the level of self-confidence among informal entrepreneurs and the belief they have upon informal sector for a brighter future (Williams and Gurtoo, 2011). Since the past decade, literature pertaining to entrepreneurship has acknowledged that many entrepreneurs operate temporarily or permanently, and partly or wholly, in the informal sector (Williams, 2006; 2008; 2009; Antonopoulos & Mitra, 2009). Hence, it is integral to improve the traits among informal entrepreneurs in order for them to exert better performance in the informal sector. In a related context, Garoma (2012) suggested that some actions are demanded to improve and to strengthen the characteristics of informal entrepreneurs, such as providing training or building capacity. Furthermore, access to capital and a common platform among the stakeholders of informal businesses should be established so as to develop entrepreneurial street vendors amidst the modern market.

FUTURE DIRECTIONS FOR DEVELOPMENT PROGRAMS AND POLICIES

Globalization helps liberalize various business activities. Undoubtedly, lack access to capital is one of the factors that impede poverty reduction. This situation also slows down the development of private initiative (Wampfler, Guérin, & Servet, 2006). Most underprivileged people, especially those poor and low-paid, are experiencing inaccessibility to credit to generate capital. These people do not have assets to make collateral, credit history, and financial records to get loans from traditional financial institutions. Then, they are hindered from participating income-generating activities actively, which will result in lower productivity and poverty. Microcredit program is popular for its attractive and practical advantages that allow underprivileged people to get access to credit for running business. This program helps developing countries to address poverty from the grass roots. In general, there are two benefits of microcredit program. The first benefit is it can create self-generating economic activities, while the second benefit is it curbs poverty and achieves economic development goals. Undeniably, microfinance is a useful instrument that alleviates poverty to minimize socio-economic disparities worldwide (Yunus and Abed, 2004). There was an increase in the use of microfinance when United Nations (UN) announced that it reduced poverty by 50% within 2015 as a Millennium Development Goals (MDG) in 2000.

Apart from that, institutions that introduce microfinance usually receive vigorous support. The governments, private enterprises, and philanthropic organizations overwhelmingly show their interests in funding microfinance projects (Ferro, 2005). At present, microcredit is one of the renowned facilities to minimize poverty issues in developing countries such as Malaysia, Bangladesh, Indonesia, Thailand, and the Philippines (Park and Ren, 2001; Rahman, Rafiq, and Momen, 2009). In Malaysia, the government has claimed that microfinance plays an essential role in reducing the disparity between poverty and income in the New Economic Policy (NEP).

The microcredit approach, which has been introduced by Professor Muhamad Yunus in Bangladesh since 1976, has the aim of alleviating poverty and expediting self-employment. In 1986, this approach commenced in Malaysia and was initiated by David Gibbons and Sukor Kasim, both are academics from University of Science Malaysia (USM). Then, a project was carried out to observe the effectiveness of Grameen Bank's microcredit approach in Malaysia. The project is named as Projek Ikhtiar and taken place in the northwestern area of Selangor. It was conducted by Centre for Policy Research, USM and financed by Islamic Economic Development Foundation of Malaysia, the Selangor State Government, and Asia-Pacific Development Centre. The purpose of Projek Ikhtiar was to identify whether microcredit can alleviate rural poverty when poor and low-income people are provided with the accessibility to microcredit through Grameen Bank's approach. This microcredit scheme intended to increase their income. The success of "Project Ikhtiar" proved that a group lending system was analogous to Grameen Bank's microcredit model and applicable to Malaysia. Since then, the operation of Amanah Ikhtiar Malaysia (AIM) started in all over Malaysia.

With the success of "Projek Ikhtiar", microcredit program began in 1987 after the establishment of AIM. AIM was institutionalized following the adoption of the Grameen Bank's microcredit model (Conroy, 2003). Undeniably, AIM brought a noteworthy change to the rural poor who were incapable of obtaining credit from the traditional financial institutions. Besides the formation of group members, AIM implemented the microcredit program with the notion of 'trust'. Besides, peer pressure is helpful in maintaining loan contracts, accountability, utilization of loans, and punctual loan repayment. Although public institutions such as Agrobank, Yayasan Usaha Maju (YUM), Koperasi Kredit Rakyat (KKR), the Economic Fund for National Entrepreneurs Group (TEKUN), and the Credit Guarantee Corporation (CGC) provide lending to small and medium enterprises, their objectives are different as compared to AIM. This is because the loan size of the public financial institutions are better than the conventional loan size granted by microfinance. Basically, the objective of AIM is to eradicate rural poverty through the provision of micro financing and allow the rural poor to engage in income-generating activities. Moreover, AIM is established to ease the difficulty of getting micro financing among rural people. It is considered as an effective means of poverty reduction (Saad and Duasa, 2011). Both the concepts of the 'center' and 'sharing liability' among members claim that the participants of AIM microcredit program have the ability to repay the loans at a lower default rate of 0.92% in 2009 (Hamdan, Othman, and Hussain, 2012).

Initially, conventional banking institutions are not allowed to take part in microcredit activities due to legislative mandate. According to (McGuire, Conroy, & Thapa, 1998) the Central Bank of Malaysia restricted the spread to 4% between the base and maximum lending rate in commercial banking system. When the lending rate is less than 4%, additional cost associated with microfinance lending is required, thus microfinance is unnecessary. Even though CGC approved some permissible loans, the spread was 2%. As a result, traditional financial institutions face challenges in participating microfinance activities and alleviating poverty. In fact, AIM has a strong institutional link with the government in terms of poverty alleviation in Malaysia. One of the contributing factors to AIM success is the government grant that helps sustain poor people in Malaysia.

AIM provides its services in Sabah, Kelantan and Kedah, which are among the poorest states in Malaysia. As of 2017, AIM had 93 branches in Peninsular Malaysia with 279,841 borrowers and the disbursement of RM10,838,854,993. The purpose of AIM is to minimize the seriousness of poverty among Malays. All impact studies that investigated the features of AIM micro financing program concluded that AIM had provided microcredit that significantly increased the borrowers' income. These studies were conducted by Social and Economic Research Unit (SERU) of the Economic Planning Unit during the period of 1990-1991, and by AIM in 1989 and during the periods of 1991-

1993 and 1994-1995. Other studies also revealed that AIM borrowers were able to increase their income and assets after receiving AIM loans (Garoma, 2012; Wampfler, Guérin, & Servet, 2006; Nor, Rashid, Nawawi, & Mohd, 2012; Al Mamun, Malarvizhi, Abdul Wahab, & Mazumder, 2011).

For instance, an impact study in 2005 confirmed that borrowers lived out of poverty after they received four loan cycles while the average loan size was RM3,500 per head. However, the impact of microcredit disbursed by AIM had a positive effect on employment. This particular study also reported that 31% of the AIM microcredit borrowers take the service of family members as workers while another 31% of them appointed non-family members as workers. Based on the above situations, it can be concluded that microcredit is instrumental in alleviating poverty and generating employment.

At the beginning, AIM offered several loans such as Ikhtiar Loan Scheme 1 (Skim Pembiayaan Ikhtiar 1-SPI 1), Ikhtiar Loan Scheme 2 (Skim Pembiayaan Ikhtiar 2-SPI 2), Ikhtiar Loan Scheme 3 (Skim Pembiyaan Ikhtiar 3-SPI 3), and Single Mother Loan Scheme (Skim Ibu Tunggal-SKIT). In addition, special education loan scheme and special housing loan scheme, which are worth RM1,000 and RM5,000 respectively, are provided for borrowers with good repayment record. In 2017, AIM micro financing programs showed a commendable collection rate of 87.3% (2001: 96.5%, 2002: 95.5%, August 2003: 95.3%, 2013: 98.6%), but not all the programs had successful repayment record. One of them was SKIT with 36% of repayment collection and another was the Fisherman Loan Scheme (SPIN).

AIM has introduced new schemes such as economic loan, social or non-economic loan and recovery loan. The economic loan consists of I-MESRA, I-SRIKANDI and I-WIBAWA. In I-MESRA, the loan is continuous with a loan size of RM1,000 to RM10, 000 and the repayment period should not exceed 50 weeks. Next, I-SRIKANDI is a continuous loan similar to I-MESRA, while I-WIBAWA is a short term loan amounting up to RM5,000 with a repayment period of 24 weeks. In contrast, the non-economic or social loan is made up of I-BISTARI and I-SEJAHTERA. Specifically, I-BISTARI is an educational loan amounting between RM1,000 and RM5,000, which should be repaid within 50 to 100 weeks. I-SEJAHTERA is a multipurpose loan with a loan size up to RM10,000 with a loan repayment period between 50 and 100 weeks. Last but not least, I-PENYAYANG is a recovery loan which offers up to RM5,000 with a repayment period between 12 to 50 weeks. This loan is given to participants who experience project failure due to health problems or natural disaster.

Undoubtedly, the success of AIM microcredit programs has been well documented in the literature. Most studies measured the success by considering the repayment rates and borrowers' life. However, AIM has to depend largely on the government or donor grants for covering its operational costs. This situation is questionable whether AIM has stable financial resources to provide loan. AIM microcredit programs are limited as compared to micro financing organizations of other countries although it replicated Grameen Bank's model. Also, administrative problems severely threaten AIM's future. In this section, we will discuss the future policies that AIM can implement for its future growth. Firstly, we will discuss about the financial viability and sustainability of the existing loan schemes. Secondly, a comparative analysis about microcredit schemes between AIM, Grameen, and BPR will be discussed. Lastly, there will be a discussion about other operational and administrative problems for limiting the AIM's outreach.

Financial viability in terms of delivery mode of microcredit program to the poor is done in an efficient and cost-effective way. Besides, financial sustainability symbolizes the capacity of AIM. This indicates that AIM is capable of running its operation with self-finance rather than seeking support from government or donor subsidies. The operational cost of AIM is higher than other microcredit financing organizations like Grameen Bank in Bangladesh, BPR in Indonesia, and SHG in India. The staff salary and administrative cost incur large proportion of operation cost to allow AIM to acquire a negligible amount of assets from its operation. However, the fixed administrative charge of 10% (previous charge was 5%) is not enough to cover the operating costs, thereby threatening AIM's sustainability and self-dependency. This kind of challenge has been common. Conroy (Conroy, 2003) asserted that AIM losses its direction since the microcredit strategies are provided to normal members, while larger loans are provided to the members and better-off borrowers.

Moreover, financial viability embodies operational and full self-sufficiency, depending on the charges AIM imposes on its members. There are two ways AIM can reduce costs. The cost of daily operation and administrative costs are to be covered by the revenues earned from microcredit programs. Therefore, there is a need to readjust the maintenance charges. Another way is that AIM needs to redesign its programs to reach a large number of people. Also, outreach microcredit programs can be extended to poor people depending on the AIM's efficiency and viability through its scale and financial leverage. On the contrary, there are other possible challenges that influence AIM's future development. These challenges are (a) to increase the quality of loan portfolio, (b) to increase the quality of services (c) to increase productivity corresponding to accelerating cost, (d) to enhance operational efficiency, and (e) to reduce the drop-out of members.

In order to achieve financial viability and sustainability, some measures should be taken by AIM. Basically, there are eight dimensions in these measures. The first dimension is to assess the structure of the overall cost including operating cost and lending cost to the borrowers. The second dimension is to determine various ratios and indicators of cost effectiveness. The third dimension is it requires the operational efficiency and productivity of loan disbursed per unit. The fourth dimension is to emphasize on an efficient and low cost delivery system. The fifth dimension is to apply a mechanism that increases the quality of loan portfolio. The sixth dimension is to give priority to the rationalization of cost structure. The seventh dimension is to identify the degree of partial and full financial self-sufficiency and return on assets. The last dimension is an analysis of benefit and cost analysis of financial self-sufficiency that determines the financial viability. A comparative analysis between the programs by AIM, Grameen, and BPR will be discussed in the next section.

The lending systems, schemes and products offered by AIM are different from Grameen Bank and BPR microcredit schemes although AIM replicated the Grameen Bank model. This model is considered the leading microfinance framework inaugurated in 1983 and practiced in many countries. When AIM is subsidized, it is different from Grameen and BPR. The microcredit programs offered by these three organizations are different. Fundamentally, Grameen Bank does not only facilitate microcredit loans, it also provides micro insurance, micro savings, and pension funds for members. Besides that, BPR encourages micro savings among borrowers in Indonesia. Since microfinance institutions in Malaysia are legally advised to take deposits from their borrowers (McGuire, Conroy, & Thapa, 1998; Siwar and Talib, 2001). AIM only offers micro credit loans. This is the only service which limits the AIM's ability to make outreach to its borrowers, thereby increasing AIM's operational cost and causing financial self-sufficiency. Several studies (Robinson, 2001; Morduch, 2000) showed that microfinance institutions that emphasize on savings are able to fulfil financial needs because savings mobilisation is used to obtain financial self-sufficiency. Nevertheless, AIM can only offer micro savings to clients, which hinders AIM from achieving financial self-sufficiency. Hence, AIM should be given an opportunity to offer this service for financial viability and sustainability.

AIM offers loans when borrowers are affected by calamities but it does not introduce micro insurance when they fail to repay the loans because of those calamities. Most importantly, micro insurance helps borrowers who are affected by natural disasters. This insurance assists them in saving the deficit accounts of uncollectible loans. It differs AIM from Grameen Bank in respect of micro financing programs. Particularly, Grameen offers pension fund and scholarships programs to the children of the borrowers, which should be made available in AIM's microfinance programs. These programs are likely to increase the borrowers' confidence in AIM and extend to poor people. In fact, offering these programs will reduce the operation cost while keeping the AIM financial account from deficit and risk of unpaid loans.

Furthermore, BPR starts a micro financing by fostering borrowers to deposit savings. The borrowers need to have some savings in their account before they are allowed to borrow. The loan they intend to borrow should be less than the amount in their savings. Borrowers can deposit their savings, which are collected by BPR staff in a daily or weekly basis. This program has been popular and successful. Thus, AIM can implement a similar program to increase revenue and encourage borrowers' savings habit concurrently.

One limitation of AIM micro financing programs and lending contracts is their inflexibility as compared to Grameen Bank and BPR. Grameen Bank adopts flexible loan to allow borrowers who are unable to pay the loan on time to reschedule their repayment period (Yunus, 2007). Regardless of the borrowers' business revenue cycle, AIM only allows them to settle loan payments weekly with only one-week grace period, which the same contract is applied to all its borrowers. In contrast, both Grameen Bank and BPR can determine the amount of loan, duration, interest rates, repayment modes, and grace periods according to the borrowers' businesses and their affordability to repay the loan. Islam (2007) posited that loan repayment systems of Grameen Bank are determined by using the borrowers' business cash flow cycle. Grameen Bank also introduces four different types of loan products at different interest rates. BPR offers similar types of micro financing programs as Grameen Bank does. Since there are many BPRs in one district, there is a strong competition to make the loan products attractive, hence different types of loans are provided at different interest rates. Also, BRP carried out a market research on the interest rates, amount of repayment, affordability, and nature of the cash flow cycle of the business to ensure that the loan contracts do not burden the borrowers.

At the beginning, Malaysian commercial banks are not allowed to offer collateral free micro financing programs. In fact, interest rate control policies by the Central Bank of Malaysia are vital. In 2007, the government authorized the commercial banks to offer these microcredit programs, but the banks did not have a division that developed the programs. The innovator of Grameen Bank microcredit system, Yunus (2007) highlighted that commercial banks that launched micro credit programs should have a special division and the management should be separated from the traditional banking system. This management structure is practiced by BPR in Indonesia and several commercial banks in Bangladesh. When commercial banks are authorized to launch micro financing programs, the AIM's outreach is limited, which is likely to increase operation cost and dependency on the government and donor grants. As a result, the government needs to extend AIM microcredit programs that are expected to reduce the operation cost, at the same time, increase the revenue.

BPR provides public shares for the villagers who receive dividends as yearly returns from the profits. It recruits skilled and qualified locals as employees. Thus, this strategy enhances the sustainability among borrowers as they rely on BPR to survive, which is similar to Grameen Bank's microcredit program because the borrowers are the shareholders who may feel the ownership. If AIM offers public shares as what BPR and Grameen Bank do, it is likely to assist AIM in facilitating sustainability.

Based on the above discussion, AIM needs to depend on the government or donor grants to address various limitations in the operation. Since the AIM's operation is subsidized by the government, AIM has limited incentives to offer attractive micro financing products to the borrowers. When AIM is unsubsidized, AIM offers several microfinance products such as micro insurance and pension funds to cover operational cost through revenue generation from the services. Besides, AIM needs to modify its products since it offers limited microcredit products as compared to BPR and Grameen Bank. AIM has to terminate standardized lending contracts and offer flexible lending contracts based on the products life cycle.

The operational and administrative challenges that limit the AIM outreach will be discussed in the next section. The AIM's charter distributes small loans to the poor households with reasonable terms and financing in order to encourage them to perform income-generating activities (Gibbons and Kasiim, 1991). However, the AIM's outreach data violates the charter by directing its activities in reducing the level of poverty among Malays. They receive the utmost attention from AIM microcredit programs. Although NEP is found to reduce the relative poverty, the issue of hardcore poverty is prevalent. Therefore, a new approach should be adopted instead of employing conventional Grameen Bank's approach without modification. Although AIM's target is feasible, it has been interfered by political elements that weaken the achievement of AIM. The service charges AIM imposes are lower than the interest rate in commercial banks in order to benefit Muslim consumers. Nevertheless, this term is not congruent with the Grameen Bank's policy of microcredit disbursement with interest rates higher than commercial banks as the cost of introducing microfinance programs is higher than conventional banking.

Basically, the difference between AIM microfinance charter and Grameen Bank's charter indicates the reason why AIM should be financed by the government grant. Besides the federal government grants, the CGC and commercial banks also contributed considerably to AIM's loan capital. However, the dependence on the Malaysian government grant (60% of AIM operational costs) and state government grant (40% of its operational costs) might have an adverse influence on AIM's self-sufficiency. With the federal and state government grants, AIM does not achieve self-sufficiency (McGuire, Conroy, & Thapa, 1998). AIM programs experienced a stunning cash-flow problem when the government decided to channel a huge grant of $7.4 million through YPEIM, which seriously suspended the expansion plan, and achievement of AIM microfinance programs (Kasim, 2000). In 1992, the cash-flow problem forced AIM to increase the loan ceiling. Then, the size of the average loan increased by 400% during the period between 1994 and 1998 with a rise in portfolio at risk (Kasim, 2000). When AIM reached 50% of its target group, it caused a significant increase in outstanding loan values instead of microcredit programs outreach to hardcore poor. In 1997, the federal government provided loan for AIM capital to increase loan ceiling. Concurrently, the operational costs and borrower dropouts also increased. The principal dropout members were mostly poor members.

Another concern AIM microcredit program faces is the disbursement of loan to the regular members. AIM disregards the fundamental Grameen principles which receive constant criticism from scholars. For example, Sukor Kasim (Kasim, 2000), one of the AIM founding members, defined this activity as a leakage of loans to the regular members. The scholar stressed that AIM should extend its outreach to women, who constitute two-third of the poverty at household level with some relaxation of terms. His argument opposed SPIN and SKIT loan programs, which are normally disbursed to fishermen and single mothers corresponding with larger loan sizes. When AIM enlarged its loan sizes and disbursement of loans to satisfy borrowers, it had actually affected the development of credit discipline and portfolio quality (Conroy, 2003). As a result, there were serious problems for maintaining a decent portfolio at risk (PAR) index for AIM. PAR index increased to 10% with an outstanding of RM100 million in which both SKIT and SPIN contributed 36% and 60% of PAR, respectively, to AIM at the end of 2000 (Mitton, 2002). However, the dropouts from the programs increased substantially when AIM decided to break its early practice of service charges by imposing 19% of interest rates on loans (Conroy, 2003) making borrowing more costly in terms of the percentage of principle. This change in AIM's decision on interest rates is consistent with movement away from subsidies and progress towards financial sustainability. Hence, higher interest rate and broader AIM outreach have a positive effect on PAR index. In response to this, AIM should be consistent with successively introduce preference based and cost-efficient operation in which there will be absence of any types of political interference and consideration. It is crucial for AIM to seek advice from political experts and solve repayment problems among AIM borrowers in northern and eastern states (Mitton, 2002).

AUTHOR CONTRIBUTIONS

All authors were involved in collecting relevant information and literature review, and writing this chapter.

CONFLICTS OF INTEREST

The authors declare no conflict of interest.

ACKNOWLEDGMENT

This research was funded by the Ministry of Higher Education, Malaysia under the grant entitled "Developing a Comprehensive Rural Entrepreneurship Model for Poverty Eradication (REMODE)" (R/NRGS/A01.00/00047A/006/2014/000149).

REFERENCES

Afrane, S. (2002). Impact assessment of microfinance interventions in Ghana and South Africa: A synthesis of major impacts and lessons. *Journal of Microfinance/ESR Review, 4*(1), 37-58.

Ahlstrom, D. (2010). Innovation and growth: How business contributes to society. *The Academy of Management Perspectives, 24*(3), 11–24.

Ahmad, N., & Seymour, R. G. (2008). *Defining entrepreneurial activity: Definitions supporting frameworks for data collection. OECD Statistics Working Papers. OECD.* Retrieved from https://ssrn.com/abstract=1090372

Ahmad, Z., & Xavier, S. R. (2012). Entrepreneurial environments and growth: Evidence from Malaysia GEM data. *Journal of Chinese Entrepreneurship, 4*(1), 50–69. doi:10.1108/17561391211200939

Al Mamun, A., Malarvizhi, C. A., Abdul Wahab, S., & Mazumder, M. N. H. (2011). Investigating the Effect of the Utilization of Microcredit on Hardcore Poor Clients Household Income and Assets. *Asian Social Science, 7*(7), 141–152. doi:10.5539/ass.v7n7p141

Amin, M. (2011). *Labor Productivity, Firm-Size and Gender: The Case of Informal Firms in Argentina and Peru. Enterprise Note 22.* Washington, DC: Enterprise Analysis Unit, World Bank Group.

Antonopoulos, G. A., & Mitra, J. (2009). The hidden enterprise of bootlegging cigarettes out of Greece: Two schemes of illegal entrepreneurship. *Journal of Small Business and Entrepreneurship, 22*(1), 1–8. doi:10.1080/08276331.2009.10593438

Audretsch, D. B. (2003). Entrepreneurship policy and the strategic management of places. In The emergence of entrepreneurship policy: Governance, start-ups, and growth in the US knowledge economy, (pp. 20-38). Cambridge University Press. doi:10.1017/CBO9780511610134.002

Audretsch, D. B., & Thurik, A. R. (2001). What's new about the new economy? Sources of growth in the managed and entrepreneurial economies. *Industrial and Corporate Change, 10*(1), 267–315. doi:10.1093/icc/10.1.267

Bangasser, P. E. (2000). *The ILO and the informal sector. ILO Employment Paper 2000/9.* Geneva: ILO.

Baumol, W. J. (1993). Formal entrepreneurship theory in economics: Existence and bounds. *Journal of Business Venturing*, *8*(3), 197–210. doi:10.1016/0883-9026(93)90027-3

Berglann, H., Moen, E. R., Røed, K., & Skogstrøm, J. F. (2011). Entrepreneurship: Origins and returns. *Labour Economics*, *18*(2), 180–193. doi:10.1016/j.labeco.2010.10.002

Bhagwati, J., & Panagariya, A. (2013). *Why growth matters: How economic growth in India reduced poverty and the lessons for other developing countries.* Hachette.

Boughzala, M., & Kouki, M. (2003). *Unemployment persistence and the informal sector*. ERF Working Paper 0326, Economic Research Forum, Cairo, Egypt.

Boz, A., & Ergeneli, A. (2014). Women entrepreneurs' personality characteristics and parents' parenting style profile in Turkey. *Procedia: Social and Behavioral Sciences*, *109*, 92–97. doi:10.1016/j.sbspro.2013.12.425

Bruton, G. D., Ketchen, D. J. Jr, & Ireland, R. D. (2013). Entrepreneurship as a solution to poverty. *Journal of Business Venturing*, *28*(6), 683–689. doi:10.1016/j.jbusvent.2013.05.002

Buehn, A. (2012). The shadow economy in German regions: An empirical assessment. *German Economic Review*, *13*(3), 275–290. doi:10.1111/j.1468-0475.2011.00557.x

Carsrud, A., & Brännback, M. (2011). Entrepreneurial Motivations: What Do We Still Need To Know? *Journal of Small Business Management*, *49*(1), 9–26. doi:10.1111/j.1540-627X.2010.00312.x

Castells, M., & Portes, A. (1989). World underneath: The origins, dynamics, and effects of the informal economy. In A. Portes, M. Castells, & L. A. Benton (Eds.), *The Informal Economy: Studies in advanced and less developed countries* (pp. 11–37). Baltimore, MD: Johns Hopkins University Press.

Chakraborty, A. B. (2010). *Studies in Indian informal sector* (Doctoral dissertation). Available from ProQuest Dissertations & Theses database. (UMI No. 3442535)

Chong, A., & Gradstein, M. (2007). Inequality and informality. *Journal of Public Economics*, *91*(1), 159–179. doi:10.1016/j.jpubeco.2006.08.001

Coleman, B. E. (2006). Microfinance in Northeast Thailand: Who benefits and how much? *World Development, 34*(9), 1612–1638. doi:10.1016/j.worlddev.2006.01.006

Conroy, J. D. (2003). *The Challenges of Micro financing in Southeast Asia*. Singapore: Institute of Southeast Asian Studies.

S. M. E. Corporation Malaysia. (2016). *SME Annual Report 2015/2016*. Retrieved December 15th, 2017 from http://www.smecorp.gov.my/index.php/en/sme-annual-report-2015-16

Corporation, S. M. E. (2017a). *SME Developments and Outlook*. SME Corporation Malaysia. Retrieved December 15th, 2017 from http://www.smecorp.gov.my/images/SMEAR/latest/Chapter2.pdf

Cumming, D., & Suret, J. M. (2011). Entrepreneurial finance and venture capital markets: Introduction. *European Financial Management, 17*(3), 420–422. doi:10.1111/j.1468-036X.2011.00610.x

Das, M. (2003). *The other side of self-employment: household enterprises in India*. Social Protection Discussion Paper Series, No. 0318. Social Protection Unit, Human Development Network, The World Bank.

Dawson, C., & Henley, A. (2012). "Push" versus "pull" entrepreneurship: An ambiguous distinction? *International Journal of Entrepreneurial Behaviour & Research, 18*(6), 697–719. doi:10.1108/13552551211268139

DeSoto, H. (1989). The Other Path: The Invisible Revolution in the Third World. New York: Harper & Row.

Du, J., Guariglia, A., & Newman, A. (2015). Do Social Capital Building Strategies Influence the Financing Behavior of Chinese Private Small and Medium-Sized Enterprises? *Entrepreneurship Theory and Practice, 39*(3), 601–631. doi:10.1111/etap.12051

Dugguh, S. I. (2014). Entrepreneurship and small business: Strategic approach to alleviating poverty and corruption in Nigeria. *GSTF Journal on Business Review, 3*(1), 57–66.

Durmaz, B., Platt, S., & Yigitcanlar, T. (2010). Creativity, culture tourism and place making: Istanbul and London film industries. *International Journal of Culture, Tourism and Hospitality Research, 4*(3), 198–213. doi:10.1108/17506181011067592

Economic Transformation Program. (2017). *Overview of ETP.* Retrieved December 12nd, 2017 from http://etp.pemandu.gov.my/About_ETP-@-Overview_of_ETP.aspx

Federation of Malaysian Manufacturer. (2010). *Views and Proposals on The New Economic Model.* Retrieved from http://www.fmm.org.my/upload/FMM_Views_and_Proposals_on_the_NEM_booklet.pdf

Ferro, N. (2005). *Value through Diversity: Microfinance and Islamic Finance, and Global Banking* (FEEM Working Paper No. 87.05). Foundazione Eni Enrico Mattei, Milan. Retrieved from http://papers.ssrn.com/sol3/papers.cfm?abstract_id=755447

Fong, C. O. (1990). Small and medium industries in Malaysia: Economic efficiency and entrepreneurship. *The Developing Economies, 28*(2), 152–179. doi:10.1111/j.1746-1049.1990.tb00179.x

Food and Fertilizer Technology Center-Asia Pacific. (2015). *Entrepreneurship Development Policy In Malaysia. Food And Fertilizer Technology Center for the Asia Pacific Region.* Retrieved December 15th, 2017 from http://ap.fftc.agnet.org/ap_db.php?id=439

Foss, N. J., & Klein, P. G. (2010). Alertness, Action, and the Antecedents of Entrepreneurship. *Journal of Private Enterprise, 25*(2), 145–164.

Garoma, B. F. (2012). *Determinants of Microenterprise Success in the Urban Informal Sector of Addis Ababa: A Multidimensional Analysis. ISS PhD Theses.* Rotterdam: Erasmus University. Retrieved from http://hdl.handle.net/1765/37927

Gerxhani, K. (2004). The informal sector in developed and less developed countries: A literature survey. *Public Choice, 120*(3-4), 267–300. doi:10.1023/B:PUCH.0000044287.88147.5e

Gibbons, D., & Kasim, S. (1991). Banking on the rural poor. Center for Policy Research, University Sains, Malaysia.

Global Entrepreneurship Monitor. (2016). Global Report 2015/2016. *Global Entrepreneurship Monitor.* Retrieved January 07th, 2018 from http://www.gemconsortium.org/report

Global Entrepreneurship Monitor. (2017). Global Report 2016/2017. *Global Entrepreneurship Monitor.* Retrieved January 07th, 2018 from http://www.gemconsortium.org/report

Hamdan, H., Othman, P., & Hussin, W. S. W. (2012). Is microfinance program in Malaysia really effective in helping the poor? *World Review of Business Research, 2*(1), 79–97.

Harris-White, B., & Sinha, A. (Eds.). (2007). *Trade liberalization and India's informal economy*. New Delhi: Oxford University Press.

Hart, K. (1973). Informal income opportunities and urban employment in Ghana. *The Journal of Modern African Studies, 11*(1), 61–89. doi:10.1017/S0022278X00008089

Idris, N. A. H., & Siwar, C. (2003). *Kemiskinan bandar dan sektor tidak formal di Malaysia*. Bangi: Penerbit Universiti Kebangsaan Malaysia.

Institut Keusahawanan Negara (INSKEN). (2017). *Scale Up Program*. Retrieved December 22nd, 2017, from http://www.insken.gov.my/insken-scale-up/

Islam, M. A., Khan, M. A., Obaidullah, A. Z. M., & Alam, M. S. (2011). Effect of entrepreneur and firm characteristics on the business success of small and medium enterprises (SMEs) in Bangladesh. *International Journal of Business and Management, 6*(3), 289–299.

Islam, T. (2007). Poverty alleviation impact on Grameen microcredit. In *Microcredit and poverty alleviation* (pp. 165–167). Hampshire, UK: Ashgate Publishing Limited.

Istrate, E. (2012). *Small Businesses, Institutions, and the Informal Economy* (Doctoral dissertation). Available from ProQuest Dissertations & Theses database. (UMI No. 3506035)

Itzigsohn, J. (2000). Immigration and the boundaries of citizenship: The institutions of immigrants' political transnationalism. *The International Migration Review, 34*(4), 1126–1154.

Jamak, A. B. S. A., Salleh, R., Sivapalan, S., & Abdullah, A. (2012). Micro business enterprise of Bumiputera Malays, Malaysia. *African Journal of Business Management, 6*(22), 6504–6510.

Johnson, S., Kaufmann, D., & Zoido-Lobaton, P. (1998). Regulatory discretion and the unofficial economy. *The American Economic Review, 88*(2), 387–392.

Jomo, K. S. (2004). *The New Economic Policy and interethnic relations in Malaysia. Identities, Conflict and Cohesion Programme Paper 7*. United Nations Research Institute for Social Development.

Kasseeah, H., & Tandrayen-Ragoobur, V. (2015). Self-employed women and their access to finance: Perspectives from the informal sector. *African Journal of Science, Technology. Innovation and Development*, *7*(4), 247–254.

Kerr, S. P., & Kerr, W. R. (2011). *Economic Impacts of Immigration: A Survey* (Working paper 16736). Cambridge, MA: National Bureau of Economic Research. Retrieved from http://www.nber.org/papers/w16736

Khandker, S. R. (2005). Microfinance and poverty: Evidence using panel data from Bangladesh. *The World Bank Economic Review*, *19*(2), 263–286. doi:10.1093/wber/lhi008

Kidd, B. (2008). A new social movement: Sport for development and peace. *Sport in Society*, *11*(4), 370–380. doi:10.1080/17430430802019268

Klassen, N. P. (2010). *State Autonomy and Population Health: The Experience of Thailand, Malaysia and South Korea During the East Asian Financial Crisis* (Doctoral dissertation). University of Regina, Canada.

Kleemans, M. (2014). *Migration choice under risk and liquidity constraints. Job Market Paper*. Berkeley, CA: University of California.

Lund, F., & Srinivas, S. (2000). *Learning from experience: A gendered approach to social protection for workers in the informal economy*. Geneva: WIEGO and ILO.

1. Malaysia Entrepreneurs. (2017). Retrieved December 15th, 2017 from http://nbos.gov.my/posts/1malaysia-entrepreneurs-(1met)

Malaysian Global Innovation & Creativity Centre. (2017). *Programs Malaysian Global Innovation & Creativity Centre*. Retrieved December 15th, 2017 from https://mymagic.my/programs/

Maloney, W. F. (2004). Informality revisited. *World Development*, *32*(7), 1159–1178. doi:10.1016/j.worlddev.2004.01.008

McGuire, P., Conroy, J., & Thapa, G. (1998). *Getting the Framework Right: Policy and Regulation for Microfinance in Asia*. Brisbane: Foundation for Development Co-operation.

Ministry of International Trade and Industry. (2017). *Entrepreneur Development*. Ministry of International Trade and Industry. Retrieved December 15th, 2017 from http://www.miti.gov.my/index.php/pages/view/2818?mid=261

Ministry of Women, Family and Community Development. (2014). *Study To Support The Development Of National Policies And Programmes To Increase And Retain The Participation Of Women In The Malaysian Labour Force: Key Finding And Recommendation*. Retrieved December 15th, 2017 from: http://www.my.undp.org/content/dam/malaysia/docs/Women%20In%20Malaysian%20Labour%20Force%20Study%20with%20UNDP-2013.pdf

Ministry of Youth and Sports. (2017). *Ministry of Youth and Sports*. Retrieved December 15th, 2017 from http://www.kbs.gov.my/en/

Mitton, T. (2002). A cross-firm analysis of the impact of corporate governance on the East Asian financial crisis. *Journal of Financial Economics*, *64*(2), 215–241. doi:10.1016/S0304-405X(02)00076-4

Mokyr, J. (2013). Cultural entrepreneurs and the origins of modern economic growth. *The Scandinavian Economic History Review*, *61*(1), 1–33. doi:10.1080/03585522.2012.755471

Morduch, J. (2000). The microfinance schism. *World Development*, *28*(4), 617–629. doi:10.1016/S0305-750X(99)00151-5

Mutalib, R. A., Arshad, R., Ismail, N. S., & Ahmad, Z. (2015). Women and entrepreneurship: An overview of women entrepreneurship programs in Malaysia. *Journal of Governance and Development*, *11*, 15–28.

Neergaard, H., Nielsen, K. T., & Kjeldsen, J. I. (2006). State of the art of women's entrepreneurship, access to financing and financing strategies in Denmark. In C. Brush, N. M. Carter, E. J. Gatewood, P. Greene, & M. Hart (Eds.), Growth oriented women entrepreneurs and their businesses: a global research perspective, (pp. 88-111). Cheltenham, UK: Edward Elgar. doi:10.4337/9781845429942.00009

Nor, N. H. M., Rashid, S. N. M., Nawawi, R., & Mohd, F. (2012). Women Enterprenuership in Micro Credit Performance: The Preliminary Study in Kelantan. In *Knowledge Management International Conference (KMICe)* (pp. 724-729). Johor Bahru. Retrieved from http://www.kmice.cms.net.my/prockmice/kmice2012/PDF/CR300.pdf

Oly Ndubisi, N., & Iftikhar, K. (2012). Relationship between entrepreneurship, innovation and performance: Comparing small and medium-size enterprises. *Journal of Research in Marketing and Entrepreneurship*, *14*(2), 214–236. doi:10.1108/14715201211271429

Park, A., & Ren, C. (2001). Microfinance with Chinese characteristics. *World Development*, *29*(1), 39–62. doi:10.1016/S0305-750X(00)00087-5

Perbadanan Kemajuan Negeri Kedah. (2017). *Pembangunan Usahawan*. Kedah State Development Corporation. Retrieved January 05th, 2018 from http://www.pknk.gov.my/index.php?option=com_content&view=article&id=613&Itemid=113

Pokrajac, S., Dondur, N., Grbić, S., & Savanović, M. (2011). Production entrepreneurship as possible way-out from economic crisis. *Ekonomski vidici, 16*(4), 719-733.

Rahman, S., Rafiq, R. B., & Momen, M. A. (2009). Impact of microcredit programs on higher income borrowers: Evidence from Bangladesh. *International Business & Economics Research Journal*, *8*(2), 119–124.

Reynolds, P., Carter, N., Gartner, W., Greene, P., & Cox, L. (2002). *The Entrepreneur Next Door, Characteristics of Individuals Starting Companies in America*. Kansas City, MO: Ewing Marion Kauffman Foundation.

Reynolds, P. D., Hay, M., Bygrave, W. D., Camp, S. M., & Autio, E. (2000). *Executive Report. Global Entrepreneurship Monitor: 2000*. Kansas City, MO: Kauffman Centre for Entrepreneurial Leadership at the Ewing Marion Kauffman Foundation.

Robinson, M. S. (2001). *The Microfinance Revolution: Sustainable Finance for the Poor*. Washington, DC: World Bank Publications. doi:10.1596/0-8213-4524-9

Saad, N. M., & Duasa, J. (2011). An economic impact assessment of a microcredit program in Malaysia: The case of Amanah Ikhtiar Malaysia (AIM). *International Journal of Business and Society*, *12*(1), 1–14.

Saini, J. S., & Gurjar, B. R. (Eds.). (2001). *Entrepreneurship & Education: Challenges & Strategies*. Jaipur, India: Rawat Publications.

Schumpeter, J. (1991). Comments on a plan for the study of entrepreneurship. In R. Swedberg (Ed.), *The economics and sociology of capitalism* (pp. 406–428). Princeton, NJ: Princeton University Press.

Shamsudin, S. F. F. B., Al Mamun, A., Nawi, N. B. C., Nasir, N. A. B. M., & Zakaria, M. N. B. (2016). Policies and practices for entrepreneurial education: The Malaysian experience. *Journal of Developing Areas*, *50*(5), 307–316. doi:10.1353/jda.2016.0053

Shaw, D., & Shiu, E. (2002). An Assessment of Ethical Obligation and Self-Identity in Ethical Consumer Decision-Making: A Structural Equation Modelling Approach. *International Journal of Consumer Studies*, *26*(4), 286–293. doi:10.1046/j.1470-6431.2002.00255.x

Siwar, C., & Talib, B. A. (2001). Micro-finance capacity assessment for poverty alleviation: Outreach, viability and sustainability. *Humanomics*, *17*(1), 116–133. doi:10.1108/eb018864

Slaughter, M. P. (1996). *Entrepreneurship: Economic Impact and Public Policy Implications: An Overview of the Field.* Kansas City, MO: Kauffman Center for Entrepreneurial Leadership.

SME Corporation Malaysia. (2017b). *SME Statistics*. Retrieved December 15th, 2017 from http://www.smecorp.gov.my/index.php/en/policies/2015-12-21-09-09-49/sme-statistics

Spring, A. (2009). Empowering women in the African entrepreneurial landscape. In M. Ndulo (Ed.), *Power, gender, and social change in Africa and the African diaspora*. Newcastle upon Tyne, UK: Cambridge Scholars.

Suhaimi, N. H. B. M., Al Mamun, A., Zainol, N. R., Nawi, N. C., Permerupan, Y., & Malarvizhi, C. A. (2016). Characteristics of informal micro-entrepreneurs in Malaysia. *Mediterranean Journal of Social Sciences*, *7*(2), 128–136.

Suruhanjaya Syarikat Malaysia. (2017). Retrieved December 15th, 2017 from http://www.ssm.com.my/

Temtime, Z. T., Chinyoka, S. V., & Shunda, J. P. W. (2004). A decision tree approach for integrating small business assistance schemes. *Journal of Management Development*, *23*(6), 563–578. doi:10.1108/02621710410541132

Van Stel, A., Carree, M., & Thurik, R. (2005). The effect of entrepreneurial activity on national economic growth. *Small Business Economics*, *24*(3), 311–321. doi:10.100711187-005-1996-6

Venkataraman, S. (1997). The distinctive domain of entrepreneurship research. *Advances in Entrepreneurship, Firm, Emergence, and Growth*, *3*(1), 119–138.

Wampfler, B., Guérin, I., & Servet, J. M. (2006). The Role of Research in Microfinance. *Revue Dialogue*, *37*, 11–25.

Webb, J. W., Bruton, G. D., Tihanyi, L., & Ireland, R. D. (2013). Research on entrepreneurship in the informal economy: Framing a research agenda. *Journal of Business Venturing*, *28*(5), 598–614. doi:10.1016/j.jbusvent.2012.05.003

Wennekers, S., Thurik, R., & Buis, F. (1997). *Entrepreneurship, Economic Growth and What Links Them Together. Research Report 97*. Zoetermeer: EIM Strategic Study, EIM Business and Policy Research.

Williams, C. C. (2006). *The Hidden Enterprise Culture: Entrepreneurship in the Underground Economy*. Cheltenham, UK: Edward Elgar. doi:10.4337/9781847201881

Williams, C. C. (2007). Entrepreneurs operating in the informal economy: Necessity or opportunity driven? *Journal of Small Business and Entrepreneurship*, *20*(3), 309–319. doi:10.1080/08276331.2007.10593402

Williams, C. C. (2008). Beyond necessity-driven versus opportunity-driven entrepreneurship: A study of informal entrepreneurs in England, Russia and Ukraine. *International Journal of Entrepreneurship and Innovation*, *9*(3), 157–166. doi:10.5367/000000008785096647

Williams, C. C. (2009). Informal entrepreneurs and their motives: A gender perspective. *International Journal of Gender and Entrepreneurship*, *1*(3), 219–225. doi:10.1108/17566260910990900

Williams, C. C., & Gurtoo, A. (2011). Women Entrepreneurs in The Indian Informal Sector: Marginalisation Dynamics or Institutional Rational Choice? *International Journal of Gender and Entrepreneurship*, *3*(1), 6–22. doi:10.1108/17566261111114953

World Bank. (2016). *Small is the New Big – Malaysian SMEs Help Energize, Drive Economy*. Retrieved December 15th, 2017 from http://www.worldbank.org/en/news/feature/2016/07/05/small-is-the-new-big---malaysian-smes-help-energize-drive-economy

Yamada, G. (1996). Urban informal employment and self-employment in developing countries: Theory and evidence. *Economic Development and Cultural Change*, *44*(2), 289–314. doi:10.1086/452214

Yunus, M. (2007). *Creating a world without poverty: Social business and the future of capitalism*. New York: Public Affairs.

Yunus & Abed. (2004). *Poverty Matters*. State of Microcredit Summit Campaign Report. Microcredit Summit.

Zengyu, H. (2013). Socio-demographic factors and network configuration among MENA entrepreneurs. *International Journal of Emerging Markets*, *8*(3), 258–281. doi:10.1108/17468801311330329

Chapter 3
Women Micro-Entrepreneurship in Malaysia

ABSTRACT

Entrepreneurship is a gateway to generate income so as to attain a more sustainable livelihood. Entrepreneurship has improved the aspect of employability among women in the Europe and Euroasia regions as they have begun to turn to self-employment and entrepreneurship as means of survival. This chapter presents a brief description regarding women micro-entrepreneurs in Malaysia followed by the socio-economic effect of women micro-entrepreneurship upon the Malaysian economy. This chapter also depicts several characteristics of micro-enterprises owned and managed by women in Malaysia and, finally, the strength and shortcomings among women micro-entrepreneurs in Malaysia.

WOMEN MICRO-ENTREPRENEURS

Entrepreneurs, regardless of their gender, have left significant footprints in the history of modern society, where entrepreneurial activity is derived from entrepreneurial talent and motivation with valid explanation for the successful growth noted in several economies (Baumol, 1993). In addition, it is an undeniable fact that entrepreneurs play a major role in contributing and developing the economy of a nation. As such, many economists and politicians hold to the belief that entrepreneurs are indeed notable contributors to economic growth and job creation, which has encouraged nearly all

DOI: 10.4018/978-1-5225-8473-5.ch003

nations to promote entrepreneurial activities (Audretsch, & Thurik, 2001; Reynolds, Camp, Bygrave, Autio, & Hay, 2001). Entrepreneurs, nevertheless, are not only associated with economic growth through new firm creation that generates new economic opportunities (Wennekers, Thurik, & Buis, 1997), but they also facilitate distribution of wealth (Saemundsson, 2003; Schumpeter, 1996) and contribute directly in eradication of poverty (Bridges, 2002; United Nation Development Program, 2001). Generally, one can say that entrepreneurship is an essential aspect that aids in developing a society, enhancing economic expansion, creating more employment opportunities, generating government income via taxation, and assisting in the well-being of consumers (Dana, 2013).

On top of all these, entrepreneurs spin social wealth out of the total economic value generated. This especially takes place when the markets fail to cater to specific social demands and when the government agencies fail to provide basic amenities, such as welfare and education, as found in third world nations (Venkataraman, 1997). In the attempt to acknowledge the role of entrepreneurship, the General Assembly of the United Nations Organization in 1993 approved a resolution that reckons entrepreneurship as an economic and social force that improves the living standards across nations. Besides, the United Nation has urged its member countries to build and to implement policies that promote and encourage entrepreneurship among their societies (Slaughter, 1996). Over the decades, women have received educational gains outpacing men in college education, whereby it has been reported that they receive 50% more Master's degrees, in comparison to their counterpart. Fresh entry workers aged between eighteen and thirty witness more women holding bachelor's degree, when compared to men. This increment in education is also reflected in entrepreneurship, where one-third of businesses established in the United States are women-owned (Robe, Coleman, and Stangler, 2014). Due to their growing potential, several other countries, such as Albania, Bosnia and Herzegovina, Croatia, and Kosovo, have begun initiating women entrepreneurship. For instance, Albania, through its National Strategy for Development and Integration 2013 – 2020, projects to increase women-owned SMEs from 26 percent in 2011 to 40 percent in 2020. Meanwhile, Bosnia and Herzegovina has set up its very first Women Entrepreneurship database in 2012, whereas Kosovo appears to be the first country to introduce a gender-based checkbox upon registration of a new business, which may emerge as important data in the future (Gender Task Force, 2014).

Since past two decades, studies have displayed that informal economy has appeared crucial for the economic survival among women trapped in poverty (Berger and Buvinic, 1989). In fact, a number of middle-income nations, such as Thailand and Turkey, have reported 76% and 80% of women involvement in informal economy, respectively, in which such substantial increment in the informal economy happens to appear vital in the transition economies, especially for women who have been retrenched from the formal labor force (Aslanbeigui, Pressman, & Summerfield, 1994; Moghadam, 1994). Additionally, informal economy offers more employment for women than that in the formal sector. The informal economy has more than 80% of workers among the low-income nations and 40% among middle-income nations both in rural and urban areas (United Nations Development Program, 2001). Since the low- and middle-income countries account for 85% of the world's population, a majority of the world's workers, approximately 61%, happen to be mostly women employed in the informal sector (Chen, 1996). As mentioned earlier, a significant increment has been noted in the number of women entrepreneurs throughout the globe and this phenomenon is further supported by individual, social, and economic factors (Raman, Anantharaman, & Jayasingam, 2008). The evident social factor includes early life experience, stage of career, personal and family backgrounds, as well as growth environment (Gibb, 1993), whereas social pressures strongly motivate women to become entrepreneurs. In essence, women become entrepreneurs in order to balance work and family (Kirk and Belovics, 2006). Among other motivating factors, social networks also turn to be a major factor that motivates women in becoming entrepreneurs (Gadar and Yunus, 2006). Apart from these factors, self-confidence in having sufficient skills and knowledge, together with the knowledge of existing opportunities, instill women a positive attitude to venture into business (Langowitz and Minniti, 2007). Although numerous motivating factors have been determined to motivate women in venturing into the entrepreneurship arena, money has never been part of it and it is a result of career dissatisfaction (Cromie, 1987). Aside from gaining greater flexibility and escaping from traditional office bureaucracy, being an entrepreneur means satisfying one's needs and also the needs of their families (Lee and Rogoff, 1997). Furthermore, many scholars have taken these motives into consideration and concluded that the motives that mainly drive these women to become entrepreneurs could be classified into two categories, which are: push and pull, where pull motivation refers to the strong desire to be self-employed based on reasons with positive connotations, such as challenges, positive work environment, independence, and flexibility; whereas push motivation are based on reasons related to negative connotations, such as losing a job, limited work opportunities, lack of positive work environment, and lack of independence (Buttner and Moore, 1997).

Furthermore, the case study conducted by Musa and his colleague found that Malaysian community perception of women micro entrepreneurs who are widows or divorcees tend to be negative. This statement illustrates the challenge:

"My neighbors always keep their eyes on me to make sure I am not talking with someone's husband. There was the case of a tomboy who came to send kitchen stuff to my house at night and they thought that she was a man". (Wan, 53 years old, mother of 4, divorcee).

Nevertheless, women entrepreneurs tend to be reliant on personal finance and only raise small scales of capital to finance. However, a typical growth-oriented firm demands substantial external capital, both in equity and debt. Therefore, the opportunity to grow is diminished, as women entrepreneurs do not seek adequate financial capital. On top of that, women-owned businesses are small in size and represent just over 30% of formal and registered businesses across nations; among which 70% are owned by women in developing countries, where they are either shut out by financial institutions or fail to receive financial aid with passable terms to meet their demands (World Bank, 2017). Furthermore, the World Bank has recorded that formal women-owned SMEs face credit deficit of approximately $300 billion annually due to these financial barriers.

ROLE OF WOMEN MICRO-ENTREPRENEURS IN MALAYSIA

SMEs have been considered as the backbone of the Malaysian economy, in which women entrepreneurs have become more evidently significant to the staggering rate in the growth of SMEs and their indirect contribution to the economy. In fact, the number of women involved in Malaysian SMEs for year 2003 was 1,122,000 or 36.8% of the total employment in SMEs and the number has escalated annually (Teoh and Chong, 2008). Economic Census 2016 reports that 98.5% of business establishments in Malaysia are of SMEs genre and among them, meanwhile, 20.6% are owned by women entrepreneurs (SME Corporation, 2017). Micro-enterprise is defined by the sales turnover that is below RM250, 000 or by the amount of employees' fewer than five full time workers. In developing countries, such as Malaysia, micro-enterprises have developed as a means to respond to the growing poverty, particularly in generating income to supplement household income. These micro-enterprises, which are mostly run by women, are more likely to be home-based, given that they are responsible for domestic labor and hence, providing flexibility for women in terms of balancing home and work responsibilities (Thompson, 2009). As such, these women entrepreneurs are mostly involved in small-scale food processing businesses. In Asia, the rural-based food processing industry constitutes almost 70% of the companies (Hicks, 2001). Micro-enterprise offers lower income holders the opportunity to develop their talents and skills, aside from improving their financial well-being. Thus, women in Malaysia have played a significant role in boosting the economic, besides stabilizing the economy during recession (Ndubisi and Kahraman, 2006).

As far as women are concerned, entrepreneurship is a gateway to generate income so as to attain a more sustainable livelihood (Spevaek, 2011). Based on the UNECE report, entrepreneurship has improved the aspect of employability among women in the Europe and Euroasia regions as they have begun to turn to self-employment and entrepreneurship as means of survival (UNECE, 2004) and women business-owners emerge as role models for the younger generation for potential female entrepreneurs to start businesses. Similarly, women in Malaysia have a significant function in enhancing the economy of the country as employees and consumers, and lately, as entrepreneurs who offer employment. Interest among women towards entrepreneurship is a positive sign for the prosperity of a nation and progression in Malaysia is strongly supported by participation and involvement among women in economic activities, which has becoming a growing importance to the country. Their huge success in contributing to the success of the nation is supported up by their courage and high level of commitment in business.

This environment is supported by a case study of Puan Siti who survived from unstable income from direct selling. Fortunately, she wake up and was confident to open stationary and gift shop (Blueberry Tree), currently, she expand the business with two new branches in Negeri Sembilan. Similarly, D'Kaz pineapple tart successfully produces the brand as one of the 1 Malaysia best products in Negeri Sembilan, West Peninsular of Malaysia (Bustamam and Padli, 2012). Nonetheless, progression among women in the entrepreneurship arena is not new in Malaysia. This is because; back in the 1970s, 18% of female labor were classified as 'own-account workers', while 2.3% were categorized as employers, and 13% were labeled as 'working proprietors of wholesale and retail trade'. This clearly indicates that many women have involved and displayed keen interest in self-employment (O'Brien, 1983).

In the past, women mostly ventured into micro-enterprises that involved hawkering, retailing, and wholesaling for these businesses do not require any special skill, labor or capital, but instead, they are simple and less risky (Daud, 1975). Additionally, a study depicted that a majority of women entrepreneurs are engaged in food and beverage businesses, clothing, retailing (Suaibah, Azlah, Hishamuddin, Rozeyta, Syaharizatul, & Rosilla, 2005) and micro-level businesses that are less intricate and only demand simple basic technology (Hoe, Isa, Hin, Hashim, Yunus, & Abdullah, 2012). This simplicity has eased women to enter into the business world and further increase in number as women entrepreneurs. According to the Companies Commission of Malaysia (CCM), women owned around 49, 554 units of business entities in year 2000, which saw further increment to 54, 626 business entities in 2001 (Mutalib, Arshad, Ismail, & Ahmad, 2015). Such progress was so invigorating that in 2002, Tun Dr Mahathir, then Prime Minister of Malaysia, congratulated women entrepreneurs for their capabilities in facing the heavy competition with the men-dominating world based on their achievements and roles played in the women entrepreneurial category. In fact, the latest data from the CCM recorded registration from 1.18 million women. This is indeed a drastic improvement in the number of women entrepreneurs throughout Malaysia.

Women balance personal life, career (Rashid and Arifin, 1992), and involvement in economic activities in the attempt to supplement family income (Hoe, Isa, Hin, Hashim, Yunus, & Abdullah, 2012). Among the Malay women entrepreneurs in Malaysia, the need for achievement correlated to entrepreneurial success, which shows that women entrepreneurs are constantly thinking about improving their businesses and they believe in hard work. Besides, the increasing number of women employment in the informal sector recorded from 427, 300 persons in 2012 to 640, 900 persons in 2013. The 2011 SME Annual Report also revealed about 88% of micro-enterprises are owned and managed by women for survival, in which their contribution goes to the economic well-being of their families, communities, and nation.

Women entrepreneurs are involved in finance, food production, general commerce, private and public services, education, training and consultancy, to name a few. This advancement is supported by the establishment of the Federation Council organization for Women Entrepreneurship, as well as other associations related to women entrepreneurs, such as *Peniagawati, Usahanita, Wawasanita*, and *Sarawak Usahanita*, which have aided women entrepreneurs tremendously to hit the global target (Mohamad and Kasuma,

2016). Food and beverage are among the top business ventures in Malaysia with 49, 554 business units owned by women in 2010 and 54, 626 units in year 2011. This increasing figure clearly exhibits that Malaysian women are strongly committed to perform in both commercial and economic activities. On top of that, home stay is an industry that women entrepreneurs excel in Malaysia. In fact, Norman and Macdonald (Norman and MacDonald, 2004) encouraged women entrepreneurs to contribute to the sustainability of home stay business, which has a positive effect upon the economy, the environment, and the social aspects of a nation (Osman, Ahmad, Ahmad, Husin, Bakar, & Tanwir, 2009). Women entrepreneurs are also involved in other sectors. Table 1 presents that in terms of distribution of establishments by size, a whopping 693, 670 establishments or 76.5% of the total SMEs in Malaysia are micro-size establishments; out of which 649,186 establishments are predominant in the Services sector with a contribution of 80.2% to the total SMEs, followed by the Manufacturing sector that has 22, 083 establishments, while the remaining 18,274 establishments are associated to Construction, Agriculture, as well as Mining and Quarrying sectors.

CHARACTERISTICS OF WOMEN-OWNED MICRO-ENTERPRISES

The characteristics of women-owned micro-enterprises play a vital role as they provide motivation and self-confidence in making the best decision for the future, apart from becoming successful women entrepreneurs in micro-enterprises (Fisher, Faritz, and Lobo, 2004). Such traits equip women involved in micro-enterprises with reference of an entrepreneur's characteristics because they share similar personalities. The traits of awareness, support, and leadership

Table 1. Micro-enterprises by Sector, 2015

	Establishments
Agriculture	736
Mining and Quarrying	217
Manufacturing	22,083
Construction	17,321
Services	649,186

Source: Economic Census, 2016 (Economic, 2016)

among women involved in micro-enterprises and the implementation of plan based on the basics of their personal characteristics, contribute to the success of business strategy (Ireland, Kuratko, and Covin, 2003).

According to Islam, Khan, Obaidullah, & Alam (2011) several characteristics, including age, education level, managerial know-how, working experience, and social skills that influence entrepreneurial performance, are essential among women micro-entrepreneurs. This outcome is supported by Hartati, Juwita, Karim, & Bayu, 2015) who asserted that age, gender, and individual background, such as education level and working experience, are instances of demographic characteristics that can influence entrepreneurial intention and effort in informal economy. Besides, an informal sector workforce survey report states that micro-entrepreneurs in Malaysia that ranged from 40 to 49-age range were more active in entrepreneurial activities in night markets or informal activities, in comparison to those from the younger age group. This is due to the increase in volume of women engaged in the informal sector from 2012 to 2013. Although involvement among women from the age range of 15 to 39 was not as high as women in the age range of 40 to 49, their business ventures displayed gradual increment. Nevertheless, the rising age range of enterprise-owners has led to the decline in the mean efficiency, hence suggesting that more young entrepreneurs should be encouraged to put in more efforts so as to raise their level of efficiency in managing business.

Many studies over the past few decades have highlighted that males were generally more likely to be engaged in business than women (Mazzarol, 1999). However, the report provided by the informal sector workforce survey report revealed that in 2013, there was not much difference for employment in the informal sector between males and females. Nonetheless, a substantial increase was discovered among females, when compared to the past year, which recorded about 213,600 persons. Furthermore, entrepreneurs should possess a certain set of capacities, mindset, cognitive ability, motivation, and competitive attitude (De Mel, McKenzie, & Woodruff, 2010; Schiebold, 2011) with a significant indicator in determining the success or failure among micro-entrepreneurs (Fisher, Maritz, and Lobo, 2014; Islam, Khan, Obaidullah, & Alam, 2011; Chittithaworn, Islam, Keawchana, & Yusuf, 2011). In addition, the level of education among enterprise owners could influence the cognitive ability that is highly significant in affecting the level of efficiency among micro-enterprises, which is important to improve both technical and allocate efficiencies. As such, a majority of entrepreneurs with elementary school education level tend to be less receptive to new technologies, as compared to those with college education (Senik, 1995).

Consequently, the entrepreneur may find it difficult to apply/adapt to new technology and improve productivity. Moreover, entrepreneurship education increases the idea of new ventures, the likelihood of self-employment, the innovation of new products, the development of high-technology businesses owned by self-employed graduates, as well as increment in the sales growth rates among emerging firms and assets. Hence, motivating girls to pursue further education is necessary to grab the opportunities available to women in the labor market, apart from increasing participation among women in the workforce as a pathway to create higher productivity and income growth, which would all together, help invest in the next generation and enhance the quality of decision-making (World Bank, 2017). In Malaysia, women involved in micro-enterprises within the informal sector who possessed secondary education were about 817,200 persons in 2013, which increased to 864200 persons in 2015. Those with primary, tertiary follow this, and nil formal education as reported in Informal Sector Workforce Survey Report, 2015).

Furthermore, based on the Economic Census 2016, women from all education background have begun venturing into the world of entrepreneurship, as presented in Table 3.

Individuals with prior entrepreneurial experience had significantly higher entrepreneurial intentions than those without such experience. In fact, a study carried out by Mazzarol, Volery, Doss, & Thein (1999) discovered that respondents with government employment experience were less likely to be successful founders of small-businesses. This notion is supported by Selamat, Razak, Gapor, & Sanusi (2011) that most entrepreneurs started with various types of occupations and the last employment before getting involved in business is being a civil servant. Furthermore, with meagre business experience and fear of no one to succeed the business have led them to retain their business activities as long as the income could sustain their lives. Alam, Jani, and Omar (2011) revealed that the highest number of entrepreneurs who started their own businesses had prior working experience, which

Table 2. Informal sector workers by education level, 2015

Education Level	2012	2013	2015
No formal Education	53.282	59.86	59.7
Primary	271.126	294.117	312.9
Secondary	629.686	817.152	864.2
Tertiary	89.885	113.095	113.095

Source: Informal Sector Workforce Survey Report, 2015 (2015)

Table 3. Number of women in SMEs by qualification, 2015

Qualification	Total	Female	Percentage (%)
SMEs	5,652,560	1,897,211	33.6
Postgraduate	50,741	15,746	31
Bachelor/Advance Diploma or Equivalent	527,791	181,774	34.4
Diploma	607,132	243,764	40.2
STPM or Equivalent	253,984	120,071	47.3
Certificate	383,363	106,697	27.8
SPM/SPM(V) or Equivalent	2,502,397	865,869	34.6
Below SPM/SPM(V) Qualification	1,327,152	363,290	27.4

Source: Economic Census 2016

motivated them to work as entrepreneurs and further expand their businesses by upgrading their entrepreneurial skills. Generally, being independent and having a positive mind-set are also part of the characteristics that should be displayed by an informal entrepreneur so as to motivate their functionality in the informal sector continuously.

In a similar vein, Epstein and O'Brian (1985) found that personal traits are dispositional characteristics that relatively endure preferences on one's part for thinking or acting in a specific manner. Thus, personal characteristics are important to explain 'why' and 'how' firms behave differently (House, Shane, & Herold, 1996). Personality traits may affect the personality dynamics of setting goals and developing strategies, consequently affecting the business and its success. This may influence specific traits, such as need for achievement, risk-taking, autonomy, locus of control, and innovativeness. According to McClelland (1987) need for achievement is one of the crucial personality characteristics among entrepreneurs for one to acquire entrepreneurial behavior. The researchers believe that entrepreneurs are proactive, highly committed, self-assured, responsible for their own decisions, and risk-takers, apart from appreciating feedback given pertaining to performance, and disliking routine or repetitive tasks. Furthermore, self-confidence and perseverance are other instances of personal qualities and traits that can influence the success or failure of a business (Glancey, Greig, & Pettigrew, 1998; Stewart, Watson, Carland, & Carland, 1998; Barakat, McLellan, & Winfield, 2011). Additionally, researchers have defined entrepreneurial orientation through independency, innovativeness, risk-taking, pro-activeness, competitive aggressiveness, as well as having self-motivation while running business (Islam, Khan, Obaidullah,

& Alam, 2011). The other characteristic is entrepreneurial readiness, which reflects self-efficacy. Self-efficacy, from the stance of social learning theory, refers to one's belief in his/her capability to perform a given task (Bandura, 1997). Individuals with higher self-efficacy are more likely to be more confident in whatever they do to attain difficult goals and tend to increase their effort when faced with a more challenging situation (Bandura, 1997). They have a strong influence on how they would act and how they would avail knowledge and skills to be utilized at full potential. Thus, they are less threatened by unpredictable situations because they believe that they can cope up with the situations that emerge and control them (Wood and Bandura, 1989). All the characteristics above serve to assist potential women entrepreneurs, which could be employed to evaluate if they also possess similar characteristics with other women who have successfully ventured into the entrepreneurship arena.

STRENGTHS AND SHORTCOMINGS OF WOMEN MICRO-ENTREPRENEURS IN MALAYSIA

The informal sector had been found to continue its contribution to the economy and also to the Gross Domestic Production (GDP), as presented in Chiba, Japan in July 2015 (Country Report for Malaysia, 2015). The engagement of women micro-entrepreneurs in informal sector has increased in an annual basis due to the strengths and advantages provided by this sector. Micro-enterprise has a strategic advantage as it can be set up at any potential area (Chong and Gradstein, 2007) for people to easily start businesses smoothly, especially in matters related to registration. Generally, micro-enterprises have flexible business structures that are organized in various genres, such as sole proprietorship, partnership, or a family enterprise, which typically consists of less than ten employees (Storey, 1994; Walls, Dowler, Cordingly, Orslene, & Greer, 2001). Since they are small, micro-enterprises seem to be more flexible and responsive to both market and customer demands (The Herman Group, 2003).

One main strength of women-owned enterprises is that it responds to issues linked to poverty, particularly in providing employment opportunities and generating income to supplement household income (Hartati, Juwita, Karim, & Bayu, 2015; Ahmad, Ibrahim, & Ismail, 2011; Baharudin, Othman, Pah, Chellamuthu, & Musa, 2011). Women micro-entrepreneurs contribute towards the economic impact in developing nations by establishing new small businesses and promoting employment for various people, regardless of gender. Furthermore, micro-entrepreneurship encourages people, along with resourcefulness and creativity, driven by the effective utilization of competencies in entrepreneurship, marketing, and innovation (Durkin and McGowan, 2001) aside from characterizing the informal sector to rapidly become an engine of growth in this sector (Loayza & Rigoloni, 2011). When people are unemployed, they find creative and alternative ways to survive Ahmad, Ibrahim, & Ismail (2011), besides incorporating technologies, for example, machines, systems, and tools, which complement the level of knowledge and the type of business (Idris and Siwar, 2003) they desire to start. The ministries and government agencies, through mentoring, provide business support services, such as technology access and research assistance to micro-enterprises. For example, SME Expert and Panel provide SMEs with experienced industrial experts to assist them in improving technological capacity and productivity, which could ultimately increase the demand for skillful and semi-skilled labor (Idris and Siwar, 2003). On top of that, the informal sector has been defined as unregistered, unobserved, and a hidden enterprise, which directly offers aid to others as well, such as local suppliers, small-scale businesses, and farmers, to support their product and to improve the local resource economy.

Conversely, although involvement of women micro-entrepreneurs has portrayed the strength to boost economic growth and to eradicate poverty, it does have its own shortcomings. For instance, a study by Pingle (2005) discovered that micro-entrepreneurs who happen to be users of micro-credit seem to be classified in the category of 'survivalist'. The study also suggests that successful performers that provide sustainable livelihood to their owners constitute only a small percentage among micro-credit users. In Malaysia, literature on the performance of micro-enterprises has described various challenges and problems faced by micro-entrepreneurs with implications on their business productivity, as well as the fact that a majority of them are survivalist (Chong, 2010; Nurbani, Chin, Yeow, & Noor Ashikin, 2011).

Some challenges faced by SMEs in Malaysia, particularly small businesses established in rural areas with low productivity are inconsistent supply of raw materials, low and inefficient production level, outdated processing methodology and equipment, poor quality of food products and product packaging, poor hygiene and sanitary practices, as well as lack of product development and marketing know-how (Hicks, 2004). In addition, some studies on SMEs in Penang reported on the challenges and struggles faced by SMEs and micro-entrepreneur operators with minimal knowledge in marketing and packaging process. Hence, although a large number of women are involved in micro-enterprises, only a handful of these women appear to be successful at generating a sustainable living from their businesses.

Furthermore, some other weaknesses noted among informal entrepreneurs are lack of access to information, skill, and technology, trapped in financial constraints, limitations of time and space, lack of infrastructure, low level of productivity, low income opportunities, and absence of legal protection. The discussion on these weaknesses appears to demonstrate the challenges and constraints faced by women micro-entrepreneurs.

Financial Constraints

Most women micro-entrepreneurs, generally, face financial constraints at the start of the business (Chong and Gradstein, 2007; Nurbani, Chin, Yeow, & Noor Ashikin, 2011). Women micro-entrepreneurs face difficulties in getting financial assistance from local micro-credit institutes due to limited knowledge on how to proceed with loan application and failure in comprehending, as well as delivering the necessary legal documentation required by the financial institution. For instance, they are unable to display proper documentation of the product they sell or the amount of capital used for monthly transactions, such as logbook and documentation of daily orders (Selamat, Razak, Gapor, & Sanusi, 2011). In reality, micro-credit ensures economic participation by women, but at the same time, it increases not only their economic difficulty due to escalating debts, but also causes stress that could lead to health related issues. Hence, women entrepreneurs become reluctant and lose confidence in applying for loans or any micro-credit schemes due to this lack of knowledge and the anxiety regarding loan repayment if their business ventures fail (leonard, 2013). Besides, access to micro-credit scheme does not normally guarantee the success of these micro-enterprises. Therefore, most of them rely on their own funds, spouse, family finance, partner, and friends by borrowing money to set up their businesses (Rao, Venkatachalm, & Joshi, 2012).

A case study conducted by Musa, Shuib, Selamat, Isa, Osman, & Abu Bakar (2016) had involved women micro entrepreneurs in Malaysian environment. This findings rose on financial issue including purchasing of raw materials, income, and expansion of business. Drawing back to the case study of Saini, 44 years old, a divorcee and a mother of two children that faced so many financial problems especially with fluctuating income in unstable economic condition. This situation become worst when the cost of electric tariff increased at her store, even though she just earn small profit. In this regards, she had to deal with a long time payment settlement and offer innovative products. Notwithstanding, she suffered from the system of group responsibility in ensuring loans payment, if her team did not make the payment. In contrast with a case study illustrates from 53 years women known as Wan, a divorcee, whose business food products managed to expand to other countries with the help of government agencies. Although she still earn small profit due to the high costs incurred and continue for business expansion.

Another case study is the terms of loan disbursement as well as repayment play an important role in business in both positive and negative sides. Every week they required attending meeting to repay loan and receive small size of loan that has no significant effect in business. Sometime, they need a large size of loan especially before Eid (Muslims celebrations) to buy clothes in economics of scale, but with current size of loan it is difficult. Therefore, they always used to borrow from other friends.

LIMITATION OF TIME AND SPACE

According to Richard (2013), women have higher labor burden and time restriction as opposed to men. This limitation makes women to struggle more both in terms of entrepreneurial productivity and family responsibilities. For example, their responsibilities towards their children (usually two or more at a time) limit their mobility and constrain their ability to generate income, particularly in less conducive environment for business. Indeed, in developing nations where women are perceived to be completely responsible for domestic duties and childcare, most women micro-entrepreneurs constantly face conflicts while managing their roles as wives, mothers, and business owners. As a result, all business operations may get postponed while prioritizing family activities.

While, another case study is involved 6 women micro entrepreneurs on the capability of decision-making that depends on their husband's decision. Most of them are reliant on husband to decide in all aspects covering business to get husband's blessing. In contrast with the other 12 women who believed that they had the right to make own decision even though they have husband. On the other hand, some of women micro entrepreneurs have a problem in terms of child care that they had to deal with. With this regards, they had to bring their child to the workplace (Grine, Fares, & Meguellati, 2015).

Lack of Training and Advisory Service

Despite the assistance offered by the government, women micro-entrepreneurs continuously face inappropriate and unsuitable training, as well as advisory services, which should help them to improve their business and technical skills. Moreover, some women entrepreneurs remain uninterested in attending training programs, even when offered. As a result, they remain less potential for success due to their lack in knowledge and skills, as required for successful start-ups and sustainable business management. Besides, women entrepreneurs being responsible in carrying out family-related duties fail to attend such training programs, particularly if the content and the method of training delivery fail to suit their context.

As training programs help to equip women micro-entrepreneurs with knowledge and skills required to expand business opportunities and to attain successful entrepreneurship (Loveline, Uchenna, & Nwanesi, 2014) women micro-entrepreneurs should, therefore, made aware of the advantages of these training programs, which can lead to increased assets and enhanced financial, operational management, innovational, networking, technology and information support skills, along with heightening morale and a positive attitude towards business. Furthermore, since participation in training programs offers opportunities for micro-enterprises to succeed via self-sufficiency; it is believed that in comparison to those who have never attended training programs, women micro-entrepreneurs with training exposure may experience less obstacles and higher business growth (Ganesan, Kaur, & Maheshwari, 2002).

High Competition

Most of them involved in the informal business tend to sell similar products, which provides customers bargaining power. As a result of the customers' bargaining power to buy from any seller who could offer them the cheapest price with the same quality, the biggest challenge among micro-entrepreneurs is the competition from their rivals within the same market selling the same product. Hence, in order to attract customers to buy their products, women micro-entrepreneurs need to struggle in providing their customers unique and quality products. However, since they lack access to information, skills, and technology; it is difficult to equip them with up-to-date skills, knowledge, and abilities in order to improve their competitive advantage over their customers (Loveline, Uchenna, & Nwanesi, 2014).

On the other hand, Alshami and his colleague provided a case study that explained the situation on sustainability of women micro-enterprises in Malaysia. This case study focuses on Hajab shop (veil), which discuss on why the profit of her shop was dropped. The reason is more competitors near her shops, especially most of the foreigners who have good suppliers. Drawing back to this case, the researcher conclude that Malay women are still weak and their right are denied from good economic opportunities as compared to other races. For example, the case studies in Melaka, which micro entrepreneurs have decided to open subway and prepared all the documents needed. However, initially the company staffs have intention to not give them the license and ask for difficult requirement. Later, the licenses have given to the other entrepreneur from their race.

Absence of Legal Protection

Those keen to venture into business, whether small or large, are obliged to register with *Suruhanjaya Syarikat Malaysia* or the Companies Commission of Malaysia (CCM), which functions as a business regulatory organization. In contrary, micro-entrepreneurs only need to register with the district council in their states to obtain a license because the CCM is only meant for formal business registrations in Malaysia. As a consequence, when an unfortunate incident befalls upon micro-enterprises, legal protection or authorities are disabled from securing these micro-entrepreneurs or their product from any harm or damage. The informal business is considered as unregistered economy, but in Malaysia, they still need to register and pay both licensing cost and operation charge to the local district known as *Majlis Perbandaran Daerah*. The operation charge is imposed to clean the location after business operations end, such as *pasar tani* and *pasar malam*.

Lack of Access to Information, Skill, and Technology

Since most women micro-entrepreneurs operate in informal sectors and generally remain detached from other networks, they are often confronted with difficulties to access information. They lack knowledge to deal with government bureaucrats and thus, are unable to acquire good location for their businesses, which further limit their growth opportunities. Such situations do not allow most of these women micro-entrepreneurs to afford sophisticated machineries and technical expertise, hence impeding their production capacity and development of competencies (Alam, Jani, and Omar, 2011). This is why micro-credit schemes are important for such entrepreneurs so as to stimulate business growth and entrepreneurial productivity.

Lack of Infrastructure, Low-Level Productivity, and Low-Income Opportunities

In Malaysia, women micro-entrepreneurs face various challenges with implications on their business productivity. In fact, they are survivalists. Apparently, this micro-enterprise business genre offers those with low-income the opportunity to develop their talents and skills towards improvising their financial well-being (Selamat, Razak, Gapor, & Sanusi, 2011). Most of these women micro-entrepreneurs belong from low-income families and do not have enough capital to start their businesses, hence forcing them to use up their own saving and utilizing equipment available to them for the business. In terms of business support, micro-enterprises do receive assistance from the local agencies, such as business premises charged on operating days only and subsidized licensing cost depending on their business location (Informal Sector Workforce Survey Report, 2015). In some situations, since micro-enterprises are smaller in size, the entrepreneurs use their own house in full capacity by using their living room or bedroom to cater to the high volume of demand from their customers. In most occasions, entrepreneurs who live in rural areas are the ones normally use their homes as their business centers. Therefore, it is important to improve the infrastructure in rural areas, as a means to develop the performance of rural micro-enterprises. Exceptional infrastructure, electricity, roads, communication, and school could contribute immensely to the growth of micro-enterprises (Kirubi, 2006), which in turn, would positively influence the economic growth and the progress of nations.

CONCLUSION

Women play a vital role in micro-enterprise, thus offering job opportunities, as well as contribute to the economy. Most of the women entrepreneurs involved in various area that supported by establish association both government and non-government to expand globally. Women entrepreneurs should possess several characteristics that influence performance in micro-enterprises. In achieving the goal of women micro-enterprise requires effective action from the related parties to ensure that women entrepreneurs are well supported and developed. The important of women micro enterprises is supported with the main strength in order to respond to issues linked in reducing poverty that explained above. On the other hand, women micro-enterprise may face various challenges and problems in various ways. Conversely, the strategies to break these weaknesses and improve the strength can help to overcome this situation.

AUTHOR CONTRIBUTIONS

All authors were involved in collecting relevant information and literature review, and writing this chapter.

CONFLICTS OF INTEREST

The authors declare no conflict of interest.

ACKNOWLEDGMENT

This research was funded by the Ministry of Higher Education, Malaysia under the grant entitled "Developing a Comprehensive Rural Entrepreneurship Model for Poverty Eradication (REMODE)" (R/NRGS/A01.00/00047A/006/2014/000149).

REFERENCES

Ahmad, W., Ibrahim, W., & Ismail, Z. (2011). Informal sector in rural areas: Socio demographic profile of traditional food industry entrepreneur in Kelantan and Terengganu, Malaysia. *International Journal of Humanities and Social Science*, *1*(5), 221–227.

Alam, S. S., Jani, M. F. M., & Omar, N. A. (2011). An empirical study of success factors of women entrepreneurs in southern region in Malaysia. *International Journal of Economics and Finance*, *3*(2), 166. doi:10.5539/ijef.v3n2p166

Aslanbeigui, N., Pressman, S., & Summerfield, G. (1994). *Women and economic transformation. In Women in the age of economic transformation: Gender impact of reforms in post-socialist and developing countries* (pp. 1–7). London: Routledge.

Audretsch, D. B., & Thurik, A. R. (2001). What's new about the new economy? Sources of growth in the managed and entrepreneurial economies. *Industrial and Corporate Change*, *10*(1), 267–315. doi:10.1093/icc/10.1.267

Baharudin, N., Othman, M., Pah, P. W. C., Chellamuthu, D., & Musa, R. (2011). Informal employment in informal sector enterprises in Malaysia. *Journal of the Department of Statistics Malaysia*, *2*, 33–45.

Bandura, A. (1977). Self-efficacy: Toward a unifying theory of behavioral change. *Psychological Review*, *84*(2), 191–215. doi:10.1037/0033-295X.84.2.191 PMID:847061

Bandura, A. (1986). The explanatory and predictive scope of self-efficacy theory. *Journal of Social and Clinical Psychology*, *4*(3), 359–373. doi:10.1521/jscp.1986.4.3.359

Barakat, S., McLellan, R., & Winfield, S. (2011). The impact of programmes for entrepreneurship: lessons from examining self-efficacy. In *Institute of Small Business and Enterprise (ISBE) Annual Conference*, London, UK.

Baumol, W. J. (1993). Formal entrepreneurship theory in economics: Existence and bounds. *Journal of Business Venturing*, *8*(3), 197–210. doi:10.1016/0883-9026(93)90027-3

Berger, M., & Buvinic, M. (Eds.). (1989). *Women's Ventures: Assistance to the Informal Sector in Latin America*. West Hartford, CT: Kumarian Press, Inc.

Bridges, B. (2002). *Supporting Entrepreneurship in Developing Countries: Survey of the field and Inventory of Initiatives*. Retrieved December 12th, 2017 from: http://www.comminit.com/africa/content/supporting-entrepreneurship-developing-countries-survey-field-and-inventory-initiatives

Bustamam, U. S. A., & Padlee, S. F. (2012). *Islamic Microcredit for Women Micro Entrepreneurs: Impact for Sahabat*. Academic Press.

Buttner, E. H., & Moore, D. P. (1997). Women's organizational exodus to entrepreneurship: Self-reported motivations and correlates with success. *Journal of Small Business Management, 35*(1), 34.

Chen, M. (1996). *Women and the informal sector: Realities, statistics and policies*. Paper presented at the Economic Policy Forum, International Center for Research on Women, Washington, DC.

Chittithaworn, C., Islam, M. A., Keawchana, T., & Yusuf, D. H. M. (2011). Factors affecting business success of small & medium enterprises (SMEs) in Thailand. *Asian Social Science, 7*(5), 180. doi:10.5539/ass.v7n5p180

Chong, A., & Gradstein, M. (2007). Inequality and informality. *Journal of Public Economics, 91*(1), 159–179. doi:10.1016/j.jpubeco.2006.08.001

Chong, F. (2010). Evaluating the credit management of micro-enterprises. *WSEAS Transactions on Business and Economics, 2*(7), 149–159.

Christy, R. D., & Dassie, W. (2000). *Entrepreneurship-Centered Economic Development: An Analysis of African American Entrepreneurship in the Southern Black Belt*. Contractor Paper, 00-10.

Country Report for Malaysia. (2015). *Country Report for Malaysia*. Retrieved November 12th, 2017 from http://www.unsiap.or.jp/e-learning/el_material/PSS/1507_Informal/cr/MLY_cr.pdf

Cromie, S. (1987). Motivations of aspiring male and female entrepreneurs. *Journal of Organizational Behavior, 8*(3), 251–261. doi:10.1002/job.4030080306

Dana, L. P. (2013). Entrepreneurship Policy, Economic Development, and Competitiveness: A Study of Culture, Public Policy, and Enterprise in the Asia-Pacific Region. *The Global Enterprise: Entrepreneurship and Value Creation*, 97.

Daud, F. (1975). *Penyertaan wanita bumiputra dalam perniagaan dan perusahaan di Kuala Lumpur* (Master's Dissertation). Universiti Malaya, Kuala Lumpur, Malaysia.

De Mel, S., McKenzie, D., & Woodruff, C. (2010). Who are the microenterprise owners? Evidence from Sri Lanka on Tokman versus DeSoto. In International differences in entrepreneurship, (pp. 63-87). University of Chicago Press.

Durkin, M., & McGowan, P. (2001). Net effect—views from the periphery: Exploring the role and importance of the Internet on marketing activity in entrepreneurial firms. *Irish Marketing Review*, *14*(1), 15–25.

Economic Census. (2016). *Economic Census 2016*. Department of Statistics Malaysia, Official Portal. Retrieved February 02nd, 2017 from https://www.dosm.gov.my/v1/index.php?r=column/cone&menu_id=UllyTnF2UTJMM1R1VmlTTlZVbk5Wdz09

Epstein, S., & O'Brian, E. J. (1985). The person-situation debate in a historical and current perspective. *Psychological Bulletin*, *98*(3), 513–537. doi:10.1037/0033-2909.98.3.513 PMID:4080897

Fisher, R., Maritz, A., & Lobo, A. (2014). Evaluating entrepreneurs' perception of success: Development of a measurement scale. *International Journal of Entrepreneurial Behaviour & Research*, *20*(5), 478–492. doi:10.1108/IJEBR-10-2013-0157

Gadar, K., & Yunus, N. K. Y. (2009). The influence of personality and socio-economic factors on female entrepreneurship motivations in Malaysia. *International Review of Business Research Papers*, *5*(1), 149–162.

Ganesan, R., Kaur, D., & Maheshwari, R. C. (2002). Women entrepreneurs: Problems and prospects. *The Journal of Entrepreneurship*, *11*(1), 75–93. doi:10.1177/097135570201100105

Gender Task Force. (Ed.). (2014). SEE Women Entrepreneurship: Best Practices 2014. In GTF, Gender Task Force, Regional Center for Gender Equality, Martina Ferk, Zagreb, Croatia.

Gibb, A. A. (1993). Enterprise culture and education: Understanding enterprise education and its links with small business, entrepreneurship and wider educational goals. *International Small Business Journal*, *11*(3), 11–34. doi:10.1177/026624269301100301

Glancey, K., Greig, M., & Pettigrew, M. (1998). Entrepreneurial dynamics in small business service firms. *International Journal of Entrepreneurial Behaviour & Research*, *4*(3), 249–268. doi:10.1108/13552559810235547

Grine, F., Fares, D., & Meguellati, A. (2015). Islamic spirituality and entrepreneurship: A case study of women entrepreneurs in Malaysia. *The Journal of Happiness & Well-Being*, *3*(1), 41–56.

Hartati, S., Juwita, R., Karim, E., & Bayu, K. (2015). Structuring models and characteristics of informal sector traders in Indonesia: Case study in informal sector Jakarta City, Indonesia. *Journal of Social and Development Sciences*, *6*(1), 24–31.

Hicks, A. (2001). Rural-Based Food Processing Industry In Asia. *Proceedings of an APO Multi-Country Study Mission.* Retrieved December 20th, 2017 from http://www.apo-tokyo.org/publications/wp-content/uploads/sites/5/agr-04-rb_fpi.pdf#page=30

Hicks, A. (2004). *Rural-Based Food Processing Industry in Asia. Report of the APO MultiCountry Study Mission on Rural-Based Food Processing Industry (SME-OS1-00).* The Asian Productivity Organization.

Hoe, C. H., Isa, F. M., Hin, C. W., Hashim, N., Yunus, J. M., & Abdullah, H. H. (2012). Development of women entrepreneurs: The case of Malaysia. *World Journal of Social Sciences*, *2*(6), 123–145.

House, R. J., Shane, S. A., & Herold, D. M. (1996). Rumors of the death of dispositional research are vastly exaggerated. *Academy of Management Review*, *21*(1), 203–224. doi:10.5465/amr.1996.9602161570

Idris, N. A. H., & Siwar, C. (2003). *Kemiskinan bandar dan sektor tidak formal di Malaysia.* Bangi: Penerbit Universiti Kebangsaan Malaysia.

Ireland, R. D., Kuratko, D. F., & Covin, J. G. (2003). Antecedents, Elements and Consequences of Corporate Entrepreneurship Strategy. *Academy of Management Proceedings*, *2003*(1), L1-L6.

Islam, M. A., Khan, M. A., Obaidullah, A. Z. M., & Alam, M. S. (2011). Effect of entrepreneur and firm characteristics on the business success of small and medium enterprises (SMEs) in Bangladesh. *International Journal of Business and Management*, *6*(3), 289.

Kirk, J., & Belovics, R. (2006). Counseling would-be entrepreneurs. *Journal of Employment Counseling*, *43*(2), 50–61. doi:10.1002/j.2161-1920.2006.tb00006.x

Kirubi, C. (2006). *How Important is Modern Energy for Micro-enterprises: Evidence from Rural Kenya.* University of California, Berkeley.

Kuehnast, K. (1993). *Women and economic changes in Kyrgyzstan: Coping mechanisms and attitudes towards social policies.* Washington, DC: The World Bank.

Langowitz, N., & Minniti, M. (2007). The entrepreneurial propensity of women. *Entrepreneurship Theory and Practice*, *31*(3), 341–364. doi:10.1111/j.1540-6520.2007.00177.x

Lee, M. S., & Rogoff, E. G. (1997). A dual path model of education effects on entrepreneurship: An empirical analysis. *Journal of Business and Entrepreneurship*, *9*(1), 99.

Leonard, E. (2013). Challenges faced by female entrepreneurs. *Journal of International Business*, *4*, 2–4.

Loayza, N. V., & Rigoloni, J. (2011). Informal Employment: Safety Net or Growth Engine? *World Development*, *39*(9), 1503–1515. doi:10.1016/j.worlddev.2011.02.003

Loveline, A. A., Uchenna, O. I., & Nwanesi, P. K. (2014). *Women Entrepreneurship in Malaysia: An Empirical Assessment of the Challenges Faced by Micro and Small Business Owners in Kuching-Sarawak*. Academic Press.

Mazzarol, T. (1999). Partnerships—A Key To Growth in Small Business. *Journal of Enterprising Culture*, *7*(02), 105–125. doi:10.1142/S021849589900008X

Mazzarol, T., Volery, T., Doss, N., & Thein, V. (1999). Factors influencing small business start-ups: A comparison with previous research. *International Journal of Entrepreneurial Behaviour & Research*, *5*(2), 48–63. doi:10.1108/13552559910274499

McClelland, D. C. (1987). Characteristics of successful entrepreneurs. *The Journal of Creative Behavior*, *21*(3), 219–233. doi:10.1002/j.2162-6057.1987.tb00479.x

Moghadam, V. M. (Ed.). (1994). *Gender and national identity: women and politics in Muslim societies*. Palgrave Macmillan.

Mohamad, M., & Kasuma, J. (2016). Identifying motivation factor involvement of Sarawak Malay women entrepreneur. *Jurnal Manajemen dan Kewirausahaan, 18*(1), 54-59.

Musa, M., Shuib, R., Selamat, N. H., Mohd Isa, S., Osman, I., & Abu Bakar, S. (2016, November). A Study Of Women Micro Entrepreneurs In Malaysia: Livelihood Strategies And Challenges. In *Proceedings of the 3rd Kanita Postgraduate International Conference on Gender Studies* (pp. 380-390). Academic Press.

Mutalib, R. A., Arshad, R., Ismail, N. S., & Ahmad, Z. (2015). Women and entrepreneurship: An overview of women entrepreneurship programs in Malaysia. *JGD Special Issue on Social Entrepreneurship*, *11*, 15–28.

Ndubisi, N. O., & Kahraman, C. (2006). Malaysian Women Entrepreneurs: Understanding the ICT usage behavior and drivers. *Journal of Enterprise Information Management*, *18*(6), 731–739.

Norman, W., & MacDonald, C. (2004). Getting to the bottom of "triple bottom line". *Business Ethics Quarterly*, *14*(2), 243–262. doi:10.5840/beq200414211

Nurbani, H., Chin, S., Yeow, J., & Noor Ashikin, M. (2011). *Financial constraints and opportunities of micro entrepreneurs: a theoretical framework*. In *International Conference on Business and Economics Research*, (Vol. 1). IACSIT Press.

O'Brien, P. (1983). The kleptomania Diagnosis: Bourgeois Women and Theft in Late Nineteenth- Century France, Journal of Social History Century. *Journal of Social History*, *17*(1), 65–77. doi:10.1353/jsh/17.1.65

Osman, I., Ahmad, Z. A., Ahmad, N. H., Husin, A., Bakar, S. A., & Tanwir, N. D. (2009). Following the Trail of Women Homestay Entrepreneurs in Malaysia: Understanding Their Motivation and Empowerment. *TEAM Journal of Hospitality & Tourism*, *6*(1), 24–35.

Pingle, V. (2005). *Micro business and sustainable livelihoods*. Paper presented at the Conference on New Frontiers of Social Policy: Development in a Globalizing World, Arusha.

Raman, K., Anantharaman, R. N., & Jayasingam, S. (2008). Motivational factors affecting entrepreneurial decision: A comparison between Malaysian women entrepreneurs and women non-entrepreneurs. *Communications of the IBIMA*, *2*(12), 85–89.

Rao, V., Venkatachalm, A., & Joshi, H. G. (2012). Challenges faced by women entrepreneurs running micro, small and medium scale fashion and apparel business: a study on fashion and apparel enterprises in Coastal Karnataka. In *International Conference on Trade, Tourism and Management (ICTTM, 2012)* (pp. 21-22). Academic Press.

Rashid, M. Z. A., & Arifin, F. (1992). Management practices of Women Entrepreneurs in Malaysia. Staff Paper No. 8, Faculty of Economics and Management, UPM, Serdang.

Reynolds, P. D., Camp, S. M., Bygrave, W. D., Autio, E., & Hay, M. (2001). GEM Global Entrepreneurship Report, 2001 Summary Report. Kauffman Center for Entrepreneurial Leadership at the Ewing Marion Kauffman Foundation.

Reynolds, P. D., Gartner, W. B., Greene, P. G., Cox, L. W., & Carter, N. M. (2002). *The entrepreneur next door: Characteristics of individuals starting companies in America: An executive summary of the Panel Study of Entrepreneurial Dynamics*. Retrieved January 12th, 2017 from: https://ssrn.com/abstract=1262320

Reynolds, P. D., Hay, M., Bygrave, W. D., Camp, S. M., & Autio, E. (2000). *Global entrepreneurship monitor: 2000 executive report*. Kansas City, MO: Kauffman Center for Entrepreneurial Leadership.

Richard, S. (2013). Challenges Faced by Women Entrepreneurs. *Journal of International Business*, *4*, 14–15.

Robb, A., Coleman, S., & Stangler, D. (2014). *Sources of Economic Hope: Women's Entrepreneurship*. Available at SSRN: https://ssrn.com/abstract=2529094

Saemundsson, R. J. (2003). *Entrepreneurship, Technology, and the Growth Process: A study of young, medium-sized technology-based firms* (PhD Thesis). University of Technology, Chalmers.

Saini, J. S. (2001). Economic Development and Entrepreneurship. In J. S. Saini & B. R. Gurjar (Eds.), *Entrepreneurship & Education: Challenges and Strategies*. Jaipur: Rawat Publications.

Schiebold, M. (2011). *Towards a Framework of Success Determinants for Micro-Entrepreneurs: The Case of Swiss WaterKiosk in Mozambique* (Bachelor Thesis). University of St. Gallen.

Schumpeter, J. A. (1993). *The Theory of Economic Development: An Inquiry into Profits, Capital, Credit, Interest, and the Business Cycle*. New Brunswick, NJ: Transaction Publishers.

Schumpeter, J. A. (1996). *Capitalism, Socialism & Democracy*. London: Routledge.

Selamat, N. H., Razak, R. R. A., Gapor, S. A., & Sanusi, Z. A. (2011). Survival through entrepreneurship: Determinants of successful micro-enterprises in Balik Pulau, Penang Island, Malaysia. *British Journal of Arts and Social Sciences, 3*(1), 23–37.

Senik, G. (1995). *Small-scale food processing enterprises in Malaysia*. Kelantan, Malaysia: ASPAC Food & Fertilizer Technology Center.

Slaughter, M. P. (1996). *Entrepreneurship: Economic Impact and Public Policy Implications: An Overview of the Field*. Kansas City, MO: Kauffman Center for Entrepreneurial Leadership.

SME Corporation. (2017). *SME Corporation*. Retrieved December 28th, 2017 from http://www.smecorp.gov.my/index.php/en/policies/2015-12-21-09-09-49/sme-statistics

Spevaek, A. (2011). *Promoting Female Sustainable Livelihoods (Employment and Entrepreneurship) in the Europe and Russia (E & E) Region. Usaid Knowledge Services Center*. KSC.

Stewart, W. H. Jr, Watson, W. E., Carland, J. A. C., & Carland, J. W. (1998). A proclivity for entrepreneurship: A comparison of entrepreneurs, small business owners, and corporate managers. *Journal of Business Venturing, 14*(2), 189–214. doi:10.1016/S0883-9026(97)00070-0

Storey, D. J. (1994). *Understanding the Small Business Sector*. London: Routledge.

Suaibah, A. B., Azlah, M. A., Hishamuddin, M. S., Rozeyta, O., Syaharizatul, N. M., & Rosilla, M. J. (2005). *Entrepreneurial activities among single mothers in the state of Johor*. University Of Technology Malaysia.

Teoh, W. M. Y., & Chong, S. C. (2008). Improving women entrepreneurs in small and medium enterprises in Malaysia: Policy recommendations. *Communication of The IBIMA, 2*, 31–38.

The Herman Group. (2003). *Micro-business will offer economic strength.* Greensboro: The Herman Trend Alert.

Thompson, E. R. (2009). Individual entrepreneurial intent: Construct clarification and development of an internationally reliable metric. *Entrepreneurship Theory and Practice, 33*(3), 669–694. doi:10.1111/j.1540-6520.2009.00321.x

UNECE. (2004). *UNECE Annual Report 2004-2005.* Available at http://www.unece.org/oes/nutshell/2004-2005/2004_2005_annual_report.html

United Nation Development Program. (2001). *New Entrepreneurship Development Project for Women in Central Vietnam.* News Report. United Nations Development Program. Retrieved December 19th, 2019 from http://www.vn.undp.org/content/vietnam/en/home/presscenter/pressreleases/2001/10/03/new-entrepreneurship-development-project-for-women-in-central-viet-nam-.html

Venkataraman, S. (1997). The distinctive domain of entrepreneurship research. *Advances in Entrepreneurship, Firm, Emergence, and Growth, 3*(1), 119–138.

Walls, R. T., Dowler, D. L., Cordingly, K., Orslene, L. E., & Greer, J. D. (2001). Micro enterprising and people with disabilities: Strategies for success and failure. *Journal of Rehabilitation, 67*(2), 29.

Wennekers, S., Thurik, R., & Buis, F. (1997). *Entrepreneurship, Economic Growth and What Links Them Together. Research.* Zoetermeer: EIM/Small Business Research and Consultancy.

Wood, R., & Bandura, A. (1989). Impact of conceptions of ability on self-regulatory mechanisms and complex decision-making. *Journal of Personality and Social Psychology, 56*(3), 407–415. doi:10.1037/0022-3514.56.3.407 PMID:2926637

World Bank. (2017). *New World Bank Group Facility to enable more than $1 billion for Women Entrepreneurship.* Press release. Retrieved December 12th, 2017 from http://www.worldbank.org/en/news/press-release/2017/07/08/new-world-bank-group-facility-to-enable-more-than-1-billion-for-women-entrepreneurship

Chapter 4
Social Capital and Micro-Entrepreneurship

ABSTRACT

Social capital has been proven in many studies to correlate with economic development and increment in standards of living in a collective manner. This chapter presents a brief description regarding social capital and micro-enterprises that narrowly focuses on the relationship between social capital theory and entrepreneurship. The chapter further portrays the varied dimensions of social capital followed by the status of social capital from the Malaysian perspective. Finally, the chapter ends with a discussion on the effect of social capital on competitive advantage, which has been presumed to be the most important aspect for micro-enterprises.

SOCIAL CAPITAL

In the arena of entrepreneurship, business networks and correlations between firms go beyond the normal and ordinary customer–supplier relationship (Drakopoulou-Dodd, Jack, & Anderson, 2006). In fact, it has been proven time and again that the entrepreneurial process is closely knitted in social networks due to its crucial role (Hoang & Antoncic, 2003). Moreover, networks appear essential to entrepreneurs mainly because they facilitate tasks, such as resource assembling and opportunity seeking.

Apart from that, specific entrepreneurial networks offer the advantage of gaining access to resources markets, knowledge, and technologies (Inkpen &

DOI: 10.4018/978-1-5225-8473-5.ch004

Tsang, 2005; Mustafa and Chen, 2010), which are highly essential to every entrepreneur. For instance, Anderson, Dodd, and Jack (2010) discovered that the networks function as a strategic alliance that contributes to creation and growth of enterprises, aside from promoting improvement among entrepreneurs.

Social capital is classified as tangible or virtual resources that one receives via association with networks (Greve and Salaff, 2003). Social Capital is also defined as Grootaert, Narayan, Jones, & Woolcock, 2004) 'the groups, networks, norms, and trust that people have available to them for productive purposes'. Meanwhile, Bourdieu (1986) defines social capital as 'the aggregate of the actual or potential resources that are linked to possession of a durable network of more or less institutionalized relationships of mutual acquaintance and recognition – or in precise, to membership in a group – to offer its members with the backing of collectively-owned capital, and a 'credential' that entitles them to credit in the various senses of the word.'

Putnam, Leonardi, & Nanetti, 1993) defined social capital as *'features of social organizations, such as trust, norms, and networks that can improve the efficiency of a society by facilitating coordinated actions'*. On the other hand, Coleman (1988) asserted that social capital is defined by its function. He further elaborated that social capital is a combination of various entities with two common elements, including certain elements of structure that facilitate actions of an individual or a group of corporate actors.

In addition, Bourdieu (1986), Coleman (1988), and Putnam, Leonardi, & Nanetti, 1993) categorized the aspect of social capital into varied levels of applications and elements. Bourdieu (1986) looks at the individual and organization levels to comprise of elements, such as network, institutionalized relationship, participation in group, durable obligations, multiplier effect, differential access to resources, as well as volume and quality of contacts. Meanwhile, Coleman (1988) views social capital from the individual, the organizational, and the community levels. He claimed that social structure, social relationships, appropriability, embeddedness, trust, obligations and expectations, norms and sanctions, responsibility and authority, closure, collective good, by-product, and context specificity are significant elements to social capital. On the other hand, Putnam et al., (1993) associated individual, organization, community, and region as social capital application levels. He embedded trust, norms and reciprocity, network of civic engagement, horizontal and vertical networks, embeddedness, bridging and bonding, self-reinforcing and cumulative, public good, under supplied, and supply increases with use into the notion of social capital.

Social capital has been proven in many studies to correlate with economic development and increment in standards of living in a collective manner (Bennet and Richardson, 2005; Hansen, 1995). Apart from the sense of economic development, poor people utilize social capital networks and trust relationship as a channel to deal with emergency situations, which reflects a way to reach available opportunity, besides participating in social events, such as festivals, weddings, and funerals (Rutherford, 2000). Social capital is also linked with increase in household assets, income per capita, and household expenditures in Indonesia and Tanzania (Grootaert, 1999; Narayan, & Pritchett, 1999). In fact, social capital was even found in the disadvantaged African American community in the early 1990s, whereby both traditional and non-traditional social capital aspects were employed to promote economic outcomes (Cook, 2011).

Generally, most studies suggest that women entrepreneurs need networks to gain advantage. Nonetheless, networks among women appear smaller and only consist of women, in comparison to that of men (Aldrich, Birley, Dubini, Greve, Johannisson, Reese, and Sakano, 1991). Some researchers also have suggested that networks among women are fragile and are not utilized to the maximum. On the contrary, a similar study revealed that women networks are as active as men's (Cooper, Folta, and Woo, 1995). In the case of women entrepreneurs, formal social capital has been proven to bring in more benefits in the sense of growth resources, such as financial resources, when compared to informal social capital (Kickul, Gundry, & Sampson, 2007). Furthermore, it was discovered that training in production/operations and planning together with formal social capital are present among women entrepreneurs with high growth resources.

On top of that, social capital in the form of social networks is known to facilitate entrepreneurs with reliable and exclusive information (Smith and Lohrke, 2008). In the long run, it generates goodwill and ultimately leads to a relationship that includes respect, gratitude, and friendship. Nevertheless, all these are built on the name of trust, which is tested through repeated exchanges in a context of goodwill (DeCarolis, & Saparito, 2006). Recently, more academicians have reckoned and agreed on the benefits of social capital. According to Carey, Lawson, and Krause (2011), a significant benefit can be derived from the correlation between buyer and supplier of a company. Based on a sample of 163 respondents, the relational social capital seemed to mediate the relationship between cognitive and structural dimensions of social capital with performance measured as innovation.

Moreover, social capital is beneficial in terms of minimising transaction cost and systematic risk, aside from boosting investment. This proof was tested by Percoco (2012) as hypothesis in Italian cities. As a result, a correlation was discovered between entrepreneurship and social capital, although this cannot be generalized, as it is only applicable to the Italian scenario. Meanwhile, Acquaah and Appiah-Nkrumah (Acquaah, & Appiah-Nkrumah, 2011) have proven that the social capital aspects of firm specific-managerial experience, bureaucratic officials, and community leader have a positive effect on performance, but social capital derived from politicians seems to display a negative effect on firm performance.

As for the Chinese life insurance industry, social capital exhibited a strong link with objective sales performance. Chen, Zhang, and Fey (2011) revealed that when HR practices failed to improve performance, the aspect of social capital served as a moderator to enhance individual performance among 984 participants from China. Meanwhile, in less developed regions of the United Kingdom, the government offered entrepreneurship scholarship. Besides, Jayawarna, Jones, and Macpherson (Jayawarna, Jones, & Macpherson, 2011) investigated performances exerted by nascent entrepreneurs and discovered that bootstrapping aided in the process, while social capital had a significant function in securing bootstrapped resources. The social capital theory can be summarized as a network of correlations that consist of valuable resources for use of social affairs. In this sense, Nahapiet and Ghoshal (1998) noted that social capital makes it possible to gain an achievement that would have been deemed as impossible without it or only achieved with extra cost.

Social capital also exhibits a positive effect on enterprise performance, as first observed by Putnam, Leonardi, & Nanetti (1993) where a positively significant relationship was displayed between economic performance and social capital. Following that, Helliwell and Putnam (1999) found a positive impact on the long-term economic growth in the Italian provinces. In addition, Pratono and Mahmood (2014) revealed the positive effect of social capital on performances displayed by Small and Medium Enterprises (SMEs) in Indonesia. The inter-firm networks and the networks of owners or managers provide firms with access to resources, for example strategic knowledge, which are vital to the value-creating processes because they allow firms to minimise transaction costs of social interaction and exchange (Bonner, Kim, & Cavusgil, 2005; Ma, Yao, & Xi, 2009). Social capital can also generate competitive advantage among micro-entrepreneurs as the trust among partners and consumers, along with networking, can enhance their ability to compete

(Nahapiet and Ghoshal, 1998), thus leading to better business performance (Fahy, 2000).

Empirical studies on social capital have presented enormous evidence of the positively significant effects of social capital on economic development and increment in life standards in a collective manner (Svendsen, 2003; Aldrich and Zimmer, 1986; Hansen, 1995). Social capital built on trust and constructive perception of group members and community appears to contribute positively to household income and net worth of productive assets (Al Mamun, 2014). The similar study probed into microcredit participants from Peninsular Malaysia and found that both social interaction and cooperation did portray an impact upon the net worth of productive assets among the participants. As a result, it was concluded that formal bonding, social capital, and household welfare indicators exemplified positively linear correlations.

Additionally, Rajennd (2016) reported empirical evidences on the effects of social capital on competitive advantage, as well as the performance of micro-enterprises owned and managed by women in Peninsular Malaysia. The study attempted to address the limitations highlighted in prior studies concerning social capital, where the focus was on a single industry (Schilling & Phelps, 2007) using only the 'membership in formal associations' as a measure of social capital (Krishna, 2008) among Microfinance Institutions (MFI) clients to measure trust, reciprocity, and social cohesion (Ahlin and Townsend, 2007), hence resulting in contradictory research outcomes in social capital and entrepreneurial performance (Park and Luo, 2001; Rowley, Behrens, & Krackhardt, 2000). The study also provided empirical evidence of social and micro-enterprise performance that blankets the manufacturing, retailing, wholesale, agriculture, and service industries. Concurrently, the study looked into three dimensions of social capital, which are: structural, relational, and cognitive social capital. Moreover, the study covered women micro-entrepreneurs who tend to be the majority in the population of women entrepreneurs and provided better representation of women entrepreneurs. Essentially, the study presented empirical evidence that supports the theory of social capital, where the social capital theory, as claimed by Nahapiet and Ghoshal (1998), is built from structural, relational, and cognitive dimensions that have an impact upon firm performance. Furthermore, the study proved that competitive advantage derived from the network relationship mediated social capital and micro-enterprise performance.

The outcomes of the study enhance one's knowledge and understanding regarding the potential benefits of social capital for women entrepreneurs, the government, and socio-economic developmental organizations. Therefore, it is crucial for women micro-entrepreneurs to realize the importance of network ties and network density, where acknowledging the right people among key business players and knowing how to reach them, together with being active in both formal and informal networks, are of great benefit. Simultaneously, understanding how other key business players carry out their day-to-day operations seems to benefit entrepreneurs. Getting used to norms, apart from sharing similar business goals and values, strengthens the cognitive capital of an entrepreneur. Women entrepreneurs should, therefore, emphasis on how to identify and reach key business players, as well as to get involved with other businesses by joining formal and informal networks. Through these, they can build trust and get close to other key players, which will eventually give them a chance to understand how other businesses operate and create a platform of value and norm sharing.

In the arena of entrepreneurship, business networks and correlations between firms go far beyond customer-supplier relationships. The entrepreneurial process, which is embedded in social networks, plays a crucial role. The networks function as a strategic alliance, which contributes to the creation, the growth, and the promotion of change among entrepreneurs. These positive effects of network and enterprise performance are well demonstrated in the literature from the stance of social capital theory. Moreover, the outcomes of this study are in line with the theory of social capital as it presents empirical evidences of the positively significant effect of social capital on competitive advantage and the performance of micro-enterprises owned and managed by women in Peninsular Malaysia. The findings also reported a medium to large effect, as well as predictive relevance of social capital, on competitive advantage and microenterprise performance.

Based on the implications of the study (Rajennd, 2016) the government and socio-economic developmental organizations in Malaysia should place their focus on building industry-specific platforms for women micro-entrepreneurs at both local and national levels. This should allow micro-entrepreneurs to share their ideas and experiences, participate in trust-building programs, refine their values and norms, as well as enhance the overall quality of the relationships among key business players. A common industry-specific platform for entrepreneurs and key business players would offer a supportive environment among women micro-entrepreneurs to build social capital and to take full advantage of it. Hence, clear understanding pertaining to the effect of social capital can encourage micro-entrepreneurs to look for ways to improve trust and quality of relationships with key business players, hence ultimately improving the performance of micro-enterprises in Malaysia.

DIMENSIONS OF SOCIAL CAPITAL

The theory of social capital reflects a theoretical point concerning the advantage gained by firms via social networks. Besides, the social capital theory depicts organizational correlations and enables the evaluation of variances in performance within and between firms supported by flow of resources (Koka and Prescott, 2002). In this research, social capital denotes 'the sum of the actual and potential resources embedded within, available through, and derived from the network of relationships that one or a social unit possess', as derived from the definition of Nahapiet and Ghoshal (1998) and further divided into three dimensions, namely, relational, structural, and cognitive.

Relational Capital

The relational dimension refers to the types of personal relationships people have built with each other through a chain of interactions (Nahapiet and Ghoshal, 1998). This dimension includes the characteristics and the qualities of individual relationships, such as shared history and trust, which are crucial. Besides, the relational dimension is strongly linked with the quality of ongoing relationships. Concurrently, the relational dimension reflects the character and the qualities of the relationship between individuals, which is often identified through trust and cooperation, along with the identification that one has within a network of relationships. As such, the relational social capital has been considered as the asset generated and distributed based on relationships built from obligations, identification, norms, and trust. Moreover, the relational dimension emphasizes on specific relationship, friendship, and respect that people have among them and how these attributes affect their behaviour.

An instance of how this dimension may come into action is observed when comparing the interactions between separate individuals with similar positions in a network of relationships, such as that portrayed in the buyer-supplier relationship. Depending on the history of bonds and trustworthiness between two individuals, the action and dynamics of the interactions differ, when compared to the interaction between the same two people without any relational ties. Such interaction is highly influenced by the relationship and the history of exchanges between the particular individuals.

The aspect of trust between actors and network is essential as it increases one's willingness to share knowledge and information (Inkpen & Tsang, 2005).

Knowledge exchange occurs after repeated transactions based on mutual knowledge and trust. In a similar vein, Kale, Singh, and Perlmutter (Kale, Singh, & Perlmutter, 2000) revealed that the stronger the relationship, more knowledge is shared. Hence, trust enables sharing of information among actors, which seems difficult to be gained outside the circle (Leana and Pil, 2006). Additionally, Uzzi (1999) found that strong ties built on trust, information sharing, and joint problem solving may enhance firm performance.

Amongst option traders, the quality of a relationship contributes to option price stability that has a direct impact upon performance (Baker, 1984). This means; entrepreneurs with strong relationship and trust with other network actors have access to knowledge and information, thus leading to better business performance. In fact, more recent works by Fornoni, Arribas, and Vila (2012) revealed that the relational dimension is strongly related to firm performance.

Cognitive Capital

The cognitive dimension refers to 'resources that provide shared representations, interpretations, and systems of meaning among parties' (Nahapiet and Ghoshal 1998). Cognitive dimension facilitates mutual understanding of goals and offers a viable method to interact with the others. This dimension of social capital, however, appears to be the least studied of the three dimensions of social capital (Nahapiet, 2008; Krause, 2007). Cognitive dimension derives from shared meanings and shared interpretations between the actors in a relationship. The cognitive dimension also includes several elements of shared norms, as well as a range of meanings and values, in which the cognitive dimension is projected to display a direct impact upon social capital creation and development of relationships. Tsai and Ghoshal (1998) suggested that the cognitive dimension is embedded in shared visions and collective goals of organizational players that are amalgamated by shared perceptions, expectations, and interpretations.

Similarly, Moran (2005) and Burt (1992) claimed that relationships built on shared norms and values appear stronger. This is proven when goals and values are mutual and combined with interpretations, which are accepted and shared within, and with organizations, hence making social capital on-going, supportive, and self-reinforcing (Weick, 1995). Meanwhile, Liker and Choi (2004) listed that unique term, interpretations of numbers, concepts, and acronyms are the aspects that communities or separate networks develop at the cognitive capital stage. As such, the cognitive dimension captures the essence of the significance of truly sharing rich information with shared meanings across network actors, and not merely passing along data or branding about fancy terms.

The cognitive dimension of social capital is integrated in norms and values of correlation, while the common goal makes it possible for the players to see the value of the exchange and the resource combination generated (Nahapiet and Ghoshal, 1998). This results in sharing of resources among the companies with similar visions.

The communication process between various actors plays a crucial role in resource exchange. A proper communication minimizes variation in meaning and context, thus signifying saying and understanding the same thing (Inkpen and Tsang, 2005). In a network relationship, relationship with other actors generates value sharing and streamlining meanings, strengthens relationship, and creates a capital beneficial for business performance (Oliveira, 2013). These shared values and understanding create common objectives and shared visions, hence contributing to performance. This means; entrepreneurs who understand their key actors can create an environment of common values, vision, and objectives, which may boost business performance.

Structural Capital

The structural dimension reflects the properties of the social system and the network of correlations as a whole (Nahapiet and Ghoshal, 1998). This dimension determines if a network tie exists between units, as well as its appearance. In precise, it probes into the density of the network structure, the hierarchy of the network, and the connectivity of the linkages. This particular dimension has been explored in depth by Burt (Burt, 1995; 2000; 2002; 2004; 2007; Butt, 1995) to relate with whom one may reach and how one may reach them. The structural dimension is comprised of network components and facets, such as the presence or the absence of ties between parties, the configuration of a network (the hierarchy within an organization), and several concepts, for instance, density of relationships and structural holes in networks.

Burt (1992) added that actors on opposite sides of structural holes operate in varied information circles, and thus, a value spans in segregating such information circles. Next, information from these separate and non-redundant flows are combined, which then offers the potential for innovation and the generation of new intellectual capital. Moreover, it is suggested that these properties cannot generate social capital, but instead, these ties facilitate social capital only when they work in conjunction with both relational and cognitive dimensions. Structural ties alone cannot bridge separated information flows effectively, for, as asserted by Burt, closure between two networks requires more than just structural ties; as bridging also demands attributes, such as facilitating trust, collaborating alignment, and sharing interpretations (Butt, 1995).

The various and vast pool of knowledge that various actors possess within a network allows them to combine and share resources, thus increasing the possibility of a firm to enhance its performance by interacting with the social network (Oliveira, 2013). Besides, the structural dimension embedded in the social capital offers the required diversity and quantity in the network, which grant access to resources. This combination boosts towards better performance (Inkpen and Tsang, 2005; Nahapiet and Ghoshal, 1998; Uzzi & Gillespie, 2002). Evidence presents that the relationship between entrepreneurs and their bankers secures them with lower loan interests (Uzzi, 1999). Besides, network density has been positively associated with profit making and network accessibility, which generates new businesses (Aldrich, Rosen, & Woodward, 1987). A study that focused on sales managers derived from Fortune 100 companies showed that network was closely linked with sales performance (Galunic and Moran, 1999). This means; entrepreneurs with adequate networks and established contacts with various actors have better access to the required resources that can be used to enhance their business performance.

Moving beyond individualism, resources generated by social capital is beneficial and improves both personal and business success. At the individual level, networks help to land a job. This is because; not all individuals secure jobs via ‘formal’ methods, such as advertisements. The practice of finding a job through networking is promoted by counsellors and outplacement consultants, whereby people tend to land better paying jobs that are satisfying, hence suggesting they stay longer at these jobs. Moreover, those with better networks are reported to have better salaries and tend to be promoted faster (Baker, 2010). At the firm level, social capital helps in securing venture capital. Based on a survey sponsored by the U.S Small Business Administration, it was discovered that a staggering 75% of new businesses and start-ups acquired financing through social networks of investors and capital seekers, such as friends, colleagues, and acquaintances (Baker, 2010). Simultaneously, social capital is linked to advertising based on word-of-mouth marketing, where this method seems to exert a better effect, as personal recommendation and referrals lead to actual purchase decision.

Hence, social capital is crucial to potential entrepreneurs who wish to embark on a start-up. The act of meeting other entrepreneurs and building good social capital is crucial to begin entrepreneurial activities. For potential entrepreneurs, joining business incubators and entrepreneurial support network appears necessary to promote and to strengthen entrepreneurship (Neira, Portela, Cancelo, & Calvo, 2013). In fact, Neira, Portela, Cancelo, and Calvo (Neira, Portela, Cancelo, & Calvo, 2013) found that the situation changes after getting involved in early-stage entrepreneurial activities and consolidated entrepreneurship, especially once when the entrepreneur has the business rolling, social trust stops to have an impact.

The Malaysian government has been promoting entrepreneurs within the nation by providing centres for instructors and advanced skills training. As such, entrepreneurs are provided skills and entrepreneur development trainings so as to improve and to seize opportunities from the job market. As for business start-ups, a total of RM65 million was allocated to Small Entrepreneur Fund in order to promote a sustainable economy. In addition, a shariah-compliant SME financing fund of RM2 billion had been allocated to strengthen and to enhance the performances among SMEs, which was carried out through 13 Islamic banks throughout the nation. Additionally, empirical studies on social capital have proven the positive effect of social capital on economic development and living standards (Svendsen, 2003; Bennet and Richardson, 2005). As such, Rutherford, 2000) suggested that social capital is the missing link in economic development.

Nonetheless, the groundbreaking contribution to the literature of social capital and its growth heightened during the 1990s with the release of a book entitled '*Making Democracy Work*' by Putnam, Leonardi, and Nanetti (1993). This book asserts a positively significant correlation between economic performance and social capital, where the latter is measured by indicators, such as the number of voluntary organizations, the number of newspaper readers, the voter turnout at polls, and the civic retardants. Following that, Helliwell and Putnam (1999) employed the similar indicators of social capital to display their positive impacts in the long run on economic growth within Italian provinces.

Based on the significance of entrepreneurship that highly contributes to the economy and the progress of a nation, studies pertaining to business failure based on several factors, such as access to finance, have been well-established. Apart from that, the variances between men and women in starting and building a business are another area of focus in entrepreneurship (Buttner and Rosen, 1998) Nonetheless, researches that emphasize on women owned businesses and factors that affect them are still scant (Hanafi, 2012).

Policymakers and scholars have begun accepting that social capital is indeed valid and relevant in adding value to communities and people. Thus, policymakers have been constantly finding ways to utilize the positive vibe of social capital to benefit communities and individuals in the economic sense. Nevertheless, the gap remains where elaboration regarding social capital is still insufficient, along with its impact upon entrepreneurship (Gailey, 2010). Apart from that, although studies by Tsai and Goshal (1998), as well as Casson and Giusta (2007), have repeatedly discussed the importance of networks in promoting entrepreneurship, the literature presents limited contribution of networks linked to business sustainability (Tsai and Goshal, 1998). Even if studies on entrepreneurship and network exist, they are mostly limited to a single industry (Schilling, & Phelps, 2007) and the preference is biased towards the manufacturing industry (Park, Shin and Kim, 2010).

SOCIAL CAPITAL IN MALAYSIA

Empirical evidences suggest that high and equally distributed levels of social capital do benefit the citizens, while unequal distribution affects economic progression (Ponzetto & Troiano, 2014). With that, Fazio and Lavecchia (2013), in a study that employed trust as a measure of social capital, discovered that variances in social capital are evident both within and across nation(s). The distribution of social capital differs among European countries (Parts, 2013). New member states, inclusive of Bulgaria, Czech Republic, Estonia, Hungary, Latvia, Lithuania, Poland, Romania, Slovak Republic, and Slovenia, happen to display lower level of social capital when compared to Western European countries, for example, Austria, Belgium, Cyprus, Denmark, Finland, Germany, France, Greece, Iceland, Ireland, Italy, Luxembourg, Malta, Netherlands, Norway, Portugal, Spain, Sweden, Switzerland, and the Great Britain. Nonetheless, a prior research carried out by Van Oorschot, Arts, and Gelissen (2006) discovered insignificant variance in regard to social capital across European countries and regions, except for Scandinavia, that reflected higher social capital. This section presents better understanding and empirical evidence on how social capital is distributed across industries and states in Malaysia.

The distribution of network density seems similar across the states in Malaysia without any statistical significance (Rajennd, Al Mamun, Permarupan, Noor Raihani, & Mohamad, 2016). The distribution of shared meaning and interpretation appeared to be at its highest in the state of Johor with a mean value of 3.8434, followed by Perak at 3.8409, while the state of Kelantan was the lowest at a mean value of 3.4719. The distribution of shared values and norms noted to be high in Penang with a mean value of 4.1250, while the lowest in the state of Kelantan with a mean value of 3.4566. As for the distribution of quality of business relationships, once again, the state of Penang recorded the highest mean value at 4.2111, while the state of Kelantan, again at its lowest at 3.5680. In addition, the state of Johor displayed the highest mean value of 3.8157, and Kelantan the lowest at 3.4388 for trust among key business players. In terms of length of business relationship, entrepreneurs from the state of Penang reported the highest mean value at 4.0083, whereas those from Kelantan scored the lowest with 3.4515 as the mean value. The state of Johor has the highest mean value for distribution of network ties with a mean value of 4.0866 and Terengganu scoring the lowest at 3.8180. as for cognitive social capital, the state of Penang is reported to have the highest mean value of 3.9542, while the state of Kelantan scored the lowest with a mean value of 3.4643. Overall, the distribution of social capital differed across the states in Malaysia. The state of Penang recorded higher social capital, in comparison to the other states, such as Perak, Selangor, Johor, Kelantan, and Terengganu. In general, Kelantan appeared to record the lowest level of social capital. The mean value for the distribution of social capital is 3.8989 for Penang, 3.8137 for Johor, 3.7659 for Selangor, 3.7530 for Perak, 3.6895 for Terengganu, and 3.5145 for Kelantan.

This study incorporated manufacturing, retailing, wholesale, agriculture, and services industries. Based on the analysis, the distribution of shared values and norms, quality of business relationship, trust among key business players, length of business relationship, network ties, network density, and social capital seem similar across the industries. It is noted that the distribution of shared meaning and interpretation, as well as cognitive social capital, differs across the industries. The mean value for distribution of shared meaning and interpretation is highest in agriculture, and followed by the wholesale industry at 4.0 and 3.8629, respectively. Meanwhile, manufacturing and retailing recorded the lowest level of shared meaning and interpretation at mean values of 3.6622 and 3.6508, respectively. As for cognitive social capital, the mean value is the highest in the agriculture industry with a mean value of 4.0000, but lowest in the retailing industry (Rajennd, Al Mamun, Permarupan, Noor Raihani, & Mohamad, 2016).

The outcomes of this study portray that the distribution of social capital is more balanced across industries, such as manufacturing, retailing wholesale, agriculture, and services (Rajennd, Al Mamun, Permarupan, Noor Raihani, & Mohamad, 2016). On the other hand, at the national level, the distribution of social capital is noted to be dissimilar among the states, especially Penang, Perak, Selangor, Johor, Terengganu, and Kelantan. The findings of social capital distribution across states are in line with those retrieved by Fazio and Lavecchia (2013). The reason for the unequal distribution of social capital across the states in Malaysia is, however, not determined in this research.

Furthermore, it is noted that the states of Kelantan and Terengganu are the lowest in social capital mean values. Relational and cognitive dimensions of social capital that consist of shared meaning and interpretation, shared values and norms, quality of business relationship, trust among key business players, and length of business relationship should reflect as the elements that may enhance social capital in both these states.

SOCIAL CAPITAL AND COMPETITIVE ADVANTAGE

Porter (1985) defines competitive advantage as attaining a superior position in performance through the application of generic strategies. Superior position can be achieved via cost leadership and via differentiation. Cost leadership refers to the ability to achieve the lowest price per unit cost in the industry, while differentiation denotes concentration on a very specific segment. Competitive advantage is also described as a position achieved by a firm so as to enhance its performance, when compared to its competitors. The aspect of competitive advantage should not be easily copied by rivals. Other sources of competitive advantage are being rare and unique, interconnected, cumulative, and renewable (Luthans & Youssef, 2004). These unique resources are difficult to imitate by rivals because they are beyond reach financially or strategically.

Social capital based on networks, norms, and trust helps to create competitive advantage. Networks connect members of a firm and units among them with the external world. These established inter-linkages permit sharing of information, knowledge, and resources so as to contribute to long term success via resources and synergies. Norms, on the other hand, generate practical mutual expectations that avoid complicated rules and regulations, aside from fostering creativity and flexibility. As a finishing touch, trust acts as a bonding agent that amalgamates networks and norms, hence leading to full potential. In total, social capital is essential in creating competitive advantage (Luthans & Youssef, 2004). As for this research, competitive advantage focuses on innovation, capability, and resources as the sources of competitive advantage.

The significance of competitive advantage has been acknowledged in the recent decade. As such, academicians and practitioners have placed their focus on the attributes that are specific to firms, how they add value to end consumers, and are transferable to a variety of industrial settings. Competitive advantage is, therefore, believed to give firms a number of advantages over others, such as lower cost structure and wages, as well as superior customer service (Coplin, 2002).

For instance, Rajennd (2016) indicated that the aspect of competitive advantage partially mediated the relationship between social capital and performance among micro-entrepreneurs. The rational justification on the positive effect of social capital on competitive advantage is because women entrepreneurs with social capital are in the state of well-connected with various types of formal and informal networks. These women entrepreneurs, through relationship based on trust, understanding, sharing of business values and norms, do get along well and are close with their suppliers, customers, and business partners, thus suggesting the possibility to have access to resources that are unavailable without the touch of social capital. The findings further display that the aspect of social capital among women entrepreneurs generates a hint of competitive advantage. Moreover, being in connection with those significant in the business arena grants access to information that may lead right to crucial resources sought by women micro-entrepreneurs.

Besides, a similar study (Rajend, 2016) found that competitive advantage positively affected the performance of micro-enterprises owned by women. The logical possible explanation for this is that the social capital aspect creates competitive advantage among micro-enterprises owned by women. Furthermore, access to resources, capabilities, and innovation are important to make a difference in the performance among the micro-enterprises. In fact, access to resources may be in the form of cheaper, better, and reliable finance, market, and raw materials. Furthermore, it is also possible to get in contact with the major industry players who may offer or introduce channels to improve capabilities and innovation into the micro-enterprises. This clearly shows that competitive advantage has a positive impact upon micro-enterprise performance.

The inter-firm networks and the networks of owners or managers provide firms with access to resources, such as strategic knowledge, which are vital to the value-creating processes for they allow firms to minimise transaction costs of social interaction and exchange (Bonner, Kim, & Cavusgil, 2005; Ma, Yao, & Xi, 2009). Social capital can also generate competitive advantage for micro-entrepreneurs as the element of trust among the partners and consumers, together with networking, can increase their ability to compete (Nahapiet and Ghoshal, 1998) hence leading towards enhanced business performance (Fahy, 2000).

Empirical studies have identified the positive effect of social capital on competitive advantage within the competitive landscape competing against networks of enterprises, as opposed to individual contenders (Hitt, Keats, & DeMarie, 1998). Firms that operate in a network have more resources that they can access in order to increase their ability to compete. In addition, recent studies pertaining to intangible resources and their impact upon sustainable competitive advantage are ingrained in the concept of social capital. In the current view, firms do not operate in isolation, but instead, are embedded in a network of relationships as they create value (Ma, Yao, and Xi, 2009). Such network of relationships with other firms, economic or social entities, as well as individuals, generates some form of intangible relational asset valuable to the firm. These intangible resources are widely known as social capital, which can potentially endow a firm with strategic resources that are essential to the creation of sustainable competitive advantage (Nahapiet and Ghoshal, 1998).

AUTHOR CONTRIBUTIONS

All authors were involved in collecting relevant information and literature review, and writing this chapter.

CONFLICTS OF INTEREST

The authors declare no conflict of interest.

ACKNOWLEDGMENT

This research was funded by the Ministry of Higher Education, Malaysia under the grant entitled "Developing a Comprehensive Rural Entrepreneurship Model for Poverty Eradication (REMODE)" (R/NRGS/A01.00/00047A/006/2014/000149).

REFERENCES

Acquaah, M., & Appiah-Nkrumah, J. (2011). Firm-specific managerial experience and the social capital--performance relationship in a sub-Saharan African transition economy. *Journal of African Business*, *12*(1), 8–30. doi:10.1080/1536710X.2011.555251

Ahlin, C., & Townsend, R. M. (2007). Using repayment data to test across models of joint liability lending. *Economic Journal (London)*, *117*(517), 11–51. doi:10.1111/j.1468-0297.2007.02014.x

Al-Mamun, A. (2014). Investigating the Development and Effects of Social Capital through Participation in Group Based Microcredit Program in Peninsular Malaysia. *Journal of Interdisciplinary Economics*, *26*(1-2), 33–59. doi:10.1177/0260107914540822

Aldrich, H., Birley, S., Dubini, P., Greve, A., Johannisson, B., Reese, P. R., & Sakano, T. (1991). *The generic entrepreneur? Insights from a multinational research project.* Paper presented at the Babson College Entrepreneurship Research Conference, Pittsburgh, PA.

Aldrich, H., Rosen, B., & Woodward, W. (1987). *The impact of social networks on business funding and profit. Frontiers of entrepreneurship research.* Wellesley, MA: Babson College.

Anderson, A. R., Dodd, S. D., & Jack, S. (2010). Network practices and entrepreneurial growth. *Scandinavian Journal of Management*, *26*(2), 121–133. doi:10.1016/j.scaman.2010.01.005

Andersson, U., Forsgren, M., & Holm, U. (2002). The strategic impact of external networks: Subsidiary performance and competence development in the multinational corporation. *Strategic Management Journal*, *23*(11), 979–996. doi:10.1002mj.267

Baker, W. (2010). *Achieving success through social capital: Tapping hidden resources in your personal and business networks*. San Francisco, CA: Jossey-Bass.

Baker, W. E. (1984). The social structure of a national securities market. *American Journal of Sociology*, *89*(4), 775–811. doi:10.1086/227944

Bennet, D., & Richardson, P. (2005). *Building Relationships and Social Capital Development*. Paper presented at the 50th ICSB World Conference, Washington, DC.

Bonner, J. M., Kim, D., & Cavusgil, S. T. (2005). Self-perceived strategic network identity and its effects on market performance in alliance relationships. *Journal of Business Research*, *58*(10), 1371–1380. doi:10.1016/j.jbusres.2004.07.002

Burt, R. S. (1992). *Structural holes: The social structure of competition*. Cambridge, MA: Harvard University Press.

Burt, R. S. (2002). The Social Capital of Structural Holes. In M. F. Guillén, R. Collins, & M. Meyer (Eds.), *The New Economic Sociology: Developments in an Emerging Field* (pp. 148–190). New York: Russell Sage Foundation.

Burt, R. S. (2004). Structural Holes and Good Ideas. *American Journal of Sociology*, *110*(2), 349–499. doi:10.1086/421787

Burt, R. S. (2007). Secondhand Brokerage: Evidence on the Importance of Local Structure for Managers, Bankers, and Analysts. *Academy of Management Journal*, *50*(1), 119–148. doi:10.5465/amj.2007.24162082

Butt, R. S. (1995). Le capital social, les trous structuraux, et 1'entrepreneur (translated by Emmanuel Lazega). *Revue Francaise de Sociologie*, *36*, 599–628. doi:10.2307/3322448

Buttner, H., & Rosen, B. (1998). Bank loan officer's perceptions of the characteristics of men and women and successful entrepreneurs. *Journal of Business Venturing*, *3*(3), 249–258. doi:10.1016/0883-9026(88)90018-3

Carey, S., Lawson, B., & Krause, D. R. (2011). Social capital configuration, legal bonds and performance in buyer--supplier relationships. *Journal of Operations Management*, *29*(4), 277–288. doi:10.1016/j.jom.2010.08.003

Casson, M., & Della Giusta, M. (2007). Entrepreneurship and social capital analysing the impact of social networks on entrepreneurial activity from a rational action perspective. *International Small Business Journal*, *25*(3), 220–244. doi:10.1177/0266242607076524

Chen, Y. Y., Zhang, Y., & Fey, C. F. (2011). When collaborative hr practices may not work well: The moderating role of social capital in the Chinese life insurance industry. *International Journal of Human Resource Management*, *22*(02), 433–456. doi:10.1080/09585192.2011.540164

Coleman, J. S. (1988). Social capital and the creation of human capital. *American Journal of Sociology*, *94*, S95–S120. doi:10.1086/228943

Cook, L. D. (2011). Inventing social capital: Evidence from African American inventors, 1843--1930. *Explorations in Economic History*, *48*(4), 507–518. doi:10.1016/j.eeh.2011.05.003

Cooper, A. C., Folta, T. B., & Woo, C. (1995). Entrepreneurial information search. *Journal of Business Venturing*, *10*(2), 107–120. doi:10.1016/0883-9026(94)00022-M

Coplin, L. C. H. (2002). *Competitive Advantages and the SMEs: The Role of Distinctive Competences as Determinants of Success, Are There Differences across Gender, Sector, And Size?* (Doctoral Dissertation). University Autonoma DeBarcelona, Barcelona, Spain.

DeCarolis, D. M., & Saparito, P. (2006). Social capital, cognition, and entrepreneurial opportunities: A theoretical framework. *Entrepreneurship Theory and Practice*, *30*(1), 41–56. doi:10.1111/j.1540-6520.2006.00109.x

Drakopoulou-Dodd, S., Jack, S., & Anderson, A. R. (2006). The mechanisms and processes of entrepreneurial networks: continuity and change. In J. Wiklund, D. Dimov, J. A. Katz & D. Shepherd (Eds.), In Entrepreneurship: Frameworks And Empirical Investigations From Forthcoming Leaders Of European Research (pp. 107-145). Bingley, UK: Emerald Group Publishing Limited.

(1986). Entrepreneurship through social networks. InAldrich, H., & Zimmer, C. (Eds.), *The Art and Science of Entrepreneurship* (pp. 3–23). New York: Ballinger.

Fahy, J. (2000). The resource-based view of the firm: some stumbling-blocks on the road to understanding sustainable competitive advantage. *Journal of European Industrial Training, 24*(2/3/4), 94-104.

Fazio, G., & Lavecchia, L. (2013). Social Capital Formation across Space: Proximity and Trust in European Regions. *International Regional Science Review, 36*(3), 296–321. doi:10.1177/0160017613484928

Fornoni, M., Arribas, I., & Vila, J. (2012). An entrepreneur's social capital and performance. *Journal of Organizational Change Management, 25*(5), 682–698. doi:10.1108/09534811211254572

Gailey, R. (2010). *Social capital and economic empowerment: A longitudinal analysis of the relationship between changes in the value of accumulate assets and measures of social capital among rural South African women* (Doctoral dissertation). University of San Diego, CA.

Galunic, C., & Moran, P. (1999). *Social capital and productive exchange: Structural and relational embeddedness and managerial performance link* (Unpublished manuscript). London Business School.

Greve, A., & Salaff, J. W. (2003). Social networks and entrepreneurship. *Entrepreneurship Theory and Practice, 28*(1), 1–22. doi:10.1111/1540-8520.00029

Grootaert, C. (1999). *Social Capital, Household Welfare, and Poverty in Indonesia* (World Bank Policy Research Working Paper No. 2148). Washington, DC: World Bank.

Grootaert, C., Narayan, D., Jones, V. N., & Woolcock, M. (2004). *Measuring Social Capital: An Integrated Questionnaire* (Working Paper No. 18). Washington, DC: World Bank.

Hanafi, N. (2012). *Learning orientation, entrepreneurial orientation, competitive advantage and business performance of women-owned SMEs in Malaysia* (Unpublished DBA dissertation). Universiti Utara Malaysia, Kedah.

Hansen, E. (1995). Entrepreneurial networks and new organization growth. *Entrepreneurship Theory and Practice, 19*(4), 7–19. doi:10.1177/104225879501900402

Helliwell, J. F., & Putnam, R. D. (1999). *Education and social capital* (NBER Working Paper No. W7121). Cambridge, MA: National Bureau of Economic Research.

Hitt, M., Keats, B., & DeMarie, S. (1998). Navigating in the new competitive landscape: Building strategic flexibility and competitive advantage in the 21st century. *The Academy of Management Perspectives*, *12*(4), 22–42. doi:10.5465/ame.1998.1333922

Hoang, H., & Antoncic, B. (2003). Network-based research in entrepreneurship: A critical review. *Journal of Business Venturing*, *18*(2), 165–187. doi:10.1016/S0883-9026(02)00081-2

Inkpen, A. C., & Tsang, E. W. (2005). Social capital, networks, and knowledge transfer. *Academy of Management Review*, *30*(1), 146–165. doi:10.5465/amr.2005.15281445

Jayawarna, D., Jones, O., & Macpherson, A. (2011). New business creation and regional development: Enhancing resource acquisition in areas of social deprivation. *Entrepreneurship and Regional Development*, *23*(9-10), 735–761. doi:10.1080/08985626.2010.520337

Kale, P., Singh, H., & Perlmutter, H. (2000). Learning and protection of proprietary assets in strategic alliances: Building relational capital. *Strategic Management Journal*, *21*(3), 217–237. doi:10.1002/(SICI)1097-0266(200003)21:3<217::AID-SMJ95>3.0.CO;2-Y

Kickul, J. R., Gundry, L. K., & Sampson, S. D. (2007). Women entrepreneurs preparing for growth: The influence of social capital and training on resource acquisition. *Journal of Small Business and Entrepreneurship*, *20*(2), 169–181. doi:10.1080/08276331.2007.10593393

Koka, B., & Prescott, J. (2002). Strategic alliances as social capital: A multidimensional view. *Strategic Management Journal*, *23*(9), 795–816. doi:10.1002mj.252

Krause, K. (2007). Social involvement and commuter students: The first-year student voice. *Journal of the First-Year Experience & Students in Transition*, *19*(1), 27–45.

Krishna, A. (2008). Social capital and economic development. In D. Castiglione, J. W. Van Deth, & G. Wolleb (Eds.), *The handbook of social capital* (pp. 438–466). New York, NY: Oxford University Press.

Leana, C. R., & Pil, F. K. (2006). Social capital and organizational performance: Evidence from urban public schools. *Organization Science*, *17*(3), 353–366. doi:10.1287/orsc.1060.0191

Liker, J. K., & Choi, T. Y. (2004). Building deep supplier relationships. *Harvard Business Review*, *82*(12), 104–113.

Luthans, F., & Youssef, C. (2004). Human, Social, and Now Positive Psychological Capital Management: Investing in people for competitive advantage. *Organizational Dynamics*, *33*(2), 143–160. doi:10.1016/j.orgdyn.2004.01.003

Ma, X., Yao, X., & Xi, Y. (2009). How do interorganizational and interpersonal networks affect a firm's strategic adaptive capability in a transition economy? *Journal of Business Research*, *62*(11), 1087–1095. doi:10.1016/j.jbusres.2008.09.008

Moran, P. (2005). Structural vs. relational embeddedness: Social capital and managerial performance. *Strategic Management Journal*, *26*(12), 1129–1151. doi:10.1002mj.486

Mustafa, M., & Chen, S. (2010). The strength of family networks in transnational immigrant entrepreneurship. *Thunderbird International Business Review*, *52*(2), 97–106. doi:10.1002/tie.20317

Nahapiet, J., & Ghoshal, S. (1998). Social Capital, Intellectual Capital, and the Organizational Advantage. *Academy of Management Review*, *23*(2), 242–266. doi:10.5465/amr.1998.533225

Narayan, D., & Pritchett, L. (1999). Cents and sociability: Household income and social capital in rural Tanzania. *Economic Development and Cultural Change*, *47*(4), 871–897. doi:10.1086/452436

Neira, I., Portela, M., Cancelo, M., & Calvo, N. (2013). Social and human capital as determining factors of entrepreneurship in the Spanish regions. *Investigaciones Regionales*, *26*, 115–139.

Oliveira, J. F. D. (2013). The influence of the social capital on business performance: An analysis in the context of horizontal business networks. *RAM. Revista de Administração Mackenzie*, *14*(3), 209–235. doi:10.1590/S1678-69712013000300009

Park, S. H., & Luo, Y. (2001). Guanxi and organisational dynamics: Organisational networking in Chinese firm. *Strategic Management Journal*, *22*(5), 455–477. doi:10.1002mj.167

Park, Y., Shin, J., & Kim, T. (2010). Firm size, age, industrial networking, and growth: A case of the Korean manufacturing industry. *Small Business Economics, 35*(2), 153–168. doi:10.100711187-009-9177-7

Parts, E. (2013). *The Dynamics and Determinants of Social Capital in the European Union and Neighbouring Countries.* Discussions on Estonian economic policy: Theory and practice of economic policy in the European Union, Working paper No. WP5/01. doi:10.2139srn.2336016

Percoco, M. (2012). Entrepreneurship, social capital and institutions: Evidence from Italy. *Spatial Economic Analysis, 7*(3), 339–355. doi:10.1080/17421772.2012.694144

Ponzetto, G. A. M., & Troiano, U. (2014). *Social Capital, Government Expenditures, and Growth.* CEPR Discussion Paper No. 9891. Available at SSRN: https://ssrn.com/abstract=2142548

Porter, M. (1985). *Competitive advantage.* New York: Free Press.

Pratono, A. H., & Mahmood, R. (2014). Social capital and firm performance: Moderating effect of environmental turbulence. *Asian Social Science, 10*(19), 59–68. doi:10.5539/ass.v10n19p59

Putnam, R. D., Leonardi, R., & Nanetti, R. (1993). *Making democracy work: Civic traditions in modern Italy.* Princeton, NJ: Princeton University Press.

Rajennd, M. (2016). *The Role of Social Capital and the Mediating effect of Competitive Advantage on Business Performance of Women Entrepreneurs in Malaysia* (Masters Thesis). Universiti Malaysia Kelantan, Kota Bharu.

Rajennd, M., Al Mamun, A., Permarupan, P., Noor Raihani, B., & Mohamad, M. (2016). Social Capital: Cross-industry and Cross-state Comparison among Malaysian Women Micro-entrepreneurs. *Mediterranean Journal of Social Sciences, 7*(1), 350–360.

Rowley, T., Behrens, D., & Krackhardt, D. (2000). Redundant government structures: An analysis of structural and relational embeddedness in the steel and semiconductor industries. *Strategic Management Journal, 21*(3), 369–386. doi:10.1002/(SICI)1097-0266(200003)21:3<369::AID-SMJ93>3.0.CO;2-M

Rutherford, S. (2000). *The poor and their money.* New Delhi: Oxford University Press.

Schilling, M. A., & Phelps, C. C. (2007). Interfirm collaboration networks: The impact of large-scale network structure on firm innovation. *Management Science*, *53*(7), 1113–1126. doi:10.1287/mnsc.1060.0624

Smith, D. A., & Lohrke, F. T. (2008). Entrepreneurial network development: Trusting in the process. *Journal of Business Research*, *61*(4), 315–322. doi:10.1016/j.jbusres.2007.06.018

(2008). Social capital and Interorganizational Relations. InNahapiet, J. (Ed.), *The Oxford Handbook of Interorganizational Relations* (pp. 580–606). Oxford, UK: Oxford University Press.

Svendsen, G. (2003). *The Political Economy of European Union: Institutions, Policy and Economic Growth*. Cheltenham, UK: Edward Elgar.

(2000). The contingent value of social capital. InBurt, R. S. (Ed.), *Knowledge and social capital: foundations and applications* (pp. 255–285). Boston: Butterworth Heinemann.

The forms of capital. (1986). InBourdieu, P. (Ed.), *Handbook of Theory and Research for the Sociology of Education* (pp. 241–258). New York: Greenwood Press.

Tsai, W., & Ghoshal, S. (1998). Social capital and value creation: The role of intrafirm networks. *Academy of Management Journal*, *41*(4), 464–476.

Uzzi, B. (1999). Embeddedness in the making of financial capital: How social relations and networks benefit firms seeking financing. *American Sociological Review*, *64*(4), 481–505. doi:10.2307/2657252

Uzzi, B., & Gillespie, J. J. (2002). Knowledge spillover in corporate financing networks: Embeddedness and the firm's debt performance. *Strategic Management Journal*, *23*(7), 595–618. doi:10.1002mj.241

VanOorschot, W., Arts, W., & Gelissen, J. (2006). Social Capital in Europe: Measurement and Social and Regional Distribution of a Multifaceted Phenomenon. *Acta Sociologica*, *49*(2), 149–167. doi:10.1177/0001699306064770

Weick, K. E. (1995). *Sensemaking in organizations*. Thousand Oaks, CA: Sage Publications.

Chapter 5
Entrepreneurial Competencies and Traits

ABSTRACT

Entrepreneurial competency is the most influential contributing factor for rapid economic progression within many developed economies. This chapter focuses on several selected entrepreneurial competencies and traits by investigating their influence on the performance and the sustainability of micro-enterprises owned and managed by low-income households. The key competencies and traits were selected after combing through a number of relevant theories and empirical studies that determined the effects of these traits and competencies on the performance and the sustainability of micro-enterprises.

INTRODUCTION

Initially, entrepreneurial activities were carried out mainly to cater to the daily needs of people. At present time, entrepreneurial activities do not only support the related households, but they also contribute to the well-being of the society, thus significantly boosting the economic growth of the nation. Entrepreneurship is defined as 'an activity involving the discovery, evaluation and exploitation of opportunities to introduce new goods and services, ways of organizing markets, processes, and raw materials through organizing efforts that previously had not existed' (Shane, Locke, and Collins, 2003). Entrepreneurship also refers to the process of creating something new, as well as assuming the associated risks and rewards. Since entrepreneurship has

DOI: 10.4018/978-1-5225-8473-5.ch005

always exhibited significantly positive impacts; most governments worldwide have taken measures to facilitate entrepreneurs by promoting entrepreneurial activities among their respective societies so as to generate employment, to eradicate poverty, and to increase economic growth.

ENTREPRENEURIAL COMPETENCIES

Several studies have highlighted both the progress and the positive impact of entrepreneurship among rapidly emerging economies, such as that in Malaysia. In the attempt of retaining the continuity of all positivity, it is pertinent for the Malaysian government to comprehend and to identify the factors that can enhance the performance of entrepreneurs towards sustenance in the present market.

Nevertheless, some gaps have been identified, particularly within the context of low-income micro-entrepreneurs in Malaysia. Wahid, Aziz, and Halim (2017) asserted that the Malaysian micro-enterprises seem to face inadequate human competency that must be addressed in order to survive and to compete in the fierce market. In order to succeed in business, entrepreneurs must acquire certain competencies that can aid them to become financially solvent (performance), as well as to attain sustenance in their entrepreneurial activities. According to Al-Mamun, Nawi, and Zainol (2016) one of the many key drivers of micro-enterprise performance is an entrepreneurial competency. Over the last century, entrepreneurial competency emerged as a crucial contributing factor for rapid economic progression within many developed economies. Studies also have proven that the correlation between individual characteristics and managerial competencies can lead to organizational success and sustainability (Gray, 2002; Jokinen, 2005). Entrepreneurial competencies further ascertain growth and survival of small- to medium-sized enterprises (Tehseen, Sajila, Ramayah, and Gadar, 2015). In particular, these small and micro businesses can only accomplish enhanced performance and continuity when their owner-managers and employees acquire knowledge, skills and entrepreneurial traits at a level of competence as required to effectively performing business activities (Nabiswa and Mukwa, 2017). Within the context of Malaysia, entrepreneurial competencies have been reckoned as strong determinants to a successful business, especially among small and medium enterprises (SMEs) (Ahmad, Ramayah, Wilson, and Kummerow, 2010) apart from exerting positive and significant effects on the performance of micro-enterprises (Al-Mamun, Nawi, and Zainol, 2016).

Entrepreneurial competencies can be defined as the characteristics that encompass personality traits, skills and knowledge, which can enhance business performances (Man, Lau, and Chan, 2002). Some studies have depicted that entrepreneurial competencies refer to a specific set of competencies that is relevant to the activities of successful entrepreneurships (Mitchelmore and Rowley, 2010). Studies have also suggested entrepreneurial competencies as skills and knowledge that can influence the abilities of entrepreneurs to perform exceptionally in their business activities (Bridge, Neill, and Martin, 2009). Furthermore, researches regarding entrepreneurial competencies have mainly focused on three aspects, namely, 1) antecedents (education, background, family, and traits), 2) processes (opportunities, organizing, and commitments), and lastly, 3) outcomes (performance, competitive advantage). Furthermore, Man, Lau and Chan (2002). identified opportunity recognition competency, organizational competency, strategic competency, relationship competency, commitment competency and conceptual competency as essential key entrepreneurial competencies, all of which are briefly discussed in the following.

TYPES OF ENTREPRENEURIAL COMPETENCIES

Opportunity recognition competency refers to the competencies possessed by entrepreneurs in recognizing, interpreting, and comprehending the environmental conditions and market opportunities through various means (Man, Lau, and Chan, 2002). These opportunity recognizing competencies guide entrepreneurs to seek opportunities that are not readily accessible through market information (using internet, personal network or media) and to embark on promotional activities, such as participating in exhibitions or advertising (Man, Lau, and Chan, 2002).

Organizational competency illustrates entrepreneurial competencies that are affiliated with the organization of various external and internal human, physical, technological, and financial resources (Man, Lau, and Chan, 2002). Organizational competencies equip entrepreneurs with knowledge and skills so as to consummate managerial duties associated to planning, organizing, motivating, leading, controlling and delegating tasks. Entrepreneurs involved in small and micro businesses need to be good at attaining various human, financial, technological, and physical resources, regardless within the perimeter of the firm or otherwise, apart from organizing them in the most efficient and systematic way possible (Man, Lau, and Chan, 2002). Nonetheless, in order to effectively execute the managerial and technical roles, entrepreneurs must possess interpersonal, conceptual, and political competencies, coupled with the ability of using tools and procedures as prerequisite in their fields of operations (Kelliher and Reini, 2009). Explicitly, from the context of micro-firms, research advocates that the accomplishments attained by a firm are largely reliant on the competency of its owner or manager to successfully mechanize inadequate resources for the progression of organizational capabilities (Kelliher and Reini, 2009).

Strategic competency is perceived as the prime competency that is essential for setting long-term direction of an organization and initiating appropriate actions towards such directions. In precise, it refers to entrepreneurial competencies linked to setting, evaluating and implementing long-term strategies of an organization in regard to vision, goal setting, budgeting, recruitment, scope and capabilities utilization, making changes, setting tactics, strategic controlling, and moving ahead in the path of the fixed goals (Man, Lau, and Chan, 2002). A competent entrepreneur does not only need to set long-term goals, but also plan realistic and achievable medium-term missions and positions as well (Man, Lau, and Chan, 2002).

Relationship competencies ascribe to interactions and communications performed via person-to-person or individual-to-group to create important contacts upon exploiting business connections and opportunities. This particular dimension of entrepreneurial competency reflects an entrepreneur's ability to build, keep, and use relationships, networks, confidence and trust of all stakeholders (suppliers, clients, family, friends, employees, partners and other business associates of the firm) by applying effective negotiation and communication skills to manage conflicts, and thereby, building consensus (Man, Lau, and Chan, 2002). Since, communication appears to be the foundation of all relationships; the micro-business environment has the tendency to embrace the informal narrative mode (Penn, Angiwa, Forster, Heydon and Richardson, 1998). Besides, micro-business owners in regular contact with their stakeholders become aware of their sentiments and conditions, thus making the micro-firms more inclined towards less internal uncertainty (Storey and Cressey, 1996).

Commitment competency refer to those entrepreneurial competencies that serve as a thrust for entrepreneurs to move forward with their businesses, aside from creating a strong commitment towards enhancing and sustaining superior performance in the long run (Man, Lau, and Chan, 2002). Nevertheless, regardless of how diverse the conditions an entrepreneur has to face, continuous dedication is vital for business progression. Besides, such commitment is emulated by the entrepreneur's strong consecration towards hard work, yearning of aiming at long-term objectives, instead of short-term accomplishments, together with the aptitude to restart their businesses even after failure for the sake of self-belief, values, and employees and also to achieve personal ambitions (Man, Lau, and Chan, 2002). *Conceptual competency* denotes entrepreneurial competencies that are associated to numerous conceptual abilities, for instance, thinking intuitively, detecting from varied viewpoints, being innovative, and considering threats, all of which fall under entrepreneurial behavior, which are essential to uncover and to analyze issues related to organizations (Man, Lau, and Chan, 2002). Considering the fact that the fate of firms, particularly micro-firms, relies almost comprehensively on the owner's intuition (Rice and Hamilton, 1979), the burden of making right decision only lies with the owner (Palvia, Means, and Jackson, 1994). Rendering to such heavy dependency, research claims that due to extensive pressure exerted on entrepreneurs; they can soar out as experts in the arena of management (Kelliher and Henderson, 2006).

FACTORS THAT AFFECT COMPETENCIES

The discussion above translates that entrepreneurial competencies have positive influence upon superior firm performance and sustainability, which in turn, contribute towards growth and development of economies. But what causes the formation and development of such required competencies? It is obvious that determining and comprehending the essential key factors may boost entrepreneurial competencies and micro-enterprise performance of low-income households who are extremely vulnerable and depend heavily on their micro-enterprise income due to lack of education and enterprise developing skills, coupled with nil or limited access to working capital and enterprise training; which appear to remain extremely significant (Al-Mamun, Nawi, and Zainol, 2016), Andrews, Sarnchez and Johansson (2011), claimed that it is crucial to identify the factors of entrepreneurial competency to predict the success or failure of businesses. Without doubt, there are several crucial factors that can affect the competencies possessed by entrepreneurs. As such, these factors have to be unraveled and channeled to entrepreneurs in order to improve their competencies. The following section depicts several prominent antecedents of entrepreneurial competencies, along with their dimensions, which could be accumulatively used to capture them.

ENTREPRENEURIAL MOTIVATION

One essential factor that affects entrepreneurial competencies is entrepreneurial motivation. Entrepreneurial motivation is perceived as a significant element in both theoretical and empirical models associated to entrepreneurial performance of small enterprises (Nhemachena and Murimbika, 2018). Since business accomplishments depend completely on entrepreneurs, their actions are considered as a result of cognitive and motivational factors. These factors are embedded within the entrepreneurs, in which their ability and willingness to act significantly may have an impact upon the entrepreneurial process (Shane, Locke, and Collins, 2003). In fact, entrepreneurial motivation can be measured in various ways. The initial dimensions include one's need for achievement, locus of control, desire for independence, vision, passion, goal setting, self-efficacy and self-drive. Later, more dimensions seemed to emerge, for instance, 'pull' or 'push' factors, one's age, sex, level of education, reward structure, as well as expected net present economic benefits in comparison to the expected gains from waged labor (Campbell, 1992; Shane, Locke, and Collins, 2003; Eijdenberg and Masurel, 2013). Some of these entrepreneurial motivational components that may influence entrepreneurial competency and enterprise sustainability amongst micro-entrepreneurs in Malaysia are elaborated in the following.

Need for achievement reflects the aspiration one craves for the sake of self-esteem instead of gaining social recognition or stature (McClelland, 1965). Early academicians endorsed that those with higher need for achievement have higher tendency to be involved in entrepreneurship, which could enhance entrepreneurial competency (McClelland, 1965; Johnson, 1990). Need for achievement among other components of entrepreneurial motivation, such as need for power and need for affiliation, are significant for performance linked to work and societal welfare (Jager, Born, and Molen, 2017).

Openness to change can be motioned as one's readiness or willingness to support change while retaining an optimistic approach regarding the probable consequences of such change (Miller, Johnson, and Grau, 1994; Wanberg and Banas, 2000). Hence, the motivational components, such as openness to new experience, self-confidence, intellectual capacity, and emotional stability, could result in regulating at a global level (Jordan and Cartwright, 1998). In the course of uncertain market condition, flexibility, openness to change, and skills can be accelerated to generate specific competencies that may facilitate entrepreneurs to grapple with the ever-changing actuality.

Since openness to change has been connoted as an aptitude to adapt swiftly to environmental changes, it can significantly trigger firm performance (Nadkarni and Herrmann, 2010).

Pull factors refer to entrepreneurial motivators that entice individuals to endeavor into doing business, similarly as detecting an exploitable opportunity (Hakim, 1989). In addition, pull factors kindle entrepreneurial motives to select, direct, and drive behaviors, which could be instigating entrepreneurial competencies towards certain aim or action that differs from the rest (Spencer and Spencer, 1993). Pull factors, which is also seen as the human capital associated to internal factors, are linked with the contributions offered by entrepreneurs towards exploitation of entrepreneurial opportunities, especially those required for business performance. Besides, these pull factors appear to originate from political, social and economic forces that 'pull' innovative technologies, hence resulting in sustainable performance (Ekpe, Mat, and Razak, 2011; Buhalis and Main, 1998).

Self-improvement is the reasoning that one provides to venture into the business arena, including pursuit of self-directed goals. Self-improvement can be deployed to initiate the abilities possessed by entrepreneurs within their entrepreneurial competencies in business towards competitive advantage from unique and inimitable resources (Barney, 1991; Grant, 1991). In fact, this is a crucial element that influences the formation of necessary economic skills and personal qualities that define social, economic, professional and informative orientation (Komelina, Mirzagalyamova, Gabbasova, Rod, Slobodyan, Esipova, Lavrentiev, and Kharisova, 2016). Furthermore, self-improvement and self-development promote competencies. As such, self-improvement is viewed to have influence over competencies and it could be advocated that self-improvement, as an individual-specific trait, may serve as a valuable and unique capability to lead firms towards superior economic, social, and environmental performance (Hart, 1995). In addition, self-improvement motivation, along with the entrepreneur's attitude, positive relationship with suppliers, and networking, can lead to sustainability (Dangi, Johari, Ismail, and Noor, 2017).

Self-confidence denotes one's ability to accumulate and to implement resources, competencies and skills in order to fulfil a certain level of accomplishment for a particular task (Shane, Lock, and Collins, 2003). Global competencies can be explained by motivational components, such as self-confidence, intellectual capacity, emotional stability and openness towards new experience (Jordan and Cartwright, 1998).

Self-confidence generates vital competencies to further motivate entrepreneurial activities (Kiggundu, 2002). Besides, completely developed self-confidence renders into business and entrepreneurial competencies (Kickul, Wilson, Marlino, and Barbosa, 2008). Sustenance of self-confidence and exceptionally significant antecedent of entrepreneur knowledge make predicting enterprise performance and growth an easy task (Omerzel and Antončič, 2008). Self-confidence is not only unique and rare, but it is also a treasured capability that is highly individual-specific, which could be molded into superior social, economic, and environmental performance (Barney, 1991; Hart, 1995).

As aforementioned above, all of these factors are close with the finding by researcher regarding on motivation of Malaysia women micro enterprise. In addition, some of researcher provided different finding based on different states in Malaysia. For examples, in Kedah, religious motivates women micro enterprises, while Johor is due to independence, interest and financial matters (Azmi, 2017). Women micro entrepreneurs in Klang Valley are highly motivated to participate in business because of opportunity to increase income and freedom. Meanwhile, independence and supportive environmental factors motivates women to involve in micro enterprise in Dungun, Terengganu (Azmi, 2017).

ENTREPRENEURIAL SKILLS

Entrepreneurial skills imply the possibility of learning and consequently, adopting specific characteristics, where individuals must focus on activities linked to the concerned entrepreneurial task that involves interactions with the social and material environment (Pyysiäinen, Anderson, McElwee, and Vesala, 2006). Entrepreneurs need to possess multiple skills in order to develop that precise competency, which is absolutely vital to successfully manage business (Phelan and Sharpley, 2012). On top of that, these entrepreneurial skills are associated with higher personal attraction and subjective norms, which are responsible in making one to feel dexterous to venture into entrepreneurship (Scherer, Brodzinski, and Wiebe, 1991). Moreover, acquiring entrepreneurial skills refurbishes one's beliefs pertaining to entrepreneurial aptitude with enlightenment of the difficulty in securing a project or an initiative off the ground (Entrialgo and Iglesias, 2016). Past researchers have proven that a skills possessed by entrepreneurs contribute to enterprise performance and growth (Bird, 1995; Mitchelmore and Rowley, 2013), which in turn, increase the profitability of firms (Kelliher and Reinl, 2009). The components of entrepreneurial skills, such as unique skills, market-sales orientation and networking activities, can facilitate micro-entrepreneurs to generate entrepreneurial competencies, thus resulting in superior enterprise performance.

Market orientation - Ali, Hilman and Gorondutse (2017) asserted that market orientation can be perceived as a firm's rare and valuable capability or resources that are inimitable in nature, thus emphasizing the placement of customer needs in the core of organizational strategy and operations. Market orientation refers to adaptive learning, wherein firms identify their respective environmental changes and responds to them in the attempt to develop required assumptions in regard to consumers and competition. Meanwhile, Narver and Slater (1990) described market orientation as an organizational culture that most efficiently generates the much-required competency so as to create superior value for buyers, thus accelerating the firm towards continuous superior performance. Grounded on the notion that stronger market orientation is essential for rapid response towards changing market needs and preferences, Boso, Story and Cadogan (Boso, Story, and Cadogan, 2013) discovered that aligning high levels of entrepreneurial and market orientation can enhance the performance of an organization. Baker and Sinkula (Baker and Sinkula, 2009) claimed that market orientation is an important factor that dictates organizational success.

Sales orientation is illustrated as the primary engagement of entrepreneurs into selling activities that highlights 'getting the sale', as much as possible from each customer (Jaramillo, Ladik, Marshall, and Mulki, 2007). The existing literature indicates that customer needs and complaints have generated a selling-oriented approach in an effort to influence certain attributes (entrepreneurial competency) that may lead to higher sales (Saxe and Weitz, 1982; OHara, Boles, and Johnston, 1991). Wachner, Plouffe and Grégoire (2009) emphasized that the selling skills exerted by a salesperson (entrepreneur in a small business) can escalate the levels of baseline competency (entrepreneurial), which further leads to superior firm performance.

Given the significance of consumer satisfaction in the present competitive business setting, coupled with the increasing expectations of consumers, entrepreneurs need to build rapport, present their services/products, and close sales in a single meeting; in the presumption that every firm needs to be engaged in some degree of sales-oriented behavior at a regular basis (Boles, Howard, and Donofrio, 2001). Boles et al., (2001) added that a non-supportive work environment could influence a greater usage of selling orientation, where managers attempt to enhance sales to improve performance. At the individual level, Jaramillo, Ladik, Marshall, and Mulki (2007) revealed that sales and customer-related orientation are significant predictors of performance, wherein firms with a larger emphasis on sales-oriented skills display better subsequent performance. In an earlier study, Churchill, Ford, Hartley, and Walker (1985) found that selling skills appeared to be the most significant determinant of performance.

Networking is defined as the ability of one in managing networks, where the networks are comprised of a focal character and all individuals or groups with whom the focal individual has direct links, as well as other parties that are indirectly introduced to the focal character by his direct associates (Aldrich, Zimmer, and Jones, 1986). Researchers discovered that networking of work contacts is an antecedent of relationship-related competencies [8, 48]. Entrepreneurial network offers the framework for varied processes that aim at organizing competencies as dictated by opportunities (Johannisson and Mønsted, 1997). Larson (1992) mentioned that entrepreneurial dyadic ties are the building blocks of networks, which are built upon a history of preconditions for exchange, inclusive of both organizational and personal competencies, together with prior links.

Furthermore, an effective networking offers opportunities for entrepreneurs to gain expertise and diverse forms of support that may lead to superior firm performance (Ahmad, Ramayah, Wilson, and Kummerow, 2010). Besides, developing social networks can benefit businesses, as connections and networks give power to entrepreneurs to take a safer route, mostly when the environment is not only demanding, but also hostile (Baum and Locke, 2004; Markman, 2007). Hence, scholars like Lee and Tsang (2001) believe that networking activities have a progressive impact upon the growth of firms. Other researchers also found that networking is an antecedent of entrepreneurial competencies, which can facilitate towards achieving higher firm profitability (Gerli, Gubitta, and Tognazzo, 2011). In the context of micro and small enterprises, Nabiswa and Mukwa (2017) pointed out that some factors, such as the existence of networking, could be applied to measure growth performance of a firm.

Conversely, Malaysia women micro enterprise that has entrepreneurial skills demonstrated success towards business development. In Malaysia, the government acts as a platform to nurture entrepreneurial skills within women micro entrepreneurs, thus providing incentives for business start up. Realize to the important of entrepreneurial skills, the Department of Women Development has initiated relevant program for women micro entrepreneur development (Jamak, Ali, and Ghazali, 2014). For example, Jejari Bestari (provide knowledge and skills in handicraft), *Inkubator Keusahawanan Wanita (I-KeuNITA)* (provide intensive skill training and assistance for low-income women), and Inkubator Kemahiran IbuTunggal (I-KIT) (Single Parent) (provide intensive skill training and assistance for single mothers).

ENTREPRENEURIAL LEADERSHIP

Entrepreneurs need to have a certain set of unique abilities and personality traits to ascertain a successful and sustainable entrepreneurship that may significantly influence in acquiring varied levels of organizational success (Beatti, 2016). In precise, the performance of SMEs depends on entrepreneurial traits and competencies, for example, leadership capabilities, managerial and networking skills, technological abilities, and education level of entrepreneurs (Odhiambo, 2013; Lateh, Hussain, and Halim, 2017). In fact, a study suggested that entrepreneurial leadership plays a vital role in business venture attainments (Lubis, 2017). Particularly for entrepreneurs of small enterprises, entrepreneurial leadership is unavoidable, mainly because in order to successfully develop their business ventures, they must portray effective leadership characteristics (Cogliser and Brigham, 2004). Moreover, the dimensions of entrepreneurial leadership, such as responsibility, accountability, analytical thinking and emotional intelligence, can facilitate entrepreneurs to articulate their respective effects in creating competencies, so as to ascertain superior firm performance and sustainability.

Responsibility reflects the habits that reinforce a leader's capacity to organize, thus expediting cooperative efforts through alertness and intelligence towards the motives and needs of others, and followed by insight into situations (Stogdill, 1948). Responsibility has also been reckoned to correlate with leadership, hence perceiving that responsibility represents the traits of a leader (Stogdill, 1948). In terms of entrepreneurship, the significance of responsibility, which is one of the many crucial traits of a leader, can be explained by the fact that entrepreneurs work within a relatively unstructured environment as they are held responsible for every aspect of the firm, such as sales, recruitment, public relations, and negotiations (Zhao and Seibert, 2006; Kuratko, 2007). Empirically, scholars have portrayed a strong and positive relationship between responsibility (environmental and social) and enterprise performance (Rodríguez and Cruz, 2007). Within the context of SMEs, a study suggested that entrepreneurial leadership is closely linked to abilities, such as team leading, whilst taking responsibilities for a task is considered as a crucial factor for the escalating growth of SMEs (Omerzel and Antončič, 2008).

Accountability in leaders denotes the informal and sociopolitical process, where one is expected or assumed to behave in a particular manner so as to maintain an appropriate social order (Hall, Blass, Ferris, and Massengale, 2004). As leadership mirrors the process of occupying one or more positions of responsibility in group activities (Stogdill, 1948), it is fundamental that accountability (socio–psychological process), as an important trait of a leader, assures that individuals are held responsible for their actions, which also controls abuse of their otherwise well-connected celebrity status (Hall, Blass, Ferris, and Massengale, 2004). Based on prior studies, accountability seems to be a significant determinant in promoting firm performance (Keay, 2016; Nuhu and Hussani, 2017). Rimvydas (2017) asserted that accountability is a key feature of sustainable organizations by highlighting its facilitating role of positioning firms in both local and international markets.

Analytical thinking has been perceived as intellectual critical thinking introversion, whereby alertness related to the surrounding environment and understanding of situations are closely linked to leadership capability (Stogdill, 1948). Empirically, such capability does not only facilitate leadership experience, but it also establishes support for leadership training (Ricketts and Rudd, 2005). According to Ibdah (2018), analytical thinking, as a means of confronting problems, as well as dealing with internal and external changes related to varied business activities, does improve the level of organizational performance. Meanwhile, Burnard and Bhamra (2011) claimed that analytical thinking supports characterizing the responses of an organization towards disruptive events, aside from facilitating organizational sustainable development by determining the essential processes deemed necessary to elicit resilient response.

Emotional intelligence is the ability of individuals in addressing their own and others' emotions, apart from using this information to assist them in decision-making and problem-solving tasks (Salovey and Mayer, 1990). Emotional intelligence can be defined as a set of cognitive capabilities and self-efficacy that enables individuals to monitor their own feelings and emotions, as well as to understand how such feelings or emotions might distinguish from the rest, and thereby, using the exhaled information to guide their emotions and thinking as they explore the available business opportunities (Petrides and Furnham, 2001; Anyanwu and Oad, 2016). According to Nanayakkara, Wickramasinghe and Samarasinghe (2017), leaders with higher levels of emotional intelligence are more likely to be highly profitable. Empirically, Nanayakkara, Wickramasinghe, and Samarasinghe (2017), revealed that emotional intelligence has a significant impact upon non-financial organizational performance, which can be translated into social and environmental dimensions of sustainability.

The women's leadership in Malaysia micro enterprises has made great improvement and effectiveness in managing business. All of the said entrepreneurial leadership is aligned with the study conducted in Malaysia, specifically in Kelantan. Particularly, entrepreneurial leadership not only affects the performance of micro enterprise, but also sustainability of micro enterprise. In Malaysia, women entrepreneurial leadership requires high commitment to run their business as micro enterprise (Jamak et al., 2014).

ENTREPRENEURIAL ORIENTATION

Entrepreneurial orientation has been highlighted as an effective mechanism that supports the capabilities deemed necessary for integrating, building and reconfiguring both external and internal competencies so as to address the rapidly changing environments in SMEs (Darwis, 2017). Entrepreneurial orientation has been widely acknowledged for its positive effect upon performance (Caseiro, and Coelho, 2018). Within the context of SMEs, Radulovich, Javalgi and Scherer (2018) empirically revealed that entrepreneurial orientation, along with relational and human capital, has a direct impact upon firm performance. Entrepreneurial orientation has also been perceived as the key determinant for growth and venture innovation (Hakala, 2013).

Entrepreneurial orientation is defined as processing, practicing, and decision-making actions, which could lead to new business ventures (Lumpkin and Dess, 1996). In terms of entrepreneurial orientation, most of the past studies have focused on the constructs of risk-taking and innovativeness as the components of entrepreneurial orientation. In addition, entrepreneurial orientation has been conceptualized in the existing literature as having anywhere between three and five dimensions, including but not limited to creativity and innovativeness, risk-taking propensity, proactiveness and autonomy (Richard, Barnett, Dwyer, and Chadwick, 2004). *Creativity and Innovativeness* - Creativity reflects the inventive ability of entrepreneurs in devising solutions that can overcome problems, especially under uncertain situations that require creativity to impress order and forward solutions, whereas innovativeness is described as the effort taken by an organization to discover novel opportunities and new solutions through involvement in experimentation and creativity, thus resulting in new products and services, or/and enhanced technical aspects of the existing products and services (Dess and Lumpkin, 1995).

In a recent study, Liu and Atuahene-Gima (2018) empirically revealed that creativity, in terms of marketing, offers better prediction regarding product innovation performance. Gong, Zhou and Chang (2013) on the other hand, displayed that core creativity of employees was positively related to firm performance, especially when the realized absorptive capacity is retained at a high level. Meanwhile, Stopford and Baden-Fuller (1994) discovered that organizational innovation and creativity serve as the key factors for entrepreneurship. In precise, innovativeness is a vital factor that epitomizes entrepreneurship (Lumpkin and Dess, 1996) and exhibits a positive relationship with firm performance (DeZubielqui, Fryges, and Jones, 2017).

Risks taking propensity reflects 'the degree to which managers are willing to make large and risky resource commitments, i.e., those with a reasonable chance of costly failures' (Miller, 1983). Organizations with entrepreneurial orientation are often exemplified by their risk-taking behavior, such as making large resource commitments or incurring heavy debt, in the interest of acquiring high returns by exploiting the existing opportunities (Lumpkin and Dess, 1996). Zhang, Yang, Xu, and Zhu, 2018) for instance, discovered that risk-taking propensity of managers significantly and positively influenced the innovation performance amongst firms.

Proactiveness can be defined as acting in anticipation of future needs, problems, or changes by relating to market opportunities, apart from exploiting initiatives (Lumpkin and Dess, 1996; 2001).

Proactiveness involves adopting initiatives in the effort to shape the environment to one's own advantage. Therefore, entrepreneurial orientation involves proactiveness in pursuing opportunities so as to aggressively respond towards competition (Lumpkin and Dess, 1996). Priyanto and Sandjojo (2005) noted that several traits, such as proactiveness, reflect mental factors that influence learning competencies, which further determine venture growth and success. In addition, Lee, Cho, Baek, and Choi (2017) empirically reported that only proactive behavior of directors significantly improved the financial performance amongst firms.

Autonomy can be defined as an individual or a team's independent action of conveying a vision or an idea into view, which is then transmitted to accomplishment by allowing an individual or a group to implement the required competencies to practice good entrepreneurship (Lumpkin and Dess, 1996). Autonomy, as the ability and willingness to take self-directed actions in the pursuit of market opportunities, permits firms to make quick and self-reliant decisions in providing new markets with novel products or services (Lee, Cho, Baek, and Choi, 2017). Empirically, Dimitratos, Liouka and Young (2014) discovered that autonomy captured distinct entrepreneurial competencies among subsidiaries of multinational companies, while Badjuri (2017) revealed that autonomy displayed a significantly positive impact on firm performance.

OTHER ENTREPRENEURIAL TRAITS

Successful and sustainable entrepreneurship requires unique abilities and personality traits; some of which have been depicted in the literature as significantly influential in acquiring the varied levels of organizational success (Beatti, 2016). Furthermore, the process of creating value, especially amidst small firms, has been reckoned to rely on the capabilities of entrepreneurs to perform their role in a successful manner (Grant, 1991). Hence, it is perceived that the connection of specific entrepreneurial traits with an entrepreneur's competencies is required to attain success among firms (Beatti, 2016). Locus of control, tolerance of ambiguity, visionary traits, persistence, and resilience are some of the other entrepreneurial traits that facilitate one in developing his/her entrepreneurial competencies, which would lead them to acquire superior enterprise performance and sustainability.

Locus of control refers to the extent to which individuals believe certain events to be consequences of their own behavior, hence potentially under their control (Lefcourt, 1976). According to Shane et al., (2003), locus of control is a significant entrepreneurial trait that has received much attention, mainly because of one's belief in the extent to which he/she perceives that personal traits or actions can affect the outcomes. Tubbs and Schulz (2006) added that locus of control, as a personality trait among individuals, determine leadership competencies. Besides, the literature exerts a significant link between locus of control and venture performance (Baum and Locke, 2004; Aldrich and Wiedenmayer, 1993).

Tolerance of ambiguity is the attraction of individuals towards ambiguous situations, whereby it is important to comprehend timely information regarding a particular situation or determining its future outcome would remain incomplete or absent (McLain, 1993). This is especially in the context of small business owners, wherein Wagener, Gorgievski and Rijsdijk (2010) stated that entrepreneurial characteristics, such as tolerance of ambiguity, enable entrepreneurs to develop competencies that facilitate business-related novelty.

Visionary denotes an individual trait, whereby one would remain single-minded and committed in the pursuit of a vision while confronting skeptic naysayers and inadequacy of external resources (Sarasvathy and Venkataraman, 2011). Visionary and self-confidence grow out of an individual's identity to drive entrepreneurial competence towards achievement. Fillis and Rentschler (2010) asserted that the generation of several alternative directions, such as creative entrepreneurial behavior and entrepreneurial competencies, can be generated through suitable visionary leadership trait. According to DeLuque, Washburn, Waldman, and House (2008) visionary leadership exhibited a positive impact upon employees' additional effort, which in turn, affected the firm performance in a positive manner.

Persistence - McClelland (1987) defined persistence as taking repeated or various actions to address obstacles. Tarabishy, Solomon, FernaldJr, and Sashkin (2005) mentioned that persistence is a significant entrepreneurial trait required by entrepreneurs to successfully operate their business activities.

Resilience has begun earning much attention recently in studies related to entrepreneurship as an individual unit of analysis from the stance of entrepreneurs as individuals who begin afresh after having failed in prior business attempts (Bullough, Renko, and Myatt, 2014). Krueger and Brazeal (1994) highlighted that resilience characterizes successfully developing communities and effectively innovating organizations. Meanwhile, Peterson, Walumbwa, Byron, and Myrowitz (2009) empirically verified that positive psychological characteristics, such as resiliency, optimism and hope, have an impact upon firm performance in an indirect manner.

Given that important competencies and traits, women micro entrepreneurs should take immediate action to improve micro-enterprise development. Malaysian government continuously cultivate and enterprising culture environment among women micro entrepreneur through increasing entrepreneurial competencies (Al Mamun, Muniady, Yukthamarani, Noor Raihani, and Mohamad, 2016). Thus, as aforementioned above, several influential keys of competencies are highlighted due to the impact towards successful women micro entrepreneur. In 1999, Masud and colleague in Peninsular Malaysia are conducted the projects that involved 319 women micro enterprise (Masud and Paim, 1999). They found that their competencies increased the ability to gained knowledge that helps to provide solution for the problems occur and successfully expand the business. While in Terengganu

(East Coast Malaysia) competencies and supportive environmental lead to the proper business setting. Accordingly, the development of competencies among Malaysian women allowed them to become more creative and innovative in producing and promoting their product or service. Moreover, in Malaysia, the research on competency and traits helps in identify appropriate planning of national policies and programs. The developing competencies among women micro entrepreneur help the government to identify the appropriate target at the startup phase and might help them to create and sustain their business ventures successfully.

CONCLUSION

The development of sustainability-driven enterprises requires competent owners (Mindt and Rieckmann, 2017). This is especially for small enterprises, where sustainability, expansion of operations, and survival highly depend on certain skill sets of their principals (Rahman, 2016). Entrepreneurial competencies form an essential ingredient for organizations to succeed, particularly amongst low-income households who rely highly on their micro-enterprise income. As such, this chapter highlights the essence of entrepreneurial competencies by outlining their significances towards successful entrepreneurship, while placing focus on the factors that could be manipulated to generate such required competency. This chapter, hence, does not only offer a theoretical stance to enhance our understanding of entrepreneurial traits and competencies required for successful and sustainable business, but also provides a tale of focus areas that could be concentrated upon by policymakers, developmental organizations, and entrepreneurs to accelerate firm performance, which would eventually lead towards greater entrepreneurial activities, thus ascertaining economic, social and environmental well-being.

AUTHOR CONTRIBUTIONS

All authors were involved in collecting relevant information and literature review, and writing this chapter.

CONFLICTS OF INTEREST

The authors declare no conflict of interest.

ACKNOWLEDGMENT

This research was funded by the Ministry of Higher Education, Malaysia under the grant entitled "Developing a Comprehensive Rural Entrepreneurship Model for Poverty Eradication (REMODE)" (R/NRGS/A01.00/00047A/006/2014/000149).

REFERENCES

Ahmad, N. H., Ramayah, T., Wilson, C., & Kummerow, L. (2010). Is entrepreneurial competency and business success relationship contingent upon business environment? A study of Malaysian SMEs. *International Journal of Entrepreneurial Behaviour & Research*, *16*(3), 182–203. doi:10.1108/13552551011042780

Al Mamun, A., Muniady, R., Yukthamarani, P. P., Noor Raihani Binti, Z., & Mohamad, M. R. (2016). Micro-enterprise development initiatives and entrepreneurial competencies, innovativeness, and social capital in Malaysia. *Development in Practice*, *26*(8), 1094–1110. doi:10.1080/09614524.2016.1228830

Al-Mamun, A., Nawi, N. B. C., & Zainol, N. R. B. (2016). Entrepreneurial Competencies and Performance of Informal Micro-Enterprises in Malaysia. *Mediterranean Journal of Social Sciences*, *7*(3), 273–281.

Aldrich, H., Zimmer, C., & Jones, T. (1986). Small business still speaks with the same voice: A replication of 'the voice of small business and the politics of survival'. *The Sociological Review*, *34*(2), 335–356. doi:10.1111/j.1467-954X.1986.tb02705.x

Aldrich, H. E., & Wiedenmayer, G. (1993). From traits to rates: An ecological perspective on organizational foundings. *Advances in Entrepreneurship, Firm, Emergence, and Growth*, *1*(3), 145–196.

Ali, G. A., Hilman, H., & Gorondutse, A. H. (2017). The effect of entrepreneurial orientation, market orientation, total quality management and organizational culture on the SMEs performance: A theoretical framework. *Journal of Business and Retail Management Research, 12*(1), 26–40. doi:10.24052/JBRMR/V12IS01/TEOEOMOTQMAOCOTSPATF

Andrews, D., Sarnchez, A. C., & Johansson, A. (2011). *Towards a Better Understanding of the Informal Economy*. OECD Economics Department Working Papers, No. 873, OECD Publishing.

Anyanwu, C., & Oad, S. (2016). Entrepreneurial Leadership and Organizational Creativity in the Collectivist Context: The moderating role of Emotional Intelligence. *International Journal of Management and Administrative Sciences, 4*(2), 1–12.

Azmi, I. A. G. (2017). Muslim women entrepreneurs' motivation in SMEs: A quantitative study in Asia Pacific Countries. *Asian Economic and Financial Review, 7*(1), 27–42. doi:10.18488/journal.aefr/2017.7.1/102.1.27.42

Badjuri, A. (2017). Pengaruh Budaya Organisasi, Pengalaman, Otonomi, Profesionalisme Dan Ambiguitas Peran Terhadap Kinerja Auditor (Studi Empiris Pada KAP di Jawa Tengah). *Students'. Journal of Accounting and Banking, 6*(2).

Baker, W. E., & Sinkula, J. M. (2009). The complementary effects of market orientation and entrepreneurial orientation on profitability in small businesses. *Journal of Small Business Management, 47*(4), 443–464. doi:10.1111/j.1540-627X.2009.00278.x

Barney, J. (1991). Firm resources and sustained competitive advantage. *Journal of Management, 17*(1), 99–120. doi:10.1177/014920639101700108

Baum, J. R., & Locke, E. A. (2004). The relationship of entrepreneurial traits, skill, and motivation to subsequent venture growth. *The Journal of Applied Psychology, 89*(4), 587–598. doi:10.1037/0021-9010.89.4.587 PMID:15327346

Baumol, W. J. (1996). Entrepreneurship: Productive, unproductive, and destructive. *Journal of Business Venturing, 11*(1), 3–22. doi:10.1016/0883-9026(94)00014-X

Beattie, S. (2016). Which Entrepreneurial Traits are the Most Critical in Determining Success? *Otago Management Graduate Review, 14*, 13–20.

Bird, B. (1995). Towards a theory of entrepreneurial competency. *Advances in Entrepreneurship, Firm, Emergence, and Growth*, *2*(1), 51–72.

Boles, J. S., Howard, W. G., & Donofrio, H. H. (2001). An investigation into the inter-relationships of work-family conflict, family-work conflict and work satisfaction. *Journal of Managerial Issues*, *13*(3), 376–390.

Boso, N., Story, V. M., & Cadogan, J. W. (2013). Entrepreneurial orientation, market orientation, network ties, and performance: Study of entrepreneurial firms in a developing economy. *Journal of Business Venturing*, *28*(6), 708–727. doi:10.1016/j.jbusvent.2013.04.001

Bridge, S., O'Neill, K., & Martin, F. (2009). *Understanding Enterprise*. Entrepreneurship.

Buhalis, D., & Main, H. (1998). Information technology in peripheral small and medium hospitality enterprises: Strategic analysis and critical factors. *International Journal of Contemporary Hospitality Management*, *10*(5), 198–202. doi:10.1108/09596119810227811

Bullough, A., Renko, M., & Myatt, T. (2014). Danger zone entrepreneurs: The importance of resilience and self-efficacy for entrepreneurial intentions. *Entrepreneurship Theory and Practice*, *38*(3), 473–499. doi:10.1111/etap.12006

Burnard, K., & Bhamra, R. (2011). Organisational resilience: Development of a conceptual framework for organisational responses. *International Journal of Production Research*, *49*(18), 5581–5599. doi:10.1080/00207543.2011.563827

Campbell, C. A. (1992). A decision theory model for entrepreneurial acts. *Entrepreneurship Theory and Practice*, *17*(1), 21–27. doi:10.1177/104225879201700103

Caruso, D. R., Mayer, J. D., & Salovey, P. (2002). *Emotional intelligence and emotional leadership*. In Kravis-De Roulet Leadership Conference, Claremont McKenna Coll, Claremont, CA.

Caseiro, N., & Coelho, A. (2018). Business Intelligence and Competitiveness: The Mediating Role of Entrepreneurial Orientation. *Competitiveness Review*, *28*(2), 213–226. doi:10.1108/CR-09-2016-0054

Churchill, G. A. Jr, Ford, N. M., Hartley, S. W., & Walker, O. C. Jr. (1985). The determinants of salesperson performance: A meta-analysis. *JMR, Journal of Marketing Research*, *22*(2), 103–118. doi:10.1177/002224378502200201

Cogliser, C. C., & Brigham, K. H. (2004). The Intersection of Leadership and Entrepreneurship: Mutual Lessons to Be Learned. *The Leadership Quarterly*, *15*(6), 771–799. doi:10.1016/j.leaqua.2004.09.004

Cooper, A. C., Gimeno-Gascon, F. J., & Woo, C. Y. (1994). Initial human and financial capital as predictors of new venture performance. *Journal of Business Venturing*, *9*(5), 371–395. doi:10.1016/0883-9026(94)90013-2

Dangi, M. R. M., Johari, R. J., Ismail, A. H., & Noor, R. M. (2017). Entrepreneurial Sustainability, Creativity and Innovation Environment of Small and Medium Enterprises (SMEs) in Malaysia. *Advanced Science Letters*, *23*(8), 7370–7373. doi:10.1166/asl.2017.9477

Darwis, G. (2017). Accelerated Transformation of Indonesian SME's: Embracing Entrepreneurial Orientation and Innovation on Achieving Dynamic Capability to Increase Competitiveness. In *3rd International Indonesian Forum for Asian Studies: Borderless communities & nations with borders, Challenges of Globalization* (pp. 1089-1101). Yogyakarta.

DeLuque, M. S., Washburn, N. T., Waldman, D. A., & House, R. J. (2008). Unrequited profit: How stakeholder and economic values relate to subordinates' perceptions of leadership and firm performance. *Administrative Science Quarterly*, *53*(4), 626–654. doi:10.2189/asqu.53.4.626

Dess, G. G., & Lumpkin, G. T. (2005). The role of entrepreneurial orientation in stimulating effective corporate entrepreneurship. *The Academy of Management Executive*, *19*(1), 147–156. doi:10.5465/ame.2005.15841975

DeZubielqui, G. C., Fryges, H., & Jones, J. (2017). Social media, open innovation & HRM: Implications for performance. *Technological Forecasting and Social Change*. doi:10.1016/j.techfore.2017.07.014

Dimitratos, P., Liouka, I., & Young, S. (2014). A missing operationalization: Entrepreneurial competencies in multinational enterprise subsidiaries. *Long Range Planning*, *47*(1-2), 64–75. doi:10.1016/j.lrp.2013.10.004

Duckett, H., & Macfarlane, E. (2003). Emotional intelligence and transformational leadership in retailing. *Leadership and Organization Development Journal*, *24*(6), 309–317. doi:10.1108/01437730310494284

Eijdenberg, E. L., & Masurel, E. (2013). Entrepreneurial motivation in a least developed country: Push factors and pull factors among MSEs in Uganda. *Journal of Enterprising Culture*, *21*(01), 19–43. doi:10.1142/S0218495813500027

Ekpe, I., Mat, N., & Razak, R. C. (2011). Attributes, environment factors and women entrepreneurial activity: A literature review. *Asian Social Science*, *7*(9), 124–130. doi:10.5539/ass.v7n9p124

Entrialgo, M., & Iglesias, V. (2016). The moderating role of entrepreneurship education on the antecedents of entrepreneurial intention. *The International Entrepreneurship and Management Journal*, *12*(4), 1209–1232. doi:10.100711365-016-0389-4

Fillis, I., & Rentschler, R. (2010). The role of creativity in entrepreneurship. *Journal of Enterprising Culture*, *18*(01), 49–81. doi:10.1142/S0218495810000501

Gerli, F., Gubitta, P., & Tognazzo, A. (2011). Entrepreneurial competencies and firm performance: an empirical study. *VIII International Workshop on Human Resource Management Conference Proceedings*.

Gong, Y., Zhou, J., & Chang, S. (2013). Core knowledge employee creativity and firm performance: The moderating role of riskiness orientation, firm size, and realized absorptive capacity. *Personnel Psychology*, *66*(2), 443–482. doi:10.1111/peps.12024

Grant, R. M. (1991). The resource-based theory of competitive advantage: Implications for strategy formulation. *California Management Review*, *33*(3), 114–135. doi:10.2307/41166664

Gray, C. (2002). Entrepreneurship, resistance to change and growth in small firms. *Journal of Small Business and Enterprise Development*, *9*(1), 61–72. doi:10.1108/14626000210419491

Hakala, H. (2013). Entrepreneurial and learning orientation: Effects on growth and profitability in the software sector. *Baltic Journal of Management*, *8*(1), 102–118. doi:10.1108/17465261311291687

Hakim, C. (1989). Identifying fast growth small firms. *Employment Gazette*, *97*, 29–41.

Hall, A. T., Blass, F. R., Ferris, G. R., & Massengale, R. (2004). Leader reputation and accountability in organizations: Implications for dysfunctional leader behavior. *The Leadership Quarterly*, *15*(4), 515–536. doi:10.1016/j.leaqua.2004.05.005

Hart, S. L. (1995). A natural-resource-based view of the firm. *Academy of Management Review*, *20*(4), 986–1014. doi:10.5465/amr.1995.9512280033

Ibdah, K. (2018). The effect of strategic thinking patterns on the efficiency of decision making process in Jordanian companies of insurance. *Archives of Business Research*, *6*(1), 67–93. doi:10.14738/abr.61.4074

Jager, S. D., Born, M., & Molen, H. V. D. (2017). Self-Other Agreement Between Employees on their Need for Achievement, Power, and Affiliation: A Social Relations Study. *Scandinavian Journal of Work, Environment & Health*, *2*(9), 1–12.

Jamak, A. B. S. A., Ali, R. M. M., & Ghazali, Z. (2014). A breakout strategy model of Malay (Malaysian indigenous) micro-entrepreneurs. *Procedia: Social and Behavioral Sciences*, *109*, 572–583. doi:10.1016/j.sbspro.2013.12.509

Jaramillo, F., Ladik, D. M., Marshall, G. W., & Mulki, J. P. (2007). A meta-analysis of the relationship between sales orientation-customer orientation (SOCO) and salesperson job performance. *Journal of Business and Industrial Marketing*, *22*(5), 302–310. doi:10.1108/08858620710773431

Johannisson, B., & Mønsted, M. (1997). Contextualizing entrepreneurial networking: The case of Scandinavia. *International Studies of Management & Organization*, *27*(3), 109–136. doi:10.1080/00208825.1997.11656715

Johnson, B. R. (1990). Toward a multidimensional model of entrepreneurship: The case of achievement motivation and the entrepreneur. *Entrepreneurship Theory and Practice*, *14*(3), 39–54. doi:10.1177/104225879001400306

Jokinen, T. (2005). Global leadership competencies: A review and discussion. *Journal of European Industrial Training*, *29*(3), 199–216. doi:10.1108/03090590510591085

Jordan, J., & Cartwright, S. (1998). Selecting expatriate managers: Key traits and competencies. *Leadership and Organization Development Journal*, *19*(2), 89–96. doi:10.1108/01437739810208665

Keay, A. R. (2016). Board Accountability and the Entity Maximization and Sustainability Approach. In B. Choudhury & M. Petrin (Eds.), *Understanding the Company: Corporate Governance and Theory*. Cambridge University Press. Retrieved from https://ssrn.com/abstract=2747398

Kelliher, F., & Henderson, J. B. (2006). A learning framework for the small businessenvironment. *Journal of European Industrial Training*, *30*(7), 512–528. doi:10.1108/03090590610704385

Kelliher, F., & Reinl, L. (2009). A resource-based view of micro-firm management practice. *Journal of Small Business and Enterprise Development*, *16*(3), 521–532. doi:10.1108/14626000910977206

Kickul, J., Wilson, F., Marlino, D., & Barbosa, S. D. (2008). Are misalignments of perceptions and self-efficacy causing gender gaps in entrepreneurial intentions among our nation's teens? *Journal of Small Business and Enterprise Development*, *15*(2), 321–335. doi:10.1108/14626000810871709

Kiggundu, M. N. (2002). Entrepreneurs and entrepreneurship in Africa: What is known and what needs to be done. *Journal of Developmental Entrepreneurship*, *7*(3), 239–258.

Komelina, V. A., Mirzagalyamova, Z. N., Gabbasova, L. B., Rod, Y. S., Slobodyan, M. L., Esipova, S. A., ... Kharisova, G. M. (2016). Features of students' economic competence formation. *International Review of Management and Marketing*, *6*(1), 53–57.

Krueger, N. F. Jr, & Brazeal, D. V. (1994). Entrepreneurial potential and potential entrepreneurs. *Entrepreneurship Theory and Practice*, *18*(3), 91–91. doi:10.1177/104225879401800307

Kuratko, D. F. (2007). Entrepreneurial leadership in the 21st century: Guest editor's perspective. *Journal of Leadership & Organizational Studies*, *13*(4), 1–11. doi:10.1177/10717919070130040201

Larson, A. (1992). Network dyads in entrepreneurial settings: A study of the governance of exchange relationships. *Administrative Science Quarterly*, *37*(1), 76–104. doi:10.2307/2393534

Lateh, M., Hussain, M. D., & Halim, M. S. A. (2017). Micro Enterprise Development and Income Sustainability for Poverty Reduction: A Literature Investigation. *International Journal of Business and Technopreneurship*, *7*(1), 23–38.

Lee, D. Y., & Tsang, E. W. (2001). The effects of entrepreneurial personality, background and network activities on venture growth. *Journal of Management Studies, 38*(4), 583–602. doi:10.1111/1467-6486.00250

Lee, E., Cho, K., Baek, H., & Choi, W. (2017). Effect of Proactive and Reactive Outside Directors' Behavior on Banks' Financial Performance. *Productivity Journal, 31*(4), 309–329.

Lefcourt, H. M. (1976). Locus of control and the response to aversive events. *Canadian Psychology, 17*(3), 202–209. doi:10.1037/h0081839

Lerner, M., & Almor, T. (2002). Relationships among strategic capabilities and the performance of women-owned small ventures. *Journal of Small Business Management, 40*(2), 109–125. doi:10.1111/1540-627X.00044

Levesque, M., Shepherd, D. A., & Douglas, E. J. (2002). Employment or self-employment: A dynamic utility-maximizing model. *Journal of Business Venturing, 17*(3), 189–210. doi:10.1016/S0883-9026(00)00063-X

Li, Y. H., Huang, J. W., & Tsai, M. T. (2009). Entrepreneurial orientation and firm performance: The role of knowledge creation process. *Industrial Marketing Management, 38*(4), 440–449. doi:10.1016/j.indmarman.2008.02.004

Liu, W., & Atuahene-Gima, K. (2018). Enhancing product innovation performance in a dysfunctional competitive environment: The roles of competitive strategies and market-based assets. *Industrial Marketing Management, 73*, 7–20. doi:10.1016/j.indmarman.2018.01.006

Lubis, R. L. (2017). Assessing entrepreneurial leadership and the law: Why are these important for graduate students in Indonesia? *The International Journal of the Arts in Society, 10*(02), 41–76.

Lumpkin, G. T., & Dess, G. G. (1996). Clarifying the entrepreneurial orientation construct and linking it to performance. *Academy of Management Review, 21*(1), 135–172. doi:10.5465/amr.1996.9602161568

Lumpkin, G. T., & Dess, G. G. (2001). Linking two dimensions of entrepreneurial orientation to firm performance: The moderating role of environment and industry life cycle. *Journal of Business Venturing, 16*(5), 429–451. doi:10.1016/S0883-9026(00)00048-3

Man, T. W., Lau, T., & Chan, K. F. (2002). The competitiveness of small and medium enterprises: A conceptualization with focus on entrepreneurial competencies. *Journal of Business Venturing*, *17*(2), 123–142. doi:10.1016/S0883-9026(00)00058-6

Markman, G. D. (2007). Entrepreneurs' competencies. In The psychology of Entrepreneurship, (pp. 67-92). Psychology Press.

Masud, J., & Paim, L. (1999). *The Economic Empowerment of Rural Women Through Involvement in Micro-enterprise*. Academic Press.

McClelland, D. C. (1965). N achievement and entrepreneurship: A longitudinal study. *Journal of Personality and Social Psychology*, *1*(4), 389–392. doi:10.1037/h0021956 PMID:14328753

McClelland, D. C. (1987). Characteristics of successful entrepreneurs. *The Journal of Creative Behavior*, *21*(3), 219–233. doi:10.1002/j.2162-6057.1987.tb00479.x

McLain, D. L. (1993). The MSTAT-I: A new measure of an individual's tolerance for ambiguity. *Educational and Psychological Measurement*, *53*(1), 183–189. doi:10.1177/0013164493053001020

Miller, D. (1983). The correlates of entrepreneurship in three types of firms. *Management Science*, *29*(7), 770–791. doi:10.1287/mnsc.29.7.770

Miller, V. D., Johnson, J. R., & Grau, J. (1994). Antecedents to willingness to participate in a planned organizational change. *Journal of Applied Communication Research*, *22*(1), 59–80. doi:10.1080/00909889409365387

Mindt, L., & Rieckmann, M. (2017). Developing competencies for sustainability-driven entrepreneurship in higher education: A literature review of teaching and learning methods. *Teoría de la Educación. Revista Interuniversitaria*, *29*(1), 129–159. doi:10.14201/teoredu291129159

Mitchelmore, S., & Rowley, J. (2010). Entrepreneurial competencies: a literature review and development agenda. *International Journal of Entrepreneurial Behavior & Research, 16*(2), 92-111.

Mitchelmore, S., & Rowley, J. (2013). Entrepreneurial competencies of women entrepreneurs pursuing business growth. *Journal of Small Business and Enterprise Development*, *20*(1), 125–142. doi:10.1108/14626001311298448

Nabiswa, F., & Mukwa, J. S. (2017). Impact of Credit Financing on Human Resource Development between Micro and Small Enterprises: A Case Study of Kimilili Sub County, Kenya. *Asian Journal of Management Science and Economics*, *4*(1), 43–53.

Nadkarni, S., & Herrmann, P. O. L. (2010). CEO pesrsonality, strategic flexibility, and firm performance: The case of the Indian business process outsourcing industry. *Academy of Management Journal*, *53*(5), 1050–1073. doi:10.5465/amj.2010.54533196

Nanayakkara, S. M., Wickramasinghe, V., & Samarasinghe, G. D. (2017, May). Emotional intelligence, technology strategy and firm's non-financial performance. *In Engineering Research Conference (MERCon)*, (pp. 467-472). IEEE. 10.1109/MERCon.2017.7980529

Narver, J. C., & Slater, S. F. (1990). The effect of a market orientation on business profitability. *Journal of Marketing*, *54*(4), 20–35. doi:10.1177/002224299005400403

Nhemachena, C., & Murimbika, M. (2018). *Motivations of sustainable entrepreneurship and their impact of enterprise performance in Gauteng Province*. Business Strategy & Development.

Nuhu, M., & Hussani, S. M. (2017). Empirical Study of the Relationship between Board of Director Mechanisms and Perceived Performance of Listed Firms in Nigeria. *Journal of Accounting and Finance in Emerging Economies*, *3*(2), 149–168. doi:10.26710/jafee.v3i2.59

O'Hara, B. S., Boles, J. S., & Johnston, M. W. (1991). The influence of personal variables on salesperson selling orientation. *Journal of Personal Selling & Sales Management*, *11*(1), 61–67.

Odhiambo, A. A. (2013). Factors influencing performance of youth owned micro, small and medium enterprises (MSME) in Kenya. *International Journal of Social Sciences and Entrepreneurship*, *1*(3), 263–272.

Omerzel, D. G., & Antončič, B. (2008). Critical entrepreneur knowledge dimensions for the SME performance. *Industrial Management & Data Systems*, *108*(9), 1182–1199. doi:10.1108/02635570810914883

Palvia, P., Means, D. B. Jr, & Jackson, W. M. (1994). Determinants of computing in very small businesses. *Information & Management*, *27*(3), 161–174. doi:10.1016/0378-7206(94)90044-2

Penn, D. W., Angiwa, W., Forster, R., Heydon, G., & Richardson, S. J. (1998). Learning in small organisations. *The Learning Organization*, *5*(3), 128–137. doi:10.1108/09696479810223400

Peterson, S. J., Walumbwa, F. O., Byron, K., & Myrowitz, J. (2009). CEO positive psychological traits, transformational leadership, and firm performance in high-technology start-up and established firms. *Journal of Management*, *35*(2), 348–368. doi:10.1177/0149206307312512

Petrides, K. V., & Furnham, A. (2001). Trait emotional intelligence: Psychometric investigation with reference to established trait taxonomies. *European Journal of Personality*, *15*(6), 425–448. doi:10.1002/per.416

Phelan, C., & Sharpley, R. (2012). Exploring entrepreneurial skills and competencies in farm tourism. *Local Economy*, *27*(2), 103–118. doi:10.1177/0269094211429654

Priyanto, S. H., & Sandjojo, I. (2005). Relationship between entrepreneurial learning, entrepreneurial competencies and venture success: Empirical study on SMEs. *International Journal of Entrepreneurship and Innovation Management*, *5*(5-6), 454–468. doi:10.1504/IJEIM.2005.006999

Pyysiäinen, J., Anderson, A., McElwee, G., & Vesala, K. (2006). Developing the entrepreneurial skills of farmers: Some myths explored. *International Journal of Entrepreneurial Behaviour & Research*, *12*(1), 21–39. doi:10.1108/13552550610644463

Radulovich, L., Javalgi, R., & Scherer, R. F. (2018). Intangible Resources Influencing the International Performance of Professional Service SMEs in an Emerging Market: Evidence from India. *International Marketing Review*, *35*(1), 113–135. doi:10.1108/IMR-06-2016-0130

Rahman, Z. (2016). The difficulties faced by micro and small enterprises in the formal market access: The case in small and micro enterprises in the cities of Makassar and Kabupaten Gowa south Sulawesi. *International Journal of the Humanities*, *4*(1), 92–103.

Rice, G. H. Jr, & Hamilton, R. E. (1979). Decision theory and the small businessman. *American Journal of Small Business*, *6*(4), 1–9. doi:10.1177/104225877900400101

Richard, O. C., Barnett, T., Dwyer, S., & Chadwick, K. (2004). Cultural diversity in management, firm performance, and the moderating role of entrepreneurial orientation dimensions. *Academy of Management Journal*, *47*(2), 255–266.

Ricketts, J. C., & Rudd, R. D. (2005). Critical thinking skills of selected youth leaders: The efficacy of critical thinking dispositions, leadership, and academic performance. *Journal of Agricultural Education*, *46*(1), 32–43. doi:10.5032/jae.2005.01032

Rimvydas, L. (2017). Key Features of Sustainable Universities: A Literature review. *Journal of Business and Management*, *13*, 56–69.

Rodríguez, F. J. G., & Cruz, Y. D. M. A. (2007). Relation between social-environmental responsibility and performance in hotel firms. *International Journal of Hospitality Management*, *26*(4), 824–839. doi:10.1016/j.ijhm.2006.08.003

Salovey, P., & Mayer, J. D. (1990). Emotional intelligence. *Imagination, Cognition and Personality*, *9*(3), 185–211. doi:10.2190/DUGG-P24E-52WK-6CDG

Sarasvathy, S. D., & Venkataraman, S. (2011). Entrepreneurship as method: Open questions for an entrepreneurial future. *Entrepreneurship Theory and Practice*, *35*(1), 113–135. doi:10.1111/j.1540-6520.2010.00425.x

Saxe, R., & Weitz, B. A. (1982). The SOCO scale: A measure of the customer orientation of salespeople. *JMR, Journal of Marketing Research*, *19*(3), 343–351. doi:10.1177/002224378201900307

Scherer, R. F., Brodzinski, J. D., & Wiebe, F. (1991). Examining the relationship between personality and entrepreneurial career preference. *Entrepreneurship and Regional Development*, *3*(2), 195–206. doi:10.1080/08985629100000013

Shane, S., Locke, E. A., & Collins, C. J. (2003). Entrepreneurial motivation. *Human Resource Management Review*, *13*(2), 257–279. doi:10.1016/S1053-4822(03)00017-2

Spencer, L. M., & Spencer, S. M. (1993). *Competence at Work: Model for Superior Performance*. New York: John Wiley and Sons.

Stogdill, R. M. (1948). Personal Factors Associated with Leadership: A Survey of the Literature. *The Journal of Psychology*, *25*(1), 35–71. doi:10.1080/00223980.1948.9917362 PMID:18901913

Stopford, J. M., & Baden-Fuller, C. W. (1994). Creating corporate entrepreneurship. *Strategic Management Journal*, *15*(7), 521–536. doi:10.1002mj.4250150703

Storey, D., & Cressy, R. (1996). Small business risk – a firm bank perspective. *The Centre for Small & Medium-sized Enterprises*, *39*, 1–16.

Tarabishy, A., Solomon, G., Fernald, L. W. Jr, & Sashkin, M. (2005). The entrepreneurial leader's impact on the organization's performance in dynamic markets. *Journal of Private Equity*, *8*(4), 20–29. doi:10.3905/jpe.2005.580519

Tehseen, S., Sajilan, S., Ramayah, T., & Gadar, K. (2015). An intra-cultural study of entrepreneurial competencies and SMEs business success in wholesale and retail industries of Malaysia: A Conceptual Model. *Review of Integrative Business and Economics Research*, *4*(3), 33–48.

Tubbs, S. L., & Schulz, E. (2006). Exploring taxonomy of global leadership competencies and meta-competencies. *The Journal of American Academy of Business, Cambridge*, *8*(2), 29–34.

Wachner, T., Plouffe, C. R., & Grégoire, Y. (2009). SOCO's impact on individual sales performance: The integration of selling skills as a missing link. *Industrial Marketing Management*, *38*(1), 32–44. doi:10.1016/j.indmarman.2007.11.003

Wagener, S., Gorgievski, M., & Rijsdijk, S. (2010). Businessman or host? Individual differences between entrepreneurs and small business owners in the hospitality industry. *Service Industries Journal*, *30*(9), 1513–1527. doi:10.1080/02642060802624324

Wahid, N. A., Aziz, N. N. A., & Halim, R. A. (2017). Networking and Innovation Performance of Micro-Enterprises in Malaysia: The Moderating Effects of Geographical Location. *Perrtanika Journal of Social Sciences & Humanities, 25*(S), 281-292.

Wanberg, C. R., & Banas, J. T. (2000). Predictors and outcomes of openness to changes in a reorganizing workplace. *The Journal of Applied Psychology*, *85*(1), 132–142. doi:10.1037/0021-9010.85.1.132 PMID:10740964

Zhang, F., Yang, J., Xu, Z., & Zhu, G. (2018). Large shareholder participation behaviors, managers' risk-taking, and firm innovation performance: A shareholder activism perspective. *Nankai Business Review International*, *9*(1), 99–115. doi:10.1108/NBRI-04-2017-0017

Zhao, H., & Seibert, S. E. (2006). The big five personality dimensions and entrepreneurial status: A meta-analytical review. *The Journal of Applied Psychology*, *91*(2), 259–271. doi:10.1037/0021-9010.91.2.259 PMID:16551182

Chapter 6
Micro-Entrepreneurship, Quality of Life and Empowerment

ABSTRACT

The intervention of grassroots development initiatives embedded with microcredit programs have seen the emergence of the relationship between socio-economic development and women empowerment, thus suggesting a solid conceptual link to women's empowerment. This chapter provides a discussion on the quality of life and women empowerment among low-income households in Malaysia. The focus is on how entrepreneurial development initiatives, rolled out by both the government and microcredit/developmental organizations, impact the quality of life and women empowerment of these households.

QUALITY OF LIFE AMONG LOW-INCOME HOUSEHOLDS IN MALAYSIA

Quality of life refers to the complete spectrum of well-being experienced by an individual. This encompasses good physical and mental health, active social life, financial solvency, as well as being satisfied and happy. Also, the individual is observed to be eating well and enjoying good family ties (Kwan, Cheung, Ngan, Ng, Lau, Leung, and Chan, 2003). In a similar context, Lee (2005) conducted a study where he concluded that the major contributory

DOI: 10.4018/978-1-5225-8473-5.ch006

factors towards better quality of life are good physical and mental health, a higher level of satisfaction, problem-free financial status, good family support, and an active social life. Examining in a financial context, both Kwan et al., (2003) and Lee (2005) emphasized having a sound financial status. Yet for low-income households, meeting daily needs and expenses is already a challenge. Therefore, being financially solvent is beyond their sight. Driven by its robust economy and developed infrastructure, Malaysia is now ranked as the region's top emerging economy. Yet one major concern remains, and that is poverty. In this thriving upper middle income nation, pockets of poverty exist and persist in specific geographies and communities where rural and urban households earn less than RM1,000 and RM1,500 per month, respectively (Nor and Azhar, 2016).

Poverty rate in Malaysia is calculated by using quantitative money-metric measures in terms of the poverty line income (PLI). Since 1976, the PLI has been calculated based on the cost of basic needs. Inside the basket of basic needs are education and recreation, transportation and communication, rent, fuel and power, clothing and footwear, as well as healthcare (Zain, 2007). To measure food, the Institute of Medical Research (IMR) develops the food requirements per household, which is based on the daily requirement of calorie intake, currently at 9,910 calories per household of five members. To measure clothing and footwear, the Department of Social Welfare evaluates and provides the minimum requirement. All other items are calculated based on the findings of the Household Expenditure Survey, which assesses the minimum level of expenditure of low-income households (Economic Transformation Programme, 2015; 2018).

Given this, poverty is defined as households whose gross monthly income fall below the mean PLI. On an annual basis, the government adjusts PLI based on the Consumer Price Index (CPI). Taking into account the regional differences in the cost of living, the government provides different PLIs for Peninsular Malaysia, and East Malaysia's Sabah and Sarawak, respectively. The Economic Transformation Programme (ETP) provides two categories of poverty: poor and extreme poverty (Economic Transformation Programme, 2015). Therefore, poor is defined as households whose average monthly income is below the mean PLI: less than RM760 (Peninsular Malaysia), less than RM1,050 (Sabah), and less than RM910 (Sarawak). Whereas hardcore poverty is defined as households whose average monthly income is approximately 60 percent of the mean PLI: less than RM460 (Peninsular Malaysia), less than

RM630 (Sabah), and less than RM590 (Sarawak) (Economic Transformation Programme, 2015).

Overall, the poverty rate (proportion of households living below PLI) in Malaysia declined dramatically after independence. In 2007, about 3.6 percent of Malaysian households lived below the PLI. However, this number was reduced to 1.7 percent in 2012, then 0.6 percent in 2014, and finally only 0.4 percent in 2016. It is noteworthy to mention that rural and urban poverty congruently declined during this period. As presented in Table 1, the incidence of poverty in rural areas first increased from 7.1 percent to 8.4 percent in 2009, but subsequently decreased from 3.4 percent in 2012 to 1.6% in 2014. It currently stands at only 1.0 percent in 2016. Nevertheless, the poorest communities in these areas are workers engaged in agriculture, hunting and forestry (Economic Planning Unit, 2008). Meanwhile, the incidence of urban poverty has always been comparatively lower, charting consistent decline from 2.0 percent (2007) to 1.7 percent (2009), then to 1.0 percent (2012), and finally to only 0.2 percent (2016).

ENTREPRENEURIAL DEVELOPMENT INITIATIVES AND QUALITY OF LIFE

One of the ways to alleviate poverty is entrepreneurship. Entrepreneurship creates jobs and boosts national economic growth. But to start a business, low-income households face multiple barriers and one of the most significant is access to finance. For these households, start-up capital is mainly sourced from personal savings or loans solicited from family and friends. These alternatives are often sought, as traditional banks require intensive documentation and collateral for loans, which these poor households are unable to furnish. In the Malaysian context, the government has successively rolled out entrepreneurial development initiatives towards diversifying sources of

Table 1. Incidence of poverty in Malaysia 2007 - 2016

	2007 %	2009 %	2012 %	2014 %	2016 %
Malaysia	3.6	3.8	1.7	0.6	0.4
Urban	2.0	1.7	1.0	0.3	0.2
Rural	7.1	8.4	3.4	1.6	1.0

Source: Economic Planning Unit (2018)

income, increasing productivity, and improving the quality of life of the poor. This crucial step was taken due to proven outcomes such as the generation of higher-paid employment opportunities, including more profitable micro and small-scale business opportunities. Thus, these poverty eradication strategies were incorporated into Malaysia's core development plans and have been benefiting the poor for decades. In order to build Malaysia as an entrepreneurial nation, the Malaysian government had embedded microcredit programs in entrepreneurial development initiatives. These initiatives are deployed at the grassroots level via tripartite partnerships with the private sectors and non-government organizations (NGOs) (Economic Planning Unit, 2010). Currently, *Amanah Ikhtiar* Malaysia (AIM), the National Entrepreneurs Economic Group Fund (TEKUN), *Bank Simpanan Nasional* (government-owned bank) and AgroBank are providing collateral-free microcredit as working capital to the poor and hardcore poor households in urban and rural Malaysia. The government also introduced niche financial programs to extend financial services to unemployed women who are living in poor households and do not have the means to borrow from banks due to their economic vulnerability (Al-shami, Razali, and Rashid, 2017). To provide a solution to this constraint, many governments embed microcredit programs at the heart of development strategies and initiatives (Abed, 2000). Harris (2009) cited Microcredit Summit Campaign's definition of microcredit as "programs to extend small loans to very poor people for self-employment projects that generate income, allowing them to care for themselves and their families." These programs have been instrumental in eradicating poverty and accelerating the quality of life among low-income households. Over the past two decades, microcredit programs have gained global attention due to its range of financial products and services that continue to provide innovative solutions to the poor, especially women in developing economies. These programs target households defined as poor and hardcore poor, who collectively comprise nearly half of the world's total population (Abed, 2000). In essence, microcredit provides productive capital, which when paired with social and human capital, enables the poor and hardcore poor households to leapfrog out of poverty (Abed, 2000; Harris, 2009).

In an effort to galvanize global synergy, the Microcredit Summit Campaign brought together microcredit practitioners, advocates, educators, trainers, donor organizations and development agencies to ensure that the 175 million of the world's poorest families, especially the women in these families, receive credit for self-employment and other financial and business services, before the end of 2015 (Harris, 2009). The potential impact in numbers was staggering. Harris (2009) estimated that by "assuming five persons per family, reaching 175 million of the world's poorest families would affect 875 million family members. When 100 million families raise their income above US$1 a day threshold, half a billion people will have left extreme poverty". Harris (2009) reported that as at December 31, 2007, a total of 3,552 microcredit institutions provided financial services to a total of 154,825,825 clients. Furthermore, the Microcredit Summit Campaign reported that microcredit programs had reached 137.5 million poorest clients at the end of 2010, and among them 113.1 million or 82.3% were women (Maes and Reed, 2012). Thus, it was not surprising that the global capacity outreach of microfinance organizations (MFOs) in providing doorstep collateral-free financial services to the targeted households had attracted the attention of academicians, donors and development policy makers all over the world (Otero, 1999; Harris, 2006).

Recent decades have seen MFOs emphasizing the need to lend to poor women. Globally, Harris (2009) reported that about 71 percent of the total borrowers are women, and among the poorest borrowers, about 84 percent are women. In the Malaysian context, there are three reasons behind the rationale of providing targeted financial services to women. First, Malaysian women have a lower economic status compared to men. For instance, only less than 16 percent of women are business owners (Omar, N. A., Nazri, M. A., Aniza, C., & Wel, C. (2014). Second, the consumption behaviour of women is motivated towards household well-being which includes children's health, nutrition and education (Samer, Majid, Rizal, Muhamad, Halim, and Rashid, 2015). Supported by the extended financial services provided to these women, documented evidence has shown significant effects on socio-economic development of low-income households. Thirdly, women borrowers have been proven to be more creditworthy than men. Microcredit programs show that poor borrowers - especially women - maintain impressive repayment rates, not to mention their willingness and ability to pay the interest rates charged by the MFOs. For example, according to a 2010 AIM report, loan repayments from women clients surpassed 99.2 percent, posthumously recording it as highest in the world (Al-Shami and Majid, 2013).

Current microcredit literature has extant evidence of the positive impact of microcredit programs on the socio-economic well-being of the borrowers, their households and communities. Well-documented and extensive studies that have shown significant impacts on poverty reduction around the world. In Bangladesh, researchers Hossain (1988), Mustafa, Ara, Banu, Hossain, Kabir, Mohsin, Yusuf, and Jahan, 1996), Khandker and Pitt (1998), Latifee (2003), Khandker (2005), Hussain and Nargis (2008), Hoque (2008), and Rahman,

Rafiq and Momen (2009) examined several MFOs' clients and noted that participation in microfinance programs improved poor households' ability to generate income. In India, Mosley (1996) found 12 percent of microcredit receivers crossed the PLI. In Sri Lanka, Hulme, Montgomery, and Bhattacharya (1996) found that one out of four microcredit program participants were no longer poor after receiving microcredit. This then boosts households' income, net working capital, fixed assets, as well as spending on food, medical services and children's education. Panda (2009) noted that the annual average income of the microcredit program participants was significantly higher (11%) than that of the non-participants in India. Besides income, he also found that the asset position of the participants is 9.75% higher than that of non-participants along with a significant growth in savings.

Additionally, microcredit literature has documented the positive impacts on poor women. Existing studies reported that poor women borrowers experienced higher economic impact after participating in microcredit programs. In Bangladesh, Khandker and Pitt (1998) found that household consumption increased by BDT18 for every BDT100 provided to women borrowers, whereas for men borrowers the rate was only BDT11. In Malaysia, Gibbons and Kasim's study in 1990 (Gibbons and Kasim, 1990) was the first to measure the impacts of AIM's microcredit programs. The findings of the study discovered a significant increase of client's monthly household income, from an average of RM142 per month, prior to participation, to RM220 which is a 55 percent increase in respondent's monthly household income. Gibbons and Kasim (1990) also showed that 84 percent of total women participants experienced an increase in monthly household income with an average of RM136. The overall average increase in income for all women clients was RM113. However, only 65 percent of the men borrowers experienced an increase of household income with an average of RM65. The overall repayment rate was 78 percent. Among the women borrowers, the repayment rate was 95 percent. However, the overall average for men borrowers was RM63, only slightly more than half of their women counterparts (Gibbons and Kasim, 1990).

In the urban areas of developing countries, low-income women are commonly relegated to household activities due to their lack of education and skills, as well as the religious/social structure. Despite operating within these limitations, studies showed that women experience higher economic impact from participation in microcredit programs, as compared to men. These overwhelming achievements allowed women to contribute to the household expenses.

Established in 1987, AIM provides small-scale financial services and training to poor households in order to improve their socio-economic condition. AIM uses a group-based Grameen Bank (a Bangladeshi MFO) model, which has been replicated by many MFO's all over the world. AIM only selects their clients based on clients' average monthly household income. Households with an average monthly household income below the PLI would be considered as poor, while households with average monthly household income below half of the PLI would be categorized as hardcore poor. AIM only selects households whose average monthly household income falls below the PLI, which includes both poor and hardcore poor households.

In 2008, AIM launched the Urban Microfinance Program (UMP). The group formation process is the same as the conventional microcredit model practiced by AIM mostly in rural areas. However, unlike the rural microcredit program, the UMP does not select their clients based on PLI. Rather they select clients with a household income of below RM2,000 or a per capita income of below RM400 a month. Moreover, an applicant's asset ownership must not exceed RM50,000 and the client's residential status in residential locality must be more than 2 years. The objectives of the UMP are: (1) to harness the potential of self-employment among the poor and low-income households; and (2) to expand AIM's microfinancing approach to the poor and lower income groups in urban areas. The participants must maintain the following terms and conditions to participate: (1) participants must agree to form a five- member group and attend basic financial training of 5 days, of one hour per day; (2) agree to form a centre; (3) attend a Centre Meeting every week; (4) agree to contribute 1 percent from economic financing to the Group Fund; (5) agree to contribute to the Group Fund in an amount of RM3 per week; (6) agree to contribute an amount of RM2 per week to the Centre Fund; (7) repayments shall be on a weekly basis; (8) contribute to the Credit Khairat Fund; and (9) pay monthly financing charges of 1 percent of the loan amount. As of 2009, AIM has extended their outreach to 93 branches in Peninsular Malaysia where it currently serves a total of 25,812 clients (Amanah Ikhtiar Malaysia, 2018), AIM is the only MFO that adopts and practices a well-established group-based microcredit model, which operates at the national level and has an outreach of more than 82 percent of the poor and hardcore poor households in Malaysia.

WOMEN EMPOWERMENT AMONG LOW-INCOME HOUSEHOLDS IN MALAYSIA

Women in Malaysia play a significant role in nation-building. Over and above economic contribution, these women safeguard the financial aspects of the household towards an improved quality of life. Yet, gender inequalities exist and persist. According to the World Economic Forum's Global Gender Gap Index [31], Malaysia is ranked extremely low (104 out of 144 countries) on gender gap in the areas of economy, education, health and political engagement. The report further presented that the gender gap score plateaued at 0.67 in 2017 as compared to 0.65 in 2006. This means that the score had increased albeit at a slower rate, thus rated as underperforming when compared to other nations. Details are given in Table 2 below.

Since the closure of gender gap has been sluggish, various achievements can adduce to the fact that Malaysian women are as progressive as their men counterparts. Approximately 16 percent of women are business owners in informal sectors and involved in low-productivity projects (Omar, Nazri, Aniza, and Wel, 2014). Additionally, these women face countless barriers throughout the business life cycle - from start-up to sustainability. Studies have shown that in most cases, women entrepreneurs suffer from lack of finance, lack of demand, and poor business location (Al-Shami, Muhammad, and Rashid, 2017; Ilhaamie, Siti Arni, Rosmawani, and Hassan Al-Banna, 2014). Furthermore, these women have to cope with the demands of marriage, which prevalent among Muslims couples, often ends in divorce. This phenomenon is supported by statistics provided by the *Syariah* Judiciary Department of Malaysia (JKSM) which shows that the number of divorces had increased among Muslim couples by 2.3 times: from 20,916 (2004) to 47,740 (2012), and to 49,311 (2013) (The Malay Mail Online, 2014). This means that divorced women bare added economic burden: coping with the demands of managing the kitchen, households expenditure, and ensuring children's continued education. Advancement in women's economic condition could led to better investments in their child's education and health and most importantly reduced household poverty (World Bank, 2012; 2013).

By definition, women's empowerment is a set of social relations with a material base that enables men to dominate women, and therefore can be thought of in terms of an improvement in intra-household gender relations (Naved, 1994; Hashemi, Schuler, and Riley, 1996). Qudrat-I-Elahi (2003) defined empowerment as authorizing someone already holding an office to

Table 2. Malaysia's global gender gaps, scores and ranks in 2006 and 2017

		2006		2017
	Rank	Score	Rank	Score
Global Gender Gap Score	72	0.651	104	0.67
Economic Participation & Opportunity	68	0.592	87	0.654
Educational Attainment	63	0.985	77	0.991
Health & Survival	80	0.970	53	0.977
Political Empowerment	90	0.056	133	0.058

Source: World Economic Forum (2017)

exercise some specific power or offering someone certain means to achieve a given end. Empowerment, as defined by Kabeer (2001) is the process by which those who previously lack the ability to make strategic life choices, acquire such ability. Kabeer (2001) also mentioned that 'strategic life choice' is a choice of livelihood, which includes whom to marry, whether to have children, where to live, etc. Banu, Farashuddin, Hossain and Akter (2001) defined women's empowerment as the capacity of women in reducing their socio-economic vulnerability and dependency on men household members. This includes improving involvement, and control over household decisions, economic activities and resources, as well as contribution to household expenses, increase of self-confidence and awareness of social issue.

Therefore, the Malaysian government established numerous financial programs targeting these deprived and low-income women with the social mission to improve household well-being and women empowerment (Al-Shami, Majid, Mohamad, and Rashid, 2017). The ultimate goal is to elevate women empowerment to transform the circumstances of the women and children among low-income households, in a way from less power and limited access to economic assets, to a situation where they experience economic advancement (Taylor and Pereznieto, 2014). Generally, the issue of women empowerment in Malaysia are often associated with the problems of living in deprivation and isolation. Hence, as technology in entrepreneurship is growing in Malaysia, women micro enterprise should applied it in their business operation. Razak has expanded the idea on how to develop women empowerment in entrepreneurship in Malaysia. He suggested the applications of e-business by single mothers (Razak and Jah, 2017). Although they run a small business, the impact on increasing standard of living is more important. In similar way, Omar proposed online digital entrepreneurship among women micro entrepreneurs in Malaysia to develop their business strategy, thus achieve women empowerment. Moreover, Osman and collaegue focus on the case study of Malaysian tourism development. Most of the women micro entrepreneurs are empowered by having the opportunity to make decision and access to training related to business operations. Therefore, Malaysian microcredit empower women micro enterprise by enabling them through their own business and gain independent income (Osman, Ahmad, Ahmad, Husin, Bakar, and Tanwir, 2010). Accordingly, women in Malaysia are empowered economically to retain sustain in the market from the viewpoint of micro enterprises. .

ENTREPRENEURIAL DEVELOPMENT INITIATIVES AND WOMEN EMPOWERMENT

The intervention of grassroots development initiatives embedded with microcredit programs have seen the emergence of the relationship between socio-economic development and women empowerment, thus suggesting a solid conceptual link to women's empowerment (Mahmud, 2003). In urban Malaysia, microcredit financing has been recognized to play a significant role in women empowerment. In their mixed mode method study, Al-Shami, Razali, Majid, Rozelan, and Rashid, 2016) scrutinized how the roles of microcredit financing have an effect on women empowerment. They found out that women with microcredit have a high authority in household decisions-making and resource control. Additionally, women who received microcredit, particularly the older borrowers with business experiences, also had the opportunity to run their businesses and contribute to their household welfare (Al-shami et al., 2016). Another study on women empowerment (Al-shami et al., 2016; Rai and Ravi, 2011) suggested that microcredit programs empower women in various aspects: (1) increases women involvement in household decisions-making and resource controlling; (2) enables women to acquire new skills that improve their business development; (3) strengthen women in their community through social capital networks; and (4) enable women to contribute to their household welfare.

In order to measure the impact of microcredit on women's empowerment, Hashemi, Schuler and Riley (1996) developed an 'empowerment index' based on eight empowerment indicators: mobility, economic security, ability to make small purchases, ability to make larger purchases, involvement in major decisions, participation in public protests and political campaigning, relative freedom from family domination, and political and legal awareness. Their analysis found that a woman contributing to her household's income is a significant contributing factor towards her empowerment. In support of previous studies, Amin and Pebley (1994) collected data from thirty six villages in Bangladesh and found that BRAC (Bangladesh Rural Advancement Committee) membership positively affect a woman's decision-making role, as well as their control over resources and mobility, but less so on their attitudes regarding marriage and education of their daughters. Naved (1994) mentioned that women participants felt that their perceived household status had improved due to the fact that they were seen as income earners for the family. After participating in microcredit programs, women were more active participants in household decision-making and had more control over household income, particularly the portion that was derived from their own earning.

Other pertinent impacts of microcredit on women empowerment were found. Zaman (1999) identified a set of indicators relating to women's control over assets and knowledge of social issues. Hussain (1998) mentioned that previously, women had no say in the income accrued from their BRAC loans when their husbands used those loans. However, through microcredit programs for women, their husbands now often consult with them about how to spend this income. Therefore, the trend is that the longer a woman participates in BRAC's microcredit programs, the more employment opportunities she receives, and the wider scope she would have to purchase large assets such as cow, land, as well as other productive and non-productive assets.

The study conducted by Pitt, Khandker and Cartwright (2003) further asserted that participation in microcredit programs helped to increase women's empowerment. Women's verdant participation in microcredit programs leads towards a greater role in household decision-making, enhanced accessibility to financial and economic resources, robust social networks, stronger bargaining power vis-à-vis their husbands, and have greater freedom of mobility. In addition, participation in microcredit programs was found to have impacted spousal communication in general, and in the areas of family planning and parenting concerns (Pitt, Khandker, and Cartwright, 2003). Mahmud (2003) mentioned that participation in microcredit programs was able to increase women's welfare and reduce men bias. Moyle, Dollard and Biswas (2006) reported that income generating activities provide support to women's personal and economic empowerment. Another supporting study conducted by Nader (2008) found that microcredit improved family health and harmony.

Recent study conducted by Al-Shami, Muhammad, and Rashid, 2017) shows that microcredit is an important tool for the livelihood of low-income households and women empowerment. It helps women to level out household expenditure and aggregate assets. In their study the researchers also revealed that extending microcredit with a productive purpose enables women to strengthen their social position in their household decision-making. Their findings suggested that microcredit is an important source of sustainable livelihood because it provides both financial and non-financial services that women can exploit the existing entrepreneurial opportunities. In Malaysia, impact studies conducted by academicians, government agencies and AIM indicated that participation in microcredit programs improves the economic conditions of the poor borrowers.

However, even though in general there are positive effects of microcredit on women empowerment and households' well-being, some studies found that microcredit programs have either no effect at all or negative effects on the reduction of households' poverty. Rooyen, Stewart, and de Wet (2012) argued that microcredit does incur harm, as well as good, to the livelihoods of the poor. Meanwhile in Vietnam, research conducted by Nghiem, Coelli, and Rao, 2012) observed the effect of microfinance on the household welfare of poor borrowers. The researchers used income and consumption per adult equivalent as proxies to measure household welfare and reported that microfinance has no effects on household welfare. Similar research was conducted by Ganle, Afriyie, and Segbefia (2015) where they examined the impact of microcredit provided to women borrowers by an NGO in rural Ghana. The findings alluded that women have little control over the use of loans. The study also revealed that some women were exposed to harassment and were worse off because of their incapability to meet loan repayments on time. Therefore, access to microcredit may not always lead to actual empowerment. On the contrary, "pretend-empowerment" emerge where sons and husbands urge their mothers and wives to gain a microcredit, thus leaving them to face the responsibility of repayment or eventual default Kabeer, 2001; Ali and Niehof, 2007). Microcredit may cause marital conflict when men force their wives to obtain microcredits for their "household" (Bekele, Bock, and Folmer, 2012). However, rather than cessation in spite of the mixed findings as mentioned, governments and development organizations should continue to formulate new and strengthen existing entrepreneurial policies and mirocredit programs, as the positive effects on quality of life and women empowerment are theoretically sound and supported. These programs would continue to enhance the quality of life of women in low-income households resulting in women empowerment, and provide relief from economic vulnerability towards better socio-economic conditions.

AUTHOR CONTRIBUTIONS

All authors were involved in collecting relevant information and literature review, and writing this chapter.

CONFLICTS OF INTEREST

The authors declare no conflict of interest.

ACKNOWLEDGMENT

This research was funded by the Ministry of Higher Education, Malaysia under the grant entitled "Developing a Comprehensive Rural Entrepreneurship Model for Poverty Eradication (REMODE)" (R/NRGS/A01.00/00047A/006/2014/000149).

REFERENCES

Abed, F. H. (2000). Micro-credit, poverty and development: the case of Bangladesh. *Behind the Headlines, 58*(2), 1-12.

Al-Shami, S. S. A., Majid, I., Mohamad, M. R., & Rashid, N. (2017). Household welfare and women empowerment through microcredit financing: Evidence from Malaysia microcredit. *Journal of Human Behavior in the Social Environment*, *27*(8), 894–910. doi:10.1080/10911359.2017.1345341

Al-Shami, S. S. A., Majid, I. B. A., Rashid, N. A., & Hamid, M. S. R. B. A. (2013). Conceptual framework: The role of microfinance on the wellbeing of poor people cases studies from Malaysia and Yemen. *Asian Social Science*, *10*(1), 230–242. doi:10.5539/ass.v10n1p230

Al-Shami, S. S. A., Muhammad, M. R., & Rashid, N. (2017). The effect of microcredit on women household decisions making and resource controlling in Malaysia. *Social Indicators Research*. doi:10.100711205-017-1632-2

Al-Shami, S. S. A., Razali, M. M., Majid, I., Rozelan, A., & Rashid, N. (2016). The effect of microfinance on women's empowerment: Evidence from Malaysia. *Asian Journal of Women's Studies*, *22*(3), 318–337. doi:10.1080/12259276.2016.1205378

Al-shami, S. S. A., Razali, R. M., & Rashid, N. (2017). The Effect of Microcredit on Women Empowerment in Welfare and Decisions Making in Malaysia. *Social Indicators Research*, 1–18.

Ali, A., & Niehof, A. (2007). Changing gender roles in household food security and rural livelihoods in Bangladesh. In R. Ruben, J. Pender & A. Kuyvenhoven (Eds.), Sustainable poverty reduction in less favoured area (pp. 228–247). Oxfordshire, UK: CABI.

Amanah Ikhtiar Malaysia. (2018). *About Amanah Ikhtier Malaysia*. Retrieved March 05th, 2018 from http://aim.gov.my/

Amin, S., & Pebley, A. R. (1994). Gender inequality within households: The impact of a women's development programme in 36 Bangladeshi villages. *Bangladesh Development Studies*, *22*(2/3), 121–154.

Banu, D., Farashuddin, F., Hossain, A., & Akter, S. (2001). Empowering women in rural Bangladesh: Impact of Bangladesh Rural Advancement Committee's (BRAC's) programme. *Journal of International Women's Studies*, *2*(3), 30–53.

Bekele, H., Bock, B., & Folmer, H. (2012). Micro finance and female empowerment: Do institutions matter? *Women's Studies International Forum*, *35*(4), 256–265. doi:10.1016/j.wsif.2012.04.001

Economic Planning Unit. (2010). *Tenth Malaysian Plan 2011-2015*. Putrajaya. Retrieved March 06th, 2018 from https://www.pmo.gov.my/dokumenattached/RMK/RMK10_Eds.pdf

Economic Planning Unit Prime Minister's Department. (2008). *Mid-term review of 9th Malaysian Plan 2006-2010*. Putrajaya. Retrieved March 06th, 2018 from http://workspace.unpan.org/sites/internet/Documents/UNPAN042517.pdf

Economic Transformation Programme (EPU). (2018). *Table 7: Incidence of Poverty by Ethnic Group, Strata and State, Malaysia, 1970-2016*. Retrieved March 06th, 2018 from http://www.epu.gov.my/en/content/table-7-incidence-poverty-ethnic-group-strata-and-state-malaysia-1970-2016

Economic Transformation Programme (ETP). (2015). *The measure of poverty*. Retrieved March 06th, 2018 from http://etp.pemandu.gov.my/Transformation_Unplugged-@-The_measure_of_poverty.aspx

Ganle, J. K., Afriyie, K., & Segbefia, A. Y. (2015). Microcredit: Empowerment and disempowerment of rural women in Ghana. *World Development*, *66*, 335–345. doi:10.1016/j.worlddev.2014.08.027

Gibbons, D. S., & Kasim, S. (1990). *Banking on the rural poor in Peninsular Malaysia*. Penang, Malaysia: Center for Policy Research, Universiti Sains Malaysia.

Harris, S. D. (2006). *State of the Microcredit Summit Campaign Report 2006*. Washington, DC: U.S. Microcredit Summit Campaign. Retrieved March 05th, 2018 from http://www.microcreditsummit.org/resource/50/state-of-the-microcredit-summit.html

Harris, S. D. (2009). *State of the Microcredit Summit Campaign Report 2009*. Washington, DC: U.S. Microcredit Summit Campaign. Retrieved March 05th, 2018 from http://www.microcreditsummit.org/uploads/resource/document/socr2009_71248.pdf

Hashemi, S. M., Schuler, S. R., & Riley, A. (1996). Rural credit programs and women's empowerment in Bangladesh. *World Development*, *24*(4), 635–653. doi:10.1016/0305-750X(95)00159-A

Hoque, S. (2008). *Does micro-credit program in Bangladesh increase household's ability to deal with economic hardships? MPRA Paper No. 6678*. Department of Economics, Monash University.

Hossain, M. (1988). *Credit for alleviation of rural poverty: The Grameen Bank in Bangladesh* (Vol. 65). Washington, DC: International Food Policy Research Institute.

Hulme, D., Montgomery, R., & Bhattacharya, D. (1996). Mutual Finance and the Poor: A Study of the Federation of Thrift and Credit Cooperatives in Sri Lanka (SANASA). In D. Hulme & P. Mosley (Eds.), *Finance Against Poverty* (pp. 228–315). London: Routledge.

Husain, A. M. M. (Ed.). (1998). *Poverty alleviation and empowerment: the second impact assessment study of BRAC's rural development program*. Dhaka: Bangladesh Rural Advancement Committee.

Hussain, A. G., & Nargis, N. (2008). *A welfare economic analysis of the impact of microfinance in Bangladesh.* Retrieved from http://economics.ca/2008/papers/0303.pdf

Ilhaamie, A. G. A., Siti Arni, B., Rosmawani, C. H., & Hassan Al-Banna, M. (2014). Challenges of muslim women entrepreneurs in Malaysian SMEs. *International Journal of Innovation, Management and Technology*, *5*(6), 428–433. doi:10.7763/IJIMT.2014.V5.553

Kabeer, N. (2001). Conflicts over credit: Re-evaluating the empowerment potential of loans to women in rural Bangladesh. *World Development*, *29*(1), 63–84. doi:10.1016/S0305-750X(00)00081-4

Kabeer, N. (2005). Gender equality and women's empowerment: A critical analysis of the third millennium development goal 1. *Gender and Development*, *13*(1), 13–24. doi:10.1080/13552070512331332273

Khandker, S. R. (2005). Microfinance and poverty: Evidence using panel data from Bangladesh. *The World Bank Economic Review*, *19*(2), 263–286. doi:10.1093/wber/lhi008

Khandker, S. R., & Pitt, M. (1998). The Impact of Group-Based Credit Programs on Poor Households in Bangladesh: Does the Gender of Participants Matter? *Journal of Political Economy*, *106*(5), 958–996. doi:10.1086/250037

Kwan, A. Y. H., Cheung, J. C. K., Ngan, R. M. N., Ng, S. H., Lau, A., Leung, E. M. F., & Chan, S. S. C. (2003). *Assessment, validation, and promotion of the quality of life and continuum of care of elderly people in Hong Kong: Research report*. Hong Kong: Department of Applied Social Studies, City University of Hong Kong.

Latifee, H. I. (2003). Financing Micro-finance programs. In International Worship on Microfinance in Poverty Reduction and the Challenges for MFIs in Vietnam, Ho Chi Minh City, Vietnam.

Lee, J. J. (2005). An exploratory study on the quality of life of older Chinese people living alone in Hong Kong. *Social Indicators Research*, *71*(1-3), 335–361. doi:10.100711205-004-8027-x

Maes, J. P., & Reed, L. R. (2012). *State of the Microcredit Summit Campaign Report 2012*. Washington, DC: U.S. Microcredit Summit Campaign. Retrieved from http://www.microcreditsummit.org/uploads/resource/document/web_socr-2012_english_62819.pdf

Mahmud, S. (2003). Actually how empowering is microcredit? *Development and Change*, *34*(4), 577–605. doi:10.1111/1467-7660.00320

Mosley, P. (1996). Metamorphosis from NGO to Commercial Bank: The Case of Bancosol in Bolivia. In D. Hulme & P. Mosley (Eds.), *Finance Against Poverty* (pp. 1–31). London: Routledge.

Moyle, T. L., Dollard, M., & Biswas, S. N. (2006). Personal and economic empowerment in rural Indian women: A self-help group approach. *International Journal of Rural Management*, *2*(2), 245–266. doi:10.1177/097300520600200207

Mustafa, S., Ara, I., Banu, D., Hossain, A., Kabir, A., Mohsin, M., ... Jahan, S. (1996). *Beacon of Hope: An Impact Assessment of BRAC's Rural Development Programme*. Dhaka, Bangladesh: Research and Evaluation Department, Bangladesh Rural Development Committee.

Nader, Y. F. (2008). Microcredit and the socio-economic wellbeing of women and their families in Cairo. *Journal of Socio-Economics*, *37*(2), 644–656. doi:10.1016/j.socec.2007.10.008

Naved, R. T. (1994). Empowerment of women: Listening to the voices of women. *Bangladesh Development Studies*, *22*(2/3), 155–178.

Nghiem, S., Coelli, T., & Rao, P. (2012). Assessing the welfare effects of microfinance in Vietnam: Empirical results from a quasi-experimental survey. *The Journal of Development Studies*, *48*(5), 619–632. doi:10.1080/00220388.2011.638051

Nor, R. M., & Azhar, S. N. F. S. (2016). 1AZAM Aiding Low-Income Households in Malaysia. *Journal of Human Resource and Sustainability Studies*, *4*(04), 293–304. doi:10.4236/jhrss.2016.44029

Omar, N. A., Nazri, M. A., Aniza, C., & Wel, C. (2014). Entrepreneurial training of low-income women micro enterprises in the service sector in Malaysia: Understanding the problems and challenges. *Journal of Social and Development Sciences*, *5*(4), 245–257.

Osman, I., Ahmad, N. H., Ahmad, Z. A., Husin, A., Bakar, S. A., & Tanwir, N. D. (2010). Understanding motivation, empowerment and sustainability outcomes of women homestay entrepreneurs in West Malaysia. A preliminary analysis. In *ICSB World Conference Proceedings* (p. 1). International Council for Small Business (ICSB).

Otero, M. (1999). Bringing development back, into microfinance. Journal of Microfinance/ESR Review, 1(1), 8-19.

Panda, K. D. (2009). Participation in the Group Based Microfmance and its Impact on Rural Households: A Quasiexperimental Evidence from an Indian State. *Global Journal of Finance and Management*, *1*(2), 171–183.

Pitt, M. M., & Khandker, S. R. (1998). The impact of group-based credit programs on poor household in Bangladesh: Does the gender of participants matter? *Journal of Political Economy*, *106*(5), 958–977. doi:10.1086/250037

Pitt, M. M., Khandker, S. R., & Cartwright, J. (2003). *Does Micro-Credit Empower Women? Evidence from Bangladesh.* World Bank Policy Research (Working Paper No. 2998). Available at SSRN: https://ssrn.com/abstract=636360

Qudrat-I-Elahi, K. (2003). Micorfinance, empowerment and Sudra women in India. *Development in Practice*, *13*(5), 570–572.

Rahman, S., Rafiq, R. B., & Momen, M. A. (2009). Impact of microcredit programs on higher income borrowers: Evidence from Bangladesh. *International Business & Economics Research Journal*, *8*(2), 119–124.

Rai, A., & Ravi, S. (2011). Do spouses make claims? Empowerment and microfinance in India. *World Development*, *39*(6), 913–921. doi:10.1016/j.worlddev.2009.10.019

Razak, N. A., & Jah, N. J. A. (2017). The e-commerce training for women entrepreneurs in facing fourth industrial revolution. *International Journal of Business, Economics and Law, 14*(5).

Reflections on the measurement of women's empowerment. (2001). InKabeer, N. (Ed.), *Discussing women's empowerment: Theory and practice*. Stockholm, Sweden: Swedish International Development Cooperation Agency.

Rooyen, C., Stewart, R., & de Wet, T. (2012). The impact of microfinance in sub-Saharan Africa: A systematic review of the evidence. *World Development*, *40*(11), 2249–2262. doi:10.1016/j.worlddev.2012.03.012

Samer, S., Majid, I., Rizal, S., Muhamad, M. R., Halim, S., & Rashid, N. (2015). The impact of microfinance on poverty reduction: Empirical evidence from Malaysian perspective. *Procedia: Social and Behavioral Sciences*, *195*, 721–728. doi:10.1016/j.sbspro.2015.06.343

Taylor, G., & Pereznieto, P. (2014). Review of evaluation approaches and methods used by interventions on women and girls' economic empowerment. London: Overseas Development Institute (ODI).

The Malay Mailonline (2014). *One divorce in Malaysia every 10 minutes.* Author.

World Bank. (2012). *World Development Report 2012: Gender equality and development*. Washington, DC: World Bank.

World Bank. (2013). *World Development Report 2013: Jobs*. Washington, DC: World Bank.

World Economic Forum. (2017). *The Global Gender Gap Report. Geneva, Switzerland: World Economic Forum.* Retrieved March 01st, 2018 from http://www3.weforum.org/docs/WEF_GGGR_2017.pdf

Zain, R. M. (2007). Understanding the formulation of the revised poverty line in Malaysia. *Akademika, 70*(1), 21–39.

Zaman, H. (1999). *Who benefits and to what extent? An evaluation of BRAC"s microcredit program* (Doctoral dissertation). Brighton, UK: University of Sussex.

Related Readings

To continue IGI Global's long-standing tradition of advancing innovation through emerging research, please find below a compiled list of recommended IGI Global book chapters and journal articles in the areas of entrepreneurship, microenterprise, and microfinance. These related readings will provide additional information and guidance to further enrich your knowledge and assist you with your own research.

Ahamad, S. S., Sastry, V. N., & Udgata, S. K. (2018). Formal Verification of Secure Payment Framework in MANET for Disaster Areas. In M. Khosrow-Pour, D.B.A. (Ed.), Entrepreneurship, Collaboration, and Innovation in the Modern Business Era(pp. 68-101). Hershey, PA: IGI Global. doi:10.4018/978-1-5225-5014-3.ch004

Al-Marri, M., & Al-Hasan, S. (2018). The Effectiveness of Financing the Marketing of Small and Medium-Sized Enterprises in Qatar and the Gulf Co-Operation Council (GCC) Countries: With a Special Focus on Advertising. In A. Woldie & B. Thomas (Eds.), *Financial Entrepreneurship for Economic Growth in Emerging Nations* (pp. 129–147). Hershey, PA: IGI Global. doi:10.4018/978-1-5225-2700-8.ch007

Almeida, R. M., Abreu, R., & Perez-Lopez, J. A. (2018). Nascent Entrepreneurship and Sustainability on the Beverage Sector. In A. Carrizo Moreira, J. Guilherme Leitão Dantas, & F. Manuel Valente (Eds.), *Nascent Entrepreneurship and Successful New Venture Creation* (pp. 215–238). Hershey, PA: IGI Global. doi:10.4018/978-1-5225-2936-1.ch010

Aninze, F., El-Gohary, H., & Hussain, J. (2018). The Role of Microfinance to Empower Women: The Case of Developing Countries. *International Journal of Customer Relationship Marketing and Management, 9*(1), 54–78. doi:10.4018/IJCRMM.2018010104

Ayopo, B. A., Isola, L. A., Niyan, T. J., & Bosede, A. V. (2018). Microfinance and Entrepreneurship in Nigeria: A Macro Analysis. In R. Das (Ed.), *Microfinance and Its Impact on Entrepreneurial Development, Sustainability, and Inclusive Growth* (pp. 65–84). Hershey, PA: IGI Global. doi:10.4018/978-1-5225-5213-0.ch004

Bandera, C., Bartolacci, M. R., & Passerini, K. (2016). Knowledge Management and Entrepreneurship: A Contradictory Recipe. *International Journal of Knowledge Management, 12*(3), 1–14. doi:10.4018/IJKM.2016070101

Baporikar, N. (2016). Entrepreneurship Culture of SMEs in India's Tourism Sector. *International Journal of Strategic Information Technology and Applications, 7*(2), 14–27. doi:10.4018/IJSITA.2016040102

Baryshev, A. A. (2017). Entrepreneurial Action as Metaphorical Process and its Metaphorics. *International Journal of Actor-Network Theory and Technological Innovation, 9*(1), 24–39. doi:10.4018/IJANTTI.2017010103

Bastida, R., & Mas-Machuca, M. (2019). Relationship Between Mission Drift and Financial Strategies in Social Enterprises. In C. Maher (Ed.), *Handbook of Research on Value Creation for Small and Micro Social Enterprises* (pp. 151–167). Hershey, PA: IGI Global. doi:10.4018/978-1-5225-6298-6.ch008

Bernardino, S., Santos, J. F., & Ribeiro, J. C. (2018). Social Entrepreneurship and Entrepreneurial Ecosystems: An Empirical Examination. In L. Carvalho (Ed.), *Handbook of Research on Entrepreneurial Ecosystems and Social Dynamics in a Globalized World* (pp. 181–210). Hershey, PA: IGI Global. doi:10.4018/978-1-5225-3525-6.ch008

Carvalho, J. M. (2018). Social Innovation, Entrepreneurship, and Sustainability. In L. Carvalho (Ed.), *Handbook of Research on Entrepreneurial Ecosystems and Social Dynamics in a Globalized World* (pp. 147–180). Hershey, PA: IGI Global. doi:10.4018/978-1-5225-3525-6.ch007

Carvalho, L. C., Vázquez, D. G., & Gil, M. T. (2018). Local Municipalities' Involvement in Promoting Entrepreneurship: An Analysis of Web Page Orientation to the Entrepreneurs in Portuguese Municipalities. In L. Carvalho (Ed.), *Handbook of Research on Entrepreneurial Ecosystems and Social Dynamics in a Globalized World* (pp. 1–19). Hershey, PA: IGI Global. doi:10.4018/978-1-5225-3525-6.ch001

Çetin, I., & Keser, H. Y. (2018). Women Entrepreneurship in MENA and Europe: Empowerment Through Microfinance. In R. Das (Ed.), *Microfinance and Its Impact on Entrepreneurial Development, Sustainability, and Inclusive Growth* (pp. 30–51). Hershey, PA: IGI Global. doi:10.4018/978-1-5225-5213-0.ch002

Chakraborty, S. (2018). Effect and Effectiveness of Microfinance in the Presence of Political Environment: A Study of Microfinance Institutions of West Bengal, India. In R. Das (Ed.), *Microfinance and Its Impact on Entrepreneurial Development, Sustainability, and Inclusive Growth* (pp. 296–307). Hershey, PA: IGI Global. doi:10.4018/978-1-5225-5213-0.ch016

Che, Y., & Zhang, B. (2019). Contextual Determinants of E-Entrepreneurship: Opportunities and Challenges. *International Journal on Semantic Web and Information Systems, 15*(3), 1–15. doi:10.4018/IJSWIS.2019070101

Cheek, R., Sale, M., & Wolverton, C. C. (2018). UX (User Experience)-Driven Website Design Utilizing Analytic Hierarchy Process (AHP) Multi-Attribute Decision Modeling. In M. Khosrow-Pour, D.B.A. (Ed.), Entrepreneurship, Collaboration, and Innovation in the Modern Business Era (pp. 121-135). Hershey, PA: IGI Global. doi:10.4018/978-1-5225-5014-3.ch006

Cîrstea, A. C. (2017). Entrepreneurship Development in Northeast Region of Romania. *International Journal of Sustainable Economies Management, 6*(3), 1–9. doi:10.4018/IJSEM.2017070101

Dalkir, K. (2018). Connecting and Sharing Tacit Knowledge: Do Social Media Help or Hinder? In M. Khosrow-Pour, D.B.A. (Ed.), Entrepreneurship, Collaboration, and Innovation in the Modern Business Era (pp. 178-193). Hershey, PA: IGI Global. doi:10.4018/978-1-5225-5014-3.ch009

Daniel, A. D., & Reis de Castro, V. (2018). Entrepreneurship Education: How to Measure the Impact on Nascent Entrepreneurs. In A. Carrizo Moreira, J. Guilherme Leitão Dantas, & F. Manuel Valente (Eds.), *Nascent Entrepreneurship and Successful New Venture Creation* (pp. 85–110). Hershey, PA: IGI Global. doi:10.4018/978-1-5225-2936-1.ch004

Dantas, J. G., Moreira, A. C., & Valente, F. M. (2018). National Culture, Societal Values, and Type of Economy: Are They Relevant to Explain Entrepreneurial Activity? In L. Carvalho (Ed.), *Handbook of Research on Entrepreneurial Ecosystems and Social Dynamics in a Globalized World* (pp. 75–103). Hershey, PA: IGI Global. doi:10.4018/978-1-5225-3525-6.ch004

Dantas, J. G., & Valente, F. M. (2018). Entrepreneurship, Non-Cognitive Skills, and Education. In A. Carrizo Moreira, J. Guilherme Leitão Dantas, & F. Manuel Valente (Eds.), *Nascent Entrepreneurship and Successful New Venture Creation* (pp. 29–57). Hershey, PA: IGI Global. doi:10.4018/978-1-5225-2936-1.ch002

Das, S. K., & Chatterjee, T. (2018). Impact of Microfinance on Consumption of Tribal Groups: A Study With a focus to Bankura Districts of West Bengal. In R. Das (Ed.), *Microfinance and Its Impact on Entrepreneurial Development, Sustainability, and Inclusive Growth* (pp. 308–321). Hershey, PA: IGI Global. doi:10.4018/978-1-5225-5213-0.ch017

de Vries, I. (2019). Exploring the Personal Drive Behind Small Social-Venture Set-Ups in the Netherlands: Encounters With Local Help and Hindrance. In C. Maher (Ed.), *Handbook of Research on Value Creation for Small and Micro Social Enterprises* (pp. 75–94). Hershey, PA: IGI Global. doi:10.4018/978-1-5225-6298-6.ch004

del Mar Miralles-Quiros, M., Miralles-Quiros, J. L., & Daza-Izquierdo, J. (2018). The Role of High-Tech Entrepreneurship on Regional Development. In A. Carrizo Moreira, J. Guilherme Leitão Dantas, & F. Manuel Valente (Eds.), *Nascent Entrepreneurship and Successful New Venture Creation* (pp. 259–271). Hershey, PA: IGI Global. doi:10.4018/978-1-5225-2936-1.ch012

Dinçer, H., Hacıoğlu, Ü., & Yüksel, S. (2018). Evaluating the Effects of Economic Imbalances on Gold Price in Turkey With MARS Method and Discussions on Microfinance. In R. Das (Ed.), *Microfinance and Its Impact on Entrepreneurial Development, Sustainability, and Inclusive Growth* (pp. 115–137). Hershey, PA: IGI Global. doi:10.4018/978-1-5225-5213-0.ch007

Doyle, G. J. (2019). Socializing Economic Development in Ireland: Social Enterprise – An Untapped Resource. In C. Maher (Ed.), *Handbook of Research on Value Creation for Small and Micro Social Enterprises* (pp. 168–187). Hershey, PA: IGI Global. doi:10.4018/978-1-5225-6298-6.ch009

Egbuta, I. C., & Gilbert, L. L. (2018). Problems Financing Small Business Enterprises in the Current Economic, Business, and Organizational Environment in Nigeria: With Recommendations for Future Support Initiatives. In A. Woldie & B. Thomas (Eds.), *Financial Entrepreneurship for Economic Growth in Emerging Nations* (pp. 111–128). Hershey, PA: IGI Global. doi:10.4018/978-1-5225-2700-8.ch006

Epepe, U. D. (2019). Small Social Enterprises and Online Advertising: Overview of Constraints in Some Selected Cities in Nigeria. In C. Maher (Ed.), *Handbook of Research on Value Creation for Small and Micro Social Enterprises* (pp. 229–253). Hershey, PA: IGI Global. doi:10.4018/978-1-5225-6298-6.ch012

Erçek, M., & Sarıtemur, M. (2018). The Dynamics of Entrepreneurial Networks: A Qualitative Assessment of University Incubator's Role in the Early Stages of Hi-Tech Startups. In A. Carrizo Moreira, J. Guilherme Leitão Dantas, & F. Manuel Valente (Eds.), *Nascent Entrepreneurship and Successful New Venture Creation* (pp. 239–258). Hershey, PA: IGI Global. doi:10.4018/978-1-5225-2936-1.ch011

Eryılmaz, M. (2019). A Discussion on the Relationship Between Information and Communication Technologies (ICT) and Entrepreneurship. *International Journal of E-Entrepreneurship and Innovation*, *9*(1), 13–22. doi:10.4018/IJEEI.2019010102

Eryılmaz, M. E., & Bektaş, O. (2018). An Examination of the Relationship Between Vision Content and Amount of Innovation in SMEs: Findings From Turkey. In L. Carvalho (Ed.), *Handbook of Research on Entrepreneurial Ecosystems and Social Dynamics in a Globalized World* (pp. 20–44). Hershey, PA: IGI Global. doi:10.4018/978-1-5225-3525-6.ch002

Farinha, L., Ferreira, J. J., Nunes, S., & Ratten, V. (2017). Conditions Supporting Entrepreneurship and Sustainable Growth. *International Journal of Social Ecology and Sustainable Development*, *8*(3), 67–86. doi:10.4018/IJSESD.2017070105

França, A., Vilares, A., Frankenbach, S., Vereb, V., & Moreira, A. C. (2018). The Challenging Dynamics of Nascent Entrepreneurship. In A. Carrizo Moreira, J. Guilherme Leitão Dantas, & F. Manuel Valente (Eds.), *Nascent Entrepreneurship and Successful New Venture Creation* (pp. 1–28). Hershey, PA: IGI Global. doi:10.4018/978-1-5225-2936-1.ch001

Ganguly, S. (2018). Micro-Finance and Poverty in India: A State-Level Analysis of Impact Assessment. In A. Woldie & B. Thomas (Eds.), *Financial Entrepreneurship for Economic Growth in Emerging Nations* (pp. 194–216). Hershey, PA: IGI Global. doi:10.4018/978-1-5225-2700-8.ch010

Giacosa, E. (2018). The Increasing of the Regional Development Thanks to the Luxury Business Innovation. In L. Carvalho (Ed.), *Handbook of Research on Entrepreneurial Ecosystems and Social Dynamics in a Globalized World* (pp. 260–273). Hershey, PA: IGI Global. doi:10.4018/978-1-5225-3525-6.ch011

Giacosa, E., & Giovando, G. (2018). Italian Tourism Sector as an Example of Entrepreneurship and Growth for Companies. In L. Carvalho (Ed.), *Handbook of Research on Entrepreneurial Ecosystems and Social Dynamics in a Globalized World* (pp. 313–331). Hershey, PA: IGI Global. doi:10.4018/978-1-5225-3525-6.ch014

Han, L., Xiang, X., & Yang, X. (2018). Emerging Economies and Financing of SMEs. In A. Woldie & B. Thomas (Eds.), *Financial Entrepreneurship for Economic Growth in Emerging Nations* (pp. 22–45). Hershey, PA: IGI Global. doi:10.4018/978-1-5225-2700-8.ch002

Hannibal, M., & Rasmussen, E. S. (2018). Digital Entrepreneurship: A Longitudinal Case Study in a Traditional Firm. In M. Khosrow-Pour, D.B.A. (Ed.), Entrepreneurship, Collaboration, and Innovation in the Modern Business Era (pp. 1-21). Hershey, PA: IGI Global. doi:10.4018/978-1-5225-5014-3.ch001

Hossain, S. F. (2019). Social Networking and Its Role in Media Entrepreneurship: Evaluating the Use of Mobile Phones in the Context of Online Shopping – A Review. *Journal of Media Management and Entrepreneurship, 1*(1), 73–86. doi:10.4018/JMME.2019010105

Huamaní, G. A., Fernández-López, S., Gómez, I. N., Rey-Ares, L., Rodríguez-Gulías, M. J., & Rodeiro-Pazos, D. (2018). The Role Models as Determinants of New Technology-Based Firms: An Exploratory Study. In A. Carrizo Moreira, J. Guilherme Leitão Dantas, & F. Manuel Valente (Eds.), *Nascent Entrepreneurship and Successful New Venture Creation* (pp. 272–288). Hershey, PA: IGI Global. doi:10.4018/978-1-5225-2936-1.ch013

Hussein, S. A., & Mswaka, W. (2018). Entrepreneurial Motives of Egyptian Entrepreneurs: Empirical Evidence From Egypt. *International Journal of Customer Relationship Marketing and Management*, *9*(1), 1–18. doi:10.4018/IJCRMM.2018010101

Jana, S. K., Karmakar, A. K., & Sarkar, K. (2018). Efficiency Analysis of Microfinance Institutions (MFIs) in India Using DEA. In R. Das (Ed.), *Microfinance and Its Impact on Entrepreneurial Development, Sustainability, and Inclusive Growth* (pp. 218–230). Hershey, PA: IGI Global. doi:10.4018/978-1-5225-5213-0.ch012

Jankelowitz, L., & Myres, K. (2019). Micro Social Enterprises in Developing Countries: The South African Experience. In C. Maher (Ed.), *Handbook of Research on Value Creation for Small and Micro Social Enterprises* (pp. 1–25). Hershey, PA: IGI Global. doi:10.4018/978-1-5225-6298-6.ch001

Kakembo, S. H., & Ahmad, A. U. (2019). Employing Islamic Microfinance in Addressing Poverty Challenges in Brunei: A Mudarabah Approach. *International Journal of Corporate Finance and Accounting*, *6*(1), 49–61. doi:10.4018/IJCFA.2019010104

Ktoridou, D., Epaminonda, E., & Karayiannis, A. (2018). Multidisciplinary Group Case-Based Learning Environment: An Education Paradigm to Cultivate Entrepreneurial Thinking. In M. Khosrow-Pour, D.B.A. (Ed.), Entrepreneurship, Collaboration, and Innovation in the Modern Business Era (pp. 262-277). Hershey, PA: IGI Global. doi:10.4018/978-1-5225-5014-3.ch013

Kulothungan, G. D., Oham, C., & Jirel, P. (2019). Managing Uncertainty in Small and Micro Social Enterprises: A Cynefin-Bricolage Framework. In C. Maher (Ed.), *Handbook of Research on Value Creation for Small and Micro Social Enterprises* (pp. 327–348). Hershey, PA: IGI Global. doi:10.4018/978-1-5225-6298-6.ch017

Kumar, A., Sikdar, P., & Alam, M. M. (2018). E-Retail Adoption in Emerging Markets: A Perspective on Predictive Constructs. In M. Khosrow-Pour, D.B.A. (Ed.), Entrepreneurship, Collaboration, and Innovation in the Modern Business Era(pp. 40-67). Hershey, PA: IGI Global. doi:10.4018/978-1-5225-5014-3.ch003

Lado-Sestayo, R., & Vivel-Bua, M. (2018). Women and Entrepreneurship: An Analysis of the Determinants in the Tourism Sector. In A. Carrizo Moreira, J. Guilherme Leitão Dantas, & F. Manuel Valente (Eds.), *Nascent Entrepreneurship and Successful New Venture Creation* (pp. 203–214). Hershey, PA: IGI Global. doi:10.4018/978-1-5225-2936-1.ch009

Lee, J. J., & Imanaka, J. L. (2018). Theorizing Virtuality in Enterprise Social Systems. In M. Khosrow-Pour, D.B.A. (Ed.), Entrepreneurship, Collaboration, and Innovation in the Modern Business Era (pp. 102-120). Hershey, PA: IGI Global. doi:10.4018/978-1-5225-5014-3.ch005

Lewis, A., Thomas, B. C., & Sanders, G. M. (2018). Attracting the Right Employees?: The Effects of Social Media as an Innovative E-Entrepreneurship Recruitment Method for Enterprises. In M. Khosrow-Pour, D.B.A. (Ed.), Entrepreneurship, Collaboration, and Innovation in the Modern Business Era (pp. 194-220). Hershey, PA: IGI Global. doi:10.4018/978-1-5225-5014-3.ch010

Lima, M. J., & Carvalho, L. C. (2018). Collaboration: The Path to SME Performance Increase – A Case Study in a Portuguese Wine Region. In L. Carvalho (Ed.), *Handbook of Research on Entrepreneurial Ecosystems and Social Dynamics in a Globalized World* (pp. 243–259). Hershey, PA: IGI Global. doi:10.4018/978-1-5225-3525-6.ch010

Liu, C. (2019). Financing Social Enterprises: A Systematic Approach. In C. Maher (Ed.), *Handbook of Research on Value Creation for Small and Micro Social Enterprises* (pp. 126–150). Hershey, PA: IGI Global. doi:10.4018/978-1-5225-6298-6.ch007

López-Cózar-Navarro, C., & Priede-Bergamini, T. (2018). Nascent Social Entrepreneurship: Economic, Legal, and Financial Framework. In A. Carrizo Moreira, J. Guilherme Leitão Dantas, & F. Manuel Valente (Eds.), *Nascent Entrepreneurship and Successful New Venture Creation* (pp. 132–152). Hershey, PA: IGI Global. doi:10.4018/978-1-5225-2936-1.ch006

Luke, B. (2019). A Review of Third Sector Reporting Frameworks: Communicating Value Created in Small and Micro Social Enterprises. In C. Maher (Ed.), *Handbook of Research on Value Creation for Small and Micro Social Enterprises* (pp. 26–45). Hershey, PA: IGI Global. doi:10.4018/978-1-5225-6298-6.ch002

Maher, C. (2018). Public Policy: Implications for Small Third Sector Social Enterprises in UK Regions. In L. Carvalho (Ed.), *Handbook of Research on Entrepreneurial Ecosystems and Social Dynamics in a Globalized World* (pp. 126–146). Hershey, PA: IGI Global. doi:10.4018/978-1-5225-3525-6.ch006

Maher, C. (2019). Social Value and Public Services Procurement. In C. Maher (Ed.), *Handbook of Research on Value Creation for Small and Micro Social Enterprises* (pp. 293–310). Hershey, PA: IGI Global. doi:10.4018/978-1-5225-6298-6.ch015

Maher, S. M. (2019). The Development of National Health Service Social Enterprises in England. In C. Maher (Ed.), *Handbook of Research on Value Creation for Small and Micro Social Enterprises* (pp. 95–108). Hershey, PA: IGI Global. doi:10.4018/978-1-5225-6298-6.ch005

Majumder, A., & Bhattacharyya, R. (2018). An Introspective Study on the Governance Practices of Major Microfinance Institutions (MFIs) in India. In R. Das (Ed.), *Microfinance and Its Impact on Entrepreneurial Development, Sustainability, and Inclusive Growth* (pp. 275–295). Hershey, PA: IGI Global. doi:10.4018/978-1-5225-5213-0.ch015

Malhotra, M. (2018). Role of Microfinance in Financial Inclusion in India. In R. Das (Ed.), *Microfinance and Its Impact on Entrepreneurial Development, Sustainability, and Inclusive Growth* (pp. 322–343). Hershey, PA: IGI Global. doi:10.4018/978-1-5225-5213-0.ch018

Mani, M. (2018). Entrepreneurship Education in Engineering Curriculum: Some Insights Into Students' Viewpoints. In M. Khosrow-Pour, D.B.A. (Ed.), Entrepreneurship, Collaboration, and Innovation in the Modern Business Era (pp. 243-261). Hershey, PA: IGI Global. doi:10.4018/978-1-5225-5014-3.ch012

Manzoor, A. (2017). Womenpreneurs in Mena Region. *International Journal of E-Entrepreneurship and Innovation*, *7*(1), 16–28. doi:10.4018/IJEEI.2017010102

Manzoor, A. (2018). High-Growth Entrepreneurship in the MENA Region. *International Journal of ICT Research in Africa and the Middle East*, *7*(1), 54–65. doi:10.4018/IJICTRAME.2018010104

Manzoor, A. (2018). Role of Microfinance Institutions in Development of India. In R. Das (Ed.), *Microfinance and Its Impact on Entrepreneurial Development, Sustainability, and Inclusive Growth* (pp. 138–155). Hershey, PA: IGI Global. doi:10.4018/978-1-5225-5213-0.ch008

Martín, I., Ramos, M., & Herrero, L. A. (2018). Intrapreneurship in Business Innovation: The Importance of Intellectual Capital Protection – Capitalize on the Commitment of Its Human Capital. In A. Carrizo Moreira, J. Guilherme Leitão Dantas, & F. Manuel Valente (Eds.), *Nascent Entrepreneurship and Successful New Venture Creation* (pp. 153–174). Hershey, PA: IGI Global. doi:10.4018/978-1-5225-2936-1.ch007

Martínez-Azúa, B. C., Mesías, F. J., & Elghannam, A. (2018). Perceptions of Extremaduran Firms Towards Innovation: Manufacturing vs. KIBS Comparative Study. In L. Carvalho (Ed.), *Handbook of Research on Entrepreneurial Ecosystems and Social Dynamics in a Globalized World* (pp. 290–312). Hershey, PA: IGI Global. doi:10.4018/978-1-5225-3525-6.ch013

Mazumdar, D., Bisai, S., & Bhattacharjee, M. (2018). Performance of SHGs in the Backward Districts of West Bengal: An Analysis. In R. Das (Ed.), *Microfinance and Its Impact on Entrepreneurial Development, Sustainability, and Inclusive Growth* (pp. 231–256). Hershey, PA: IGI Global. doi:10.4018/978-1-5225-5213-0.ch013

Moreira, A. C., & Freitas da Silva, P. M. (2018). Internationalization in Business-to-Business Markets: The Importance of New Product Development. In L. Carvalho (Ed.), *Handbook of Research on Entrepreneurial Ecosystems and Social Dynamics in a Globalized World* (pp. 460–487). Hershey, PA: IGI Global. doi:10.4018/978-1-5225-3525-6.ch020

Mukherjee, A., & Das, R. C. (2018). Impact of Microfinance on Investment Decision and Consumption Smoothing: A Theoretical Approach. In R. Das (Ed.), *Microfinance and Its Impact on Entrepreneurial Development, Sustainability, and Inclusive Growth* (pp. 52–64). Hershey, PA: IGI Global. doi:10.4018/978-1-5225-5213-0.ch003

Mukhopadhyay, P., Sinha, M., Chaudhury, A. R., & Sengupta, P. P. (2018). Microfinance, Micro-Entrepreneurial Activities Through Self-Help Groups, and Socio-Economic Empowerment of Women: A Study of Burdwan District of West Bengal, India. In R. Das (Ed.), *Microfinance and Its Impact on Entrepreneurial Development, Sustainability, and Inclusive Growth* (pp. 85–102). Hershey, PA: IGI Global. doi:10.4018/978-1-5225-5213-0.ch005

Murphy, L. J., Abdulai, A., Anwar, K., Abdullah, A., & Thomas, B. C. (2018). Financial Entrepreneurship in Three Emerging Economies: A Comparative Study of Ghana, Pakistan, and Yemen. In A. Woldie & B. Thomas (Eds.), *Financial Entrepreneurship for Economic Growth in Emerging Nations* (pp. 1–21). Hershey, PA: IGI Global. doi:10.4018/978-1-5225-2700-8.ch001

Natário, M. M. (2018). Evaluating the Determinants of Nascent Entrepreneurship Among Countries. In A. Carrizo Moreira, J. Guilherme Leitão Dantas, & F. Manuel Valente (Eds.), *Nascent Entrepreneurship and Successful New Venture Creation* (pp. 326–342). Hershey, PA: IGI Global. doi:10.4018/978-1-5225-2936-1.ch016

Ndinguri, E., Machtmes, K., Machtmes, R. J., & Hill, J. I. (2018). Entrepreneurs and Technology: Use and Access of Technology for Idea Generation. In M. Khosrow-Pour, D.B.A. (Ed.), Entrepreneurship, Collaboration, and Innovation in the Modern Business Era (pp. 22-39). Hershey, PA: IGI Global. doi:10.4018/978-1-5225-5014-3.ch002

Nisha, N., Iqbal, M., & Rifat, A. (2018). Service Quality and Knowledge as Determinants of Mobile Health Services: Empirical Investigation and Further Considerations. In M. Khosrow-Pour, D.B.A. (Ed.), Entrepreneurship, Collaboration, and Innovation in the Modern Business Era (pp. 151-177). Hershey, PA: IGI Global. doi:10.4018/978-1-5225-5014-3.ch008

O'Reilly, K. A., Kelley, B. M., & Lancendorfer, K. M. (2018). Leveraging Virtual Communities to Enhance Brand Equity: A Case Study. In M. Khosrow-Pour, D.B.A. (Ed.), Entrepreneurship, Collaboration, and Innovation in the Modern Business Era (pp. 136-150). Hershey, PA: IGI Global. doi:10.4018/978-1-5225-5014-3.ch007

Oham, C. (2019). Faith-Based Social Enterprise and Value Creation in Communities. In C. Maher (Ed.), *Handbook of Research on Value Creation for Small and Micro Social Enterprises* (pp. 109–125). Hershey, PA: IGI Global. doi:10.4018/978-1-5225-6298-6.ch006

Oncioiu, I., Duca, I., Postole, M. A., & Ciobanasu, M. (2018). A Comparative Study of Financing Innovation Capacity for Romanian SMEs in a Global Economy. In A. Woldie & B. Thomas (Eds.), *Financial Entrepreneurship for Economic Growth in Emerging Nations* (pp. 69–84). Hershey, PA: IGI Global. doi:10.4018/978-1-5225-2700-8.ch004

Patra, S. (2018). Determinants of Participation and Impact of Microfinance: An Econometric Analysis. In R. Das (Ed.), *Microfinance and Its Impact on Entrepreneurial Development, Sustainability, and Inclusive Growth* (pp. 156–184). Hershey, PA: IGI Global. doi:10.4018/978-1-5225-5213-0.ch009

Pego, A., & Bernardo, M. D. (2018). Decision Making in Rural Tourism Management: The Case of Algarve. In L. Carvalho (Ed.), *Handbook of Research on Entrepreneurial Ecosystems and Social Dynamics in a Globalized World* (pp. 274–289). Hershey, PA: IGI Global. doi:10.4018/978-1-5225-3525-6.ch012

Piccarozzi, M., Silvestri, C., & Stefanoni, A. (2018). Positive Effects of the Innovative Start-Up on University Spin-Offs: A Recent Italian Legislation. In A. Carrizo Moreira, J. Guilherme Leitão Dantas, & F. Manuel Valente (Eds.), *Nascent Entrepreneurship and Successful New Venture Creation* (pp. 289–307). Hershey, PA: IGI Global. doi:10.4018/978-1-5225-2936-1.ch014

Pjero (Beqiraj), E., & Kordha, E. (2019). Social Enterprises and Fundraising Challenge: Crowd Funding as an Innovative Solution for Developing Countries – Best Practices in Albania. In C. Maher (Ed.), Handbook of Research on Value Creation for Small and Micro Social Enterprises (pp. 271-292). Hershey, PA: IGI Global. doi:10.4018/978-1-5225-6298-6.ch014

Potts, M., & Puia, G. M. (2018). The Divergence of Entrepreneurial Landscapes in the European Union. In M. Khosrow-Pour, D.B.A. (Ed.), Entrepreneurship, Collaboration, and Innovation in the Modern Business Era (pp. 291-307). Hershey, PA: IGI Global. doi:10.4018/978-1-5225-5014-3.ch015

Preto, M. T., & Farlens, T. (2018). Creativity, Entrepreneurship, and Labor Dynamics: The Role of Creative Workers in Portugal. In L. Carvalho (Ed.), *Handbook of Research on Entrepreneurial Ecosystems and Social Dynamics in a Globalized World* (pp. 488–502). Hershey, PA: IGI Global. doi:10.4018/978-1-5225-3525-6.ch021

Raghunath, K. M., Patro, C. S., & Sirisha, K. (2019). Paraphernalias of Entrepreneurship – A Contemplating Outlook. *International Journal of E-Entrepreneurship and Innovation*, *9*(1), 47–62. doi:10.4018/IJEEI.2019010105

Ratten, V., & Dana, L. (2017). Sustainable Entrepreneurship, Family Farms and the Dairy Industry. *International Journal of Social Ecology and Sustainable Development*, *8*(3), 114–129. doi:10.4018/IJSESD.2017070108

Razzaque, S. (2018). Effects of Peer Monitoring and Contract Choice on Repayment Rates Under Group Liability Lending: A Laboratory Microfinance Experiment From Australia. *International Journal of Applied Behavioral Economics*, *7*(3), 1–33. doi:10.4018/IJABE.2018070101

Rego, M. D., Lucas, M. R., Vieira, C., & Vieira, I. (2018). Entrepreneurial Ecosystems in Low-Density Regions: Business Incubation Practices in Alentejo. In L. Carvalho (Ed.), *Handbook of Research on Entrepreneurial Ecosystems and Social Dynamics in a Globalized World* (pp. 45–74). Hershey, PA: IGI Global. doi:10.4018/978-1-5225-3525-6.ch003

Rohlfer, S. (2018). The Ambiguous Role of Trade Unions in Startup Formation. In A. Carrizo Moreira, J. Guilherme Leitão Dantas, & F. Manuel Valente (Eds.), *Nascent Entrepreneurship and Successful New Venture Creation* (pp. 308–325). Hershey, PA: IGI Global. doi:10.4018/978-1-5225-2936-1.ch015

Rua, O. L., & Correia, M. J. (2018). Analysing Innovation in Healthcare Organizations: An Empirical Study From Portugal. In L. Carvalho (Ed.), *Handbook of Research on Entrepreneurial Ecosystems and Social Dynamics in a Globalized World* (pp. 212–242). Hershey, PA: IGI Global. doi:10.4018/978-1-5225-3525-6.ch009

Rwamigabo, E. R. (2019). Challenges and Opportunities of Micro or Small Social Enterprises in Rwanda. In C. Maher (Ed.), *Handbook of Research on Value Creation for Small and Micro Social Enterprises* (pp. 254–270). Hershey, PA: IGI Global. doi:10.4018/978-1-5225-6298-6.ch013

Sahu, K. K. (2018). Sustainability of Microfinance Institutions in India. In R. Das (Ed.), *Microfinance and Its Impact on Entrepreneurial Development, Sustainability, and Inclusive Growth* (pp. 257–274). Hershey, PA: IGI Global. doi:10.4018/978-1-5225-5213-0.ch014

Saiz-Alvarez, J. M., Colvin-Díez, J., & Cuñado, J. H. (2017). Digital Entrepreneurial Charity, Solidarity, and Social Change. *International Journal of E-Entrepreneurship and Innovation, 7*(1), 29–48. doi:10.4018/IJEEI.2017010103

Sana, A. K., & Biswas, B. (2018). Risk Management Practices in Indian Microfinance Sector: A Study of Some Selected Institutions in West Bengal. In R. Das (Ed.), *Microfinance and Its Impact on Entrepreneurial Development, Sustainability, and Inclusive Growth* (pp. 1–29). Hershey, PA: IGI Global. doi:10.4018/978-1-5225-5213-0.ch001

Sánchez-García, J. C., & Hernández-Sánchez, B. R. (2018). Nascent Entrepreneurs, Psychological Characteristics, and Sociocultural Background: Psycho-Sociocultural Background of Nascent Entrepreneurs. In A. Carrizo Moreira, J. Guilherme Leitão Dantas, & F. Manuel Valente (Eds.), *Nascent Entrepreneurship and Successful New Venture Creation* (pp. 111–131). Hershey, PA: IGI Global. doi:10.4018/978-1-5225-2936-1.ch005

Sánchez-García, J. C., Rodriguez-Gómez, E., Hernández-Sánchez, B. R., & Pérez-Díaz, J. M. (2018). Entrepreneurship Education as a Key Antecedent to Boost Nascent Entrepreneurs. In A. Carrizo Moreira, J. Guilherme Leitão Dantas, & F. Manuel Valente (Eds.), *Nascent Entrepreneurship and Successful New Venture Creation* (pp. 58–84). Hershey, PA: IGI Global. doi:10.4018/978-1-5225-2936-1.ch003

Siakas, K. V., Georgiadou, E., & Siakas, D. (2018). Knowledge Sharing in Distributed Teams: Influence of National and Organizational Culture. In M. Khosrow-Pour, D.B.A. (Ed.), Entrepreneurship, Collaboration, and Innovation in the Modern Business Era (pp. 221-242). Hershey, PA: IGI Global. doi:10.4018/978-1-5225-5014-3.ch011

Sinha, M., Mukhopadhyay, P., Chaudhury, A. R., & Sengupta, P. P. (2018). Capturing the Performances of Self-Help Groups Across Indian States: A Dynamic Quantitative Exploration. In R. Das (Ed.), *Microfinance and Its Impact on Entrepreneurial Development, Sustainability, and Inclusive Growth* (pp. 207–217). Hershey, PA: IGI Global. doi:10.4018/978-1-5225-5213-0.ch011

Snoussi, W., & Béjaoui, A. (2018). The Influence of Specific Criteria of Emerging Markets on SME Financing in MENA Markets. In A. Woldie & B. Thomas (Eds.), *Financial Entrepreneurship for Economic Growth in Emerging Nations* (pp. 46–68). Hershey, PA: IGI Global. doi:10.4018/978-1-5225-2700-8.ch003

Sousa, M. A., Palacios, T. B., & Martínez-Azúa, B. C. (2018). Factors Affecting Internationalization Degree of Higher Education Institutions in Portugal and Spain. In L. Carvalho (Ed.), *Handbook of Research on Entrepreneurial Ecosystems and Social Dynamics in a Globalized World* (pp. 348–377). Hershey, PA: IGI Global. doi:10.4018/978-1-5225-3525-6.ch016

Tambunan, T. T. (2018). MSMEs and Access to Financing in a Developing Economy: The Indonesian Experience. In A. Woldie & B. Thomas (Eds.), *Financial Entrepreneurship for Economic Growth in Emerging Nations* (pp. 148–172). Hershey, PA: IGI Global. doi:10.4018/978-1-5225-2700-8.ch008

Teixeira, N., Pardal, P. N., & Rafael, B. G. (2018). Internationalization, Financial Performance, and Organizational Challenges: A Success Case in Portugal. In L. Carvalho (Ed.), *Handbook of Research on Entrepreneurial Ecosystems and Social Dynamics in a Globalized World* (pp. 379–423). Hershey, PA: IGI Global. doi:10.4018/978-1-5225-3525-6.ch017

Tomaževič, N., & Cantele, S. (2019). Social Entrepreneurship and Social Enterprises in Slovenia: Strengths and Weaknesses From an Analysis of the Institutional Framework. In C. Maher (Ed.), *Handbook of Research on Value Creation for Small and Micro Social Enterprises* (pp. 207–228). Hershey, PA: IGI Global. doi:10.4018/978-1-5225-6298-6.ch011

Vargas-Hernández, J. G., & Bhattacharjee, K. (2018). Microfinance and Rural Entrepreneurship in Mexico: A Budget Study for PROMUSAG. In R. Das (Ed.), *Microfinance and Its Impact on Entrepreneurial Development, Sustainability, and Inclusive Growth* (pp. 103–114). Hershey, PA: IGI Global. doi:10.4018/978-1-5225-5213-0.ch006

Vargas-Hernández, J. G., & Ortiz, C. L. (2018). Impacts of Microfinance Strategic Management and Social Capital on Women Entrepreneurship in Rural Mexico. In R. Das (Ed.), *Microfinance and Its Impact on Entrepreneurial Development, Sustainability, and Inclusive Growth* (pp. 185–205). Hershey, PA: IGI Global. doi:10.4018/978-1-5225-5213-0.ch010

Vargas-Hernández, J. G., & Ortiz, C. L. (2019). Social Capital as a Factor of Success in Mexican Cooperatives: Case – Cooperativa "Las Chiquihuitecas" Producer of Grana Cochinilla. In C. Maher (Ed.), *Handbook of Research on Value Creation for Small and Micro Social Enterprises* (pp. 311–326). Hershey, PA: IGI Global. doi:10.4018/978-1-5225-6298-6.ch016

Vázquez, D. G. (2018). Improvement in Higher Education: The Role of Chairs in University Social Responsibility. In L. Carvalho (Ed.), *Handbook of Research on Entrepreneurial Ecosystems and Social Dynamics in a Globalized World* (pp. 333–347). Hershey, PA: IGI Global. doi:10.4018/978-1-5225-3525-6.ch015

Vecco, M., & Srakar, A. (2018). Nascent Cultural and Creative Entrepreneurship: Between Entrepreneurial Economics and Institutional Entrepreneurship. In A. Carrizo Moreira, J. Guilherme Leitão Dantas, & F. Manuel Valente (Eds.), *Nascent Entrepreneurship and Successful New Venture Creation* (pp. 175–202). Hershey, PA: IGI Global. doi:10.4018/978-1-5225-2936-1.ch008

Wale-Oshinowo, B. A., Uba, C. D., Adeyeye, M. M., & Omobowale, A. O. (2019). Understanding Social Entrepreneurship in the African Context: An Exploratory Review of Evidence From Nigeria. In C. Maher (Ed.), *Handbook of Research on Value Creation for Small and Micro Social Enterprises* (pp. 188–206). Hershey, PA: IGI Global. doi:10.4018/978-1-5225-6298-6.ch010

Watson, E. S., & Roberts, P. (2019). Applying a Cross-Cultural Health Systems Strengthening Diagnostic Tool: The Experiences of a Small Social Enterprise Delivering Health Care Services in England. In C. Maher (Ed.), *Handbook of Research on Value Creation for Small and Micro Social Enterprises* (pp. 46–74). Hershey, PA: IGI Global. doi:10.4018/978-1-5225-6298-6.ch003

Woldie, A., Hagshenas, H., & Thomas, B. C. (2018). The Qualitative Relationship Between Banks and SMEs in Wales. In A. Woldie & B. Thomas (Eds.), *Financial Entrepreneurship for Economic Growth in Emerging Nations* (pp. 86–110). Hershey, PA: IGI Global. doi:10.4018/978-1-5225-2700-8.ch005

Woldie, A., & Ubrurhe, U. (2018). Small and Medium Enterprises' Challenges of Accessing Microfinance in Nigeria. In A. Woldie & B. Thomas (Eds.), *Financial Entrepreneurship for Economic Growth in Emerging Nations* (pp. 229–253). Hershey, PA: IGI Global. doi:10.4018/978-1-5225-2700-8.ch012

Yang, J. G. (2018). The Advantages and Disadvantages of Internet Commerce in China. In M. Khosrow-Pour, D.B.A. (Ed.), Entrepreneurship, Collaboration, and Innovation in the Modern Business Era (pp. 278-290). Hershey, PA: IGI Global. doi:10.4018/978-1-5225-5014-3.ch014

Yıldırım, İ. (2018). Access to Finance: Developing Microinsurance Market in Turkey. In A. Woldie & B. Thomas (Eds.), *Financial Entrepreneurship for Economic Growth in Emerging Nations* (pp. 217–228). Hershey, PA: IGI Global. doi:10.4018/978-1-5225-2700-8.ch011

Index

M

N

P

Q

R

S

T

W

Y

www.ingramcontent.com/pod-product-compliance
Lightning Source LLC
LaVergne TN
LVHW081322300926
849161LV00008B/1855